Konstantin Petrovich Pobedonostsev, R. E. C. (Robert Edward Crozier)
Long

Reflections of a Russian Statesman

Konstantin Petrovich Pobedonostsev, R. E. C. (Robert Edward Crozier) Long

Reflections of a Russian Statesman

ISBN/EAN: 9783337167226

Printed in Europe, USA, Canada, Australia, Japan

Cover: Foto ©ninafisch / pixelio.de

More available books at **www.hansebooks.com**

REFLECTIONS OF A RUSSIAN STATESMAN

BY

K. P. POBYEDONOSTSEFF

PROCURATOR OF THE HOLY SYNOD OF RUSSIA

TRANSLATED FROM THE RUSSIAN

BY

ROBERT CROZIER LONG

WITH A PREFACE BY

OLGA NOVIKOFF

LONDON

GRANT RICHARDS

9 HENRIETTA STREET, COVENT GARDEN, W.C.

1898

PREFACE

SEVERAL years ago, Mr Kinglake, the author of the "Crimean War," whom we, his friends, generally called "Eothen," wrote to me suggesting that I should make a study of the Decay of Parliamentarism. Here is a part of his letter:

"Now I am going 'to set you a subject,' as your governess would have said in the days of the schoolroom.

"I think it might suit your position to write on the 'Fall of Parliamentary Government.' You would please Moscow, please Petersburg, please your Emperor, and though not exactly *pleasing* England, you would win her attention, and perhaps put her on her mettle, and teach her to mend her ways. Let me know what you think of this, and if I hear that you incline to the subject I will revert to it."

Mr Froude urged me to do the same, but the task to which I was invited was far beyond my power. Besides, I should only have repeated what was so much better said by Carlyle, Sir Henry Maine, Mr Lecky, and others. But that difficult duty was undertaken by a Russian, who possesses all the scientific qualifications for such an examination. The book, which Mr Pobyedonostseff published in Russian, and which was immediately, translated into German, French, and Italian referring principally to that subject, has been extensively circulated on the Continent. It has not until now been translated into English.

b   v

In securing its appearance in the present form, I
feel as if I were in some measure, though vicariously,
carrying out the wish of my two departed friends,
Kinglake and Froude.

Of the author of this remarkable and pregnant
volume of reflections upon the grandest problems
of Church and State, it is not necessary for me
to say more than a single word.

That word is his name, a name familiar throughout Europe. It stands for Religion as opposed to
Atheism, for Orthodoxy as opposed to Romanism on
one hand and Protestantism on the other, and for
Authority as opposed to Anarchy.

In him all the irreligious forces of modern Nihilism,
as well as the theological quacks, with their sham
remedies for the ills of the soul, have long recognised
the supreme embodiment of all the principles against
which they wage unceasing war.

It is not his habit to descend into the arena.
For the most part of his long and remarkable
career he has been a silent witness, working, not
talking, serving his Emperor and his country in
the sphere to which he has been called.

As tutor to our late Emperor he had much to
do with implanting in the heart and soul of
Alexander III. those profound religious convictions
which made him afterwards so famous as the man
who, in his private life and in his policy, was dominated by an almost fanatical hatred of all lies, and
who earned for himself the noble title of the Peace-
keeper of Europe by his not less passionate
detestation of war.

To train a pupil who, on the greatest of Imperial

thrones, should never forget to hate a lie, and to regard as his most coveted ambition to keep the peace—that was the first merit of Mr Pobyedonostseff.

Even the democratic West would not grudge him that laurel, especially to-day when the French Republic, organised on all the principles of free thought and equality, clings to the Russian alliance as the anchor of all its confidence in the present, and its hopes for the future.

But after fulfilling the duty of tutorship to the Grand Duke, who, at the much-lamented death of his beloved brother, became the heir to the throne, Mr Pobyedonostseff was called to a post of great difficulty and importance, that of Procurator of the Holy Synod — a post tantamount to that of Cabinet Minister.

It is not for me to speak here of the many questions with which he has had to deal during the tenure of his office. I am not writing a history of Russia under Alexander II., Alexander III., and Nicholas II. I only refer to the subject in order to assert, what even his worst enemies will not deny, that during the whole of his life, Mr Pobyedonostseff has never even been accused of acting on any other than the loftiest political and religious principles. He certainly has carried out his convictions with honest pertinacity. He is not a man of compromise. He is a man of principle, and he has been true to his convictions.

What his convictions are he has plainly stated with characteristic frankness in this volume of reflections upon the subjects which underlie all modern political discussions. That they will be endorsed by readers in England and America, I do not pretend to expect; on the contrary, I am afraid they will probably produce the effect of a spray of iced water suddenly turned upon molten lead. It is hardly to be expected that English critics will be otherwise than scandalised by the calm declaration of the typical Russian statesman of our time that "the Parliamentary comedy is the supreme political lie which dominates our age."

Nevertheless, considering the exceeding liberality with which many Englishmen have showered upon us criticisms of Russian institutions, which, for the most part, have not even been studied or understood at all, it is allowable to hope that modern Democracy, carefully investigated by the most scientific Russian authority, should get the same hearing secured to it as in Germany and France.

To those who insist upon asserting that the Russian views expressed in this volume belong to the dark Middle Ages, and have nothing in common with the "last word of civilisation," I should like to say, "Strike, but hear." Mr Pobyedonostseff, by his deep learning and his lofty character, has secured for himself one of the highest positions in an Empire which even the blindest now begin to see is the dominating power in Europe and Asia. He is not afraid of speaking his mind freely to his Emperor, and he is just as unbiassed in appealing to the masses of his readers.

His worst foes cannot deny the perfect frankness and honesty which permeate his book.

The opinions of a statesman who, for many years, has held such a position in an Empire like Russia are surely well worth the attention of the Western nations.

Mr Pobyedonostseff is the critic in the stalls. To him, as to all of us Russians, the parliamentary theatre of the Western world performs a long tragi-comedy, which occasionally ascends to tragedy and sometimes sinks into farce. We can observe it dispassionately, critically, and sometimes even sympathetically.

However you may deplore the fact, we are outside of it, and have never shown less disposition than to-day to enrol ourselves in the Democratic troupe.

Even Count Leon Tolstoi, who may, perhaps, be regarded as the most extreme and privileged critic in Russia, treats Constitutionalism with the same supercilious contempt as all the other forms of government.

We have no parliamentary party in Russia. No one, even in the abstract, as a matter of theory, would wish to inoculate the Muscovite politician with the passion of parliamentary faction; hence the observations of Mr Pobyedonostseff have an independence and a detachment from things impossible to those who are themselves in the movement, and who have to consider in all they write and speak the effect which their action may have upon their own future relations to the multitude.

It is not for me to follow every step of the Procurator of the Holy Synod over the wide field which he traverses with such a steady tread. My task is done when, in these few words, I introduce his book to the attention of English readers.

But I cannot resist the temptation of noting especially the prescient words of Mr Pobyedonostseff as to the impossibility of reconciling the pretensions of Nationality and Democracy. The recent developments in Austria have signally justified the grave warnings of the Russian publicist, which were written years before the conflict of national passions which has made parliamentary government impossible in the Cis-Leithan State.

In conclusion, I may remind those who protest against giving a hearing to an advocate of autocracy, that Her Most Gracious Majesty Queen Victoria, even in the sixty-first year of her reign, has not deemed it expedient, or even possible, to govern more than a mere fraction of her subjects on Democratic principles. The government of three-fourths of the British Empire is as autocratic and as free from the *chinoiseries* of representative government as the government of Russia itself.

OLGA NOVIKOFF.

(" O. K.")

April 1898.

CONTENTS

CHURCH AND STATE

I

THE conflict between religious and political principles is one of the most remarkable phenomena of
our time. When discord once appears in the sphere
of religious and spiritual principles it is impossible
to predict by what limits it will be confined, what
elements it will involve, and whither will flow the
stream of passions aroused by the clash of convictions and beliefs. Where the religious convictions of
a people are concerned, it is essential that the State
shall establish its demands and regulations with
especial caution to avoid such collision with their
sentiments and spiritual necessities as would be
resented by the masses. For, however powerful
the State may be, its power is based alone upon
identity of religious profession with the people ;
the faith of the people sustains it ; when discord once appears to weaken this identity, its
foundations are sapped, its power dissolves away.
In spiritual sympathy with its rulers a people may
bear many heavy burdens, may concede much, and
surrender many of its privileges and rights. In one
domain alone the State must not demand concession, or the people concede, and that is the domain
where every believer, and all together, sink the foundations of their spiritual existence and bind them-

A

selves with eternity. There are depths in this domain
to which the secular power dare not, and must not,
descend, lest it strike at the roots of faith in each
and all.

The prime cause of the misunderstandings which
now exist, and which threaten to increase, between
the people and its rulers is the artificial theory,
popularly held, of the relations of Church to State.
In the course of events in Western Europe—events
indissolubly bound up with the development of the
Roman Catholic Church—there originated and took
root, as an element in political construction, the idea
of the Church as a religious and political institution,
with a power which, in opposition to the State,
carried on with it a political conflict, the incidents
of which crowd the pages of history in Western
Europe. This conception of the political mission
of the Church has driven into the background its
simple, true, and natural conception as a congregation of Christians organically bound by identity of
faith in divine alliance. Yet this innate conception
lies concealed in the depths of the popular conscience,
corresponding with the essential aspiration of the
human soul — the aspiration to faith and identity
of faith with others. In this sense the Church, as
a community of believers, cannot and must not
detach itself from the State, as a society united by
a civil bond. Whatever perfection theories based
on the separation of Church and State may attain
in the minds of logicians, they do not satisfy the
simple sentiments of the mass of believers. They
may indeed content the political mind which sees
in them the best of all possible compromises, and

a perfect construction of philosophic ideas; but
in the depths of the soul which feels the living
necessity of faith, and of unity of faith with life,
these artificial theories are irreconcilable with truth.
The spiritual life needs and seeks above all things
spiritual unity; to this it aspires as the ideal of its
existence, but when this ideal is realised in duality,
it scorns to accept it and turns away. By its nature
faith is uncompromising, and tolerates no accommo-
dations in its ideals. It is true that the actual life
of all and each of us is an uninterrupted history
of failure and duality, a melancholy discord between
thought and work, between faith and life; but in this
ceaseless struggle the human soul is sustained by
nothing so much as by faith in an ideal ultimate unity,
a faith which it cherishes as the strongest sanctuary of
existence. Reduce a believer to the recognition of
this duality, he will be humiliated. Reveal to him
that end of all duality to which his soul aspires,—he
lifts his head, he feels his life renewed, and marches
onward armed with faith. Tell him that life and
faith are independent of one another, and his soul
rejects the thought with the abhorrence with which
it would reject the thought of ultimate annihilation.

It may be objected that this is a question of
personal belief. But the faith of individuals can in
no way be distinguished from the faith of the
Church, for its essential need is community, and
of this need it finds satisfaction only in the
Church.

The struggle between Church and State in
Western Europe has now endured for many years.
The last word in this struggle has not yet been

spoken, and what that word will be is still unknown. Each party still measures its strength and
assembles its forces around it. The State relies
upon the forces of intelligence; the Church relies
upon the faith of the people, and upon the recognition of its spiritual authority. There can be no
doubt that in the end the victory will belong to
that party which displays the most perfect unity
in a living and spiritual faith. The intelligence of
the partisans of the State is in any case confronted with a delicate task, the task of alluring
to its side and binding with it in firm alliance
the popular faith. But, to gain the sympathy
and alliance of faith, intelligence alone is vain.
The State must show in itself a living faith. *Si
vis me flere dolendum est primum ipsi tibi.* The
popular mind is suspicious, and may not be seduced
by appearances of faith, or drawn by compromise;
for the living faith accepts no compromise, and
rejects the authority of rational logic. Though
"faith" is vulgarly considered as identical with
"conviction," the conviction of reason must not be
confounded with the conviction of faith; and the
forces of intellect are sadly mistaken if they assume
in themselves the necessary elements of spiritual
force, independently of faith which is their very
essence.

This confusion of ideas is a great danger to
the State in its struggle with the Church. When,
at the time of the Reformation in Germany, the
State set itself at the head of the movement
against the old ecclesiastical power, and built a
new organisation for the Church, it possessed

actually the spiritual force of faith. The movement
which it led had its origin among the people; it
was animated by the deepest and strongest faith;
its first leaders represented the highest intelligence
of the community, and glowed with the fire of a
sincere faith uniting them with the people. Thus
in this movement were concentrated immense
spiritual forces, which, after many years of struggle,
compelled the surrender of the ancient faith.

To-day conditions differ altogether. From the
side of the State discord has arisen between the
religion of the people and the political organisation
of the Church. From the other quarter of intelligence has sprung a still more striking disunion
between religion and its scientific construction.
Theological science—no longer restricted to its
original function of studying and comprehending
religious beliefs—threatens to absorb all belief by
submitting it as a phenomenon and external object
of investigation to the unsparing critical analysis
of reason. Political science has established a carefully elaborated doctrine of the definite severance
of Church from State, in consequence of which, by
the operation of a law admitting no division of
supreme power, the Church inevitably appears as
an institution subordinate to the State. Together
with this, the State appears, according to the new
conception, as an institution detached from every
religion and indifferent to all. It is natural that,
from this point of view, the Church appears merely
as an institution satisfying one of the needs of the
population recognised by the State—namely, the
need of religion; and the modern State, while

exercising over this institution control and super-
vision, in no way troubles about religion itself. For
the State, as the supreme political institution, such a
theory is attractive : it assures it complete autonomy,
the elimination of opposition, and the simplification
of all the operations of its ecclesiastical policy. But
such assurances are delusive; for this theory, evolved
in the studies of ministers and scholars, the conscience of the people will not accept. In all that
relates to religion the masses demand simplicity
and completeness, which satisfy their minds, and
they reject all artificial ideas, instinctively discerning
their diversity from truth. Political theorists will
accept the retention of their offices by priests and
professors who — as unhappily often occurs in
Germany — publicly declare their disbelief in the
divinity of our Saviour. The conscience of the
people will never accept such an interpretation of
the priestly office, but will reject it with abhorrence
as a falsehood. Unhappy and hopeless is the
position of the ruling power when in its dispositions
in matters of religion the masses everywhere detect
falsehood and infidelity.

II

The separation of Church and State was treated
remarkably by the ex-priest Hyacinthe in his public
lectures delivered in Geneva, in the spring of 1863
War to the knife with the Church—this is the fancy
of the revolutionary party, or, at least, of its extreme representatives, who in politics call themselves

Jacobins, and in the domain of religious ideas propagate materialism and infidelity. These men are armed with two weapons, sophistry and violence. They have long lost the confidence of men; they are blind; they lack the strength to continue the struggle, because they confound all among their adversaries, distinguish nothing, and exaggerate beyond measure their importance.

The aim of the French Revolution was to regenerate society, but regeneration could only succeed through the application to civil society of Christian principles. A struggle began between the Revolution and the Roman theocracy, for the Revolution confounded this theocracy with the Catholic Church, the universe which surrounds all believing Christians, the Evangel itself, and the person of Christ. Thus war was declared, not only with Rome, but with the kingdom of Christ on earth. In the heart of Christendom these men began to persecute the very religious feeling which, for nigh two thousand years, had been inseparably associated with Christianity. Such was the adversary they challenged to battle, arming themselves with two weapons—base and dishonoured both—the axe of the headsman and the living word of the sophist.

Thanks to the Abbé freethinkers who thronged the court, thanks to the admitted levity of contemporary morals, Catholicism in France was in an evil state. Suddenly, it was summoned, awakened, and dragged to prison. In its name ascended the scaffold priests, young girls, and peasants, side by side with distinguished nobles, with poets, and with statesmen, as in the epoch of the early Caesars.

Till then its robes had been stained by the blood of
St Bartholomew's night, and traces of parents' and
orphans' tears caused by the revocation of the Edict of
Nantes : yet all these traces were suddenly effaced,
nothing was seen save the blood from its own veins,
the traces of its own tears.   From this the Church
soon arose again to a great and stainless glory.   For
this glory her executioners had prepared her.

Thus acted the sophist-philosophers also.   They
opened questions which modern science declares insoluble ; they unveiled the secrets of death, seeing in
it only fantasy and delusion ; they strove to pierce
to the origin of humanity, and instead of the Adam
of our Bibles, called to its cradle some unknown
being, slowly developed from animal life, an ape at
first, and then a man.   Having placed this man both
as to his origin and as to his end in an animal
medium, having degraded him to the limits of corruption, they changed their tone and began to glorify
his greatness : " How great art thou, man !" they
cried. "How great art thou in thy atheism and in thy
materialism, and in thy freedom, submitting to nothing
in morals !" But in the glory of this strange greatness
man seemed crushed with grief.   He had forsaken
God, but he kept the need of religion.   So imperious
is this need that religion may exist even without
God—such is Buddhism, a religion numbering its
millions of adherents.   But what if it were true that
man first sprang from an animal matter? this in
no way changes the case of faith.   In the Book of
Genesis man was made from a material baser still—
mud and dust, a handful of earth.   It is not the
envelope that makes the man.   He took from his

Creator a living soul, a breath of religious and moral life, of which, whatever he may wish, he cannot be rid. And this forbids him ever to cut himself loose from the Christian religion.

The Church must be separated from the State, we are told. These are only words, expressing no distinct idea, for the word separation may express many things. We must first understand in what the separation consists. If it consist in the clearer delimitation of religious and secular society — a sincere and permanent delimitation effected without craft or violence—all men will approve of such separation. If, from a practical standpoint, it is demanded that the State shall abdicate its right of appointing the ministers of the Church, and shall repudiate its responsibility for their maintenance, the concession of this demand would establish a most desirable, an ideal state of affairs, for which it is necessary to prepare under favourable circumstances and in legal form. When this question matures, the State, if it wishes so to decide it, is bound to restore to the proper parties the right to elect priests and bishops ; in such case, it will be impossible to surrender to the Pope that which belongs to the clergy and to the people by historical and apostolic right. The State is merely depository of this right, which in no way belongs to it.

We are told that this separation is to be understood in the widest sense. Able and learned men define it thus : the State has no concern with the Church, or the Church with the State. Thus humanity is to revolve in two great circles. In one circle will be the body, in the other the soul ; and between these circles will be a void as between heaven and earth. But this is impossible. The body cannot separate itself from its soul—soul and body live a single life.

Can we expect that the Church—I do not speak of the Catholic Church in particular, but of the universal Church — will consent to abdicate its interest in civil society, in family society, human society—all, in short, that is understood by the State? Since when has it been supposed that the function of the Church is to train ascetics, to people monasteries, to display in temples the poetry of its ceremonies and processions? No; these are but a little part of the duties entrusted to the Church. To it was appointed another mission : to teach all peoples. That is its work. Its duty is to train the peoples of the earth that from the midst of the earthly city and earthly family they may be not altogether unworthy to step into the heavenly city and the heavenly communion. At birth, at marriage, at death, in the supreme moments of human existence, the Church appears with its three solemn sacraments. And yet we are told that the Church has no concern with family life! Its duty is to inspire the people with respect for the law and for power, and to inspire in power respect for human freedom. Yet we are told that the Church has no concern with society.

No; the moral principle is indivisible. It cannot be apportioned to provide one system of morals for individuals, another for society—one for the body, another for the soul. In a single moral principle are embraced all the relations of life—personal, domestic, and political ; and no church which retains

the consciousness of its own worthiness will ever
surrender its lawful influence on the family or on
civil society. To demand that the Church shall
abstain from intervention in civil affairs is scarcely
to give it new strength.

The State, we are told, has no concern with the
Church. Civil society was first established on the
basis of the primitive family, every head of a family
being a citizen : in that age the society of believers
was indistinguishable from the family or from the
entire people. In the course of time the structure
of civil society was perfected, and an universal
Christianity arose, embracing both families and
people. How can we justly say to the father and
the citizen : You and the Church are independent
of one another ? Unhappily both father and citizen
have long ago said this to themselves. The father
has grown indifferent to the tendencies and sentiments of religion in his family circle. He can find
no answer when his wife turns to him with her
doubts ; when his child with childish simplicity asks,
"Who is this God ? And why dost thou not pray
to him ? And what is this death that comes and
bears children away ?" If the father answers
nothing to these questions, what answer will the
child devise ? And if the father finds an answer,
the child hears in it a fable, and not the voice of
the living faith. The consequence is that children
become sceptical as their fathers, or superstitious as
their mothers and their confessors. Thus operates
the separation of the Church and State in the family
circle. In the place of the father is introduced into
the house a strange priest, in the capacity of a

spiritual guide, and the guardian of consciences, under aspect of a teacher. For this the priests without doubt are to be blamed ; but still more guilty are the parents, for permitting the priest to take their places at the domestic hearth. With these conditions, the citizens and the civil power must not be surprised if the edifice they have erected tumbles, and crushes them with its ruins. Such is the consequence of the separation of Church and State.

III

When, early in the forties, the king of Prussia learnt that some of the citizens of Berlin had forsaken the Christian Church, he expressed surprise, and asked with a smile : " What church, then, they were about to join ? " In the west of Europe, this question would be meaningless, nowadays. Half-a-century ago it was believed that he who abandoned Christianity had left the firm ground to live suspended in space. But, nowadays, to be without religion is a symptom of steadfastness, not of levity.

In the Middle Ages an unbeliever was regarded as a madman ; a madman at the same time so repulsive and dangerous that he was delivered to the stake.

At that time there was no place for unbelieving citizens, but there were believers deprived of the right of citizenship, vagabonds and outlaws to whom the State refused the protection of the law, and who sought the protection of their feudal lords, those mighty vassals who repudiated the authority of the State, and might even enter upon conflict with their suzerains.

In our time a subject who declared himself independent of the State, who refused to pay taxes, to render military service, and to recognise authority, in short, to be his own government, would, as unbelievers in the Middle Ages, be declared insane ; but, instead of being burnt at the stake, would either be forced to submit to the lawful authorities or be expelled his country. He might be transported to other territories, where also he would be reduced to submission or expelled.

At the present day we may freely reject religion and the Church, but we must not deny the State. The State guarantees the enjoyment of social life in all its plenitude, while the Church no longer rules over social life as it ruled before. Our time is distinguished by an attempt to subject all human relations to the power of the State. If the Church were to pretend to dominion over even half of them, it would meet from all sides with obstacles and opposition.

Notwithstanding the liberty everywhere extolled, we tend in all things to fall under the power of the State. We establish laws and regulations for every important condition of our social life ; many formally demand complete centralisation, and the assimilation of individual conditions by legislative measures. If but a shoe pinches we demand regulation by the State ; if half-a-dozen individuals complain of a burden, they must seek redress in a petition to the Government. In former times they would have sought redress in the Church. The doctrine that all individual life must be absorbed in the life of the community, and that the life of the community must be concentrated in the State, and regulated by it, is the chief motive of the Socialist ideal; and as this doctrine in a distinct or indistinct form has taken root in the strongest minds, the simplest man is often unconsciously in sympathy with the Socialist.

It is impossible to ignore that a change has taken place in the relationship of the Church to the community of believers which sustains it. The people will no longer admit of the re-establishment of the old relationship of the Church to its flock with its interference in individual and domestic life, in the life of the community, in politics, and in the economy of society. The State establishes law after law; the Church not only no longer promulgates no new dogmas, but cannot as before insist formally and rigorously upon the interpretation and application of its teachings.

In appearance, therefore, the Church has lost all authority, as contrasted with the disproportionate powers usurped by the State. In reality, however, this is not so, for the Church relies on the spiritual forces of the people (*Riehl*).

IV

The oldest and most familiar system of relationship of Church to State is the system of Established or State Churches. Out of the multitude of religions, the State adopts and recognises as the true faith one, which it maintains and protects exclusively, to the prejudice of all remaining Churches and religions. This prejudice in general means that the remaining Churches are not recognised as true, or entirely true, but practically it is expressed in many forms, with innumerable shadows, from non-recognition and alienation to persecution. In all cases where this system is in force the estranged faiths submit to more or less diminution in honour and prerogative as compared with the established faith. The State must not be the representative of the material interests of society alone; were it so, it would deprive itself of religious forces and would abandon its spiritual community with the people. The stronger will the State be, the more important in the eyes of the masses, the more firmly it stands as their spiritual representative.

Under these conditions alone will the sentiment of respect for the law, and of confidence in the power of the State, be maintained and strengthened among the people. No considerations for the safety of the State, for its prosperity and advantage, no moral principle even, is itself sufficient to strengthen the bonds between the people and its rulers; for the moral principle is never steadfast, and it loses its fundamental base when it is bereft of the sanction of religion. This force of cohesion will, without doubt, be lost to that State which, in the name of impartial relationship to every religious belief, cuts itself loose from all. The confidence of the people in its rulers is founded on faith—that is, not only on identity of religious profession, but on the simple conviction that its rulers have faith them-

selves and rule according to it. Even the heathen
and Mahometan peoples have more confidence and
respect for a Government which stands on the firm
principles of faith—whatever that faith may be—
than for a Government which acknowledges no faith,
and is indifferent to all.

Such is the indisputable superiority of the Established Church.   Nevertheless, in the course of
centuries the circumstances in which this system
established itself have changed, and new conditions
have arisen which combine to make its operation
more difficult than before. When the first foundations of European civilisation and politics were laid,
the Christian State was strong by its whole and
indissoluble alliance with the united Christian
Church.   Since then the Christian Church has
broken up into innumerable sects and religions, each
of which pretends to be the only true doctrine and
the only true Church.   By such means the State
was confronted with many different doctrines, which
divided the support of the people.   With the
destruction of universal communion in a single
faith, the time must come when the dominant
Church supported by the State becomes the Church
of an insignificant minority, and loses sympathy
with, or is deprived of the sympathy of, the mass of
the people.   When this condition has once been
realised, grave troubles inevitably arise in the definition of the relationship of the State and its Established Church to the Churches to which the majority
of the people belongs.

At the end of the eighteenth century there began in Western Europe a change from the ancient system to the system of equalisation of Christian beliefs before the State, with the exception, however, from this equality of sectarians and Jews. The State accepted Christianity as the essential base of its being and of social order, and adherence to one or another of the Churches or religions became obligatory for every citizen.

Since 1848 this relation of the State and Church has essentially changed; the rising waves of Liberalism have overthrown the ancient rampart, and threaten to undermine the foundations of the Christian State. The separation of Church and State is advocated everywhere; the State has no concern with the Church—all men are free to believe what they will, or not to believe at all. The fundamental principles (*Grundrechte*) promulgated by the Frankfort Parliament in 1848-9, are the embodiment of this doctrine, and, although they soon ceased to be operative legislation served and serve to-day as the ideal for the establishment of Liberal principles in the legislation of Western Europe in modern times.

Political and civil rights no longer depend upon religion, or even upon adherence to one or another of the Churches or sects. Concerning religion the State asks no questions. The solemnisation of marriage, and other acts of the civil condition, no longer appertain to the Church. The full freedom of

mixed marriages is proclaimed, and the religious principle of the indissolubility of marriage is destroyed
by facility of divorce, removed from the jurisdiction
of the ecclesiastical courts.

In view of all these changes, which in France
have gone so far as the official renunciation of faith,
and even so far as violence against the Church,
we may well ask: Can the modern State be
called a Christian State? But here we observe the
inconsistency which we have noticed in individuals who, having severed their organic alliance
with the Christian Church, at the same time lead
a life in accordance with its principles. The
modern State, while severing its organic alliance
with the Christian Church, cannot dispense with
the forms and ceremonies which it practises. The
Churches and their ministers are maintained out
of the treasury of the State; the army and all
public institutions are provided with spiritual
directors; the Christian festivals are civil holidays:
in the public service, in the courts of justice, the
oath retains its obligatory force. In Germany there
is no State Church, nevertheless, the supre-
macy (Kirchenhoheit) in the Evangelical Church
appertains to the chief of the State; in Parliament, and in all social affairs the government may
not ignore the parties with their different religious
professions. In England with its absolute equality
of all religions on Liberal principles, not only the
sovereign but the greatest dignitaries of State must
belong to the Anglican Church. In the United
States also perfect religious equality obtains. To all
Churches, to all religious communities, the relations

of the State are identical with its relations to private corporations. In the State schools the study of the Law of God, and the obligatory reading of the Scriptures are forbidden. Yet Congress opens its sessions with prayer, with the participation of an ecclesiastic. The State maintains ministers of religion in the army and on the fleet. From time to time the President appoints days for thanksgiving and repentance. A stern law upholds the sanctity of the Sabbath. In certain States the severest punishments are ordained for swearing and blasphemy.

Does it not follow then that the atheist State is no more than an impossible Utopia, infidelity being negation of the State? Religion and, above all, Christianity is the source of every right in political and civil life, and of all true culture. It is for this reason, then, that those political parties the most inimical to social order, parties radically denying the State, are the first to declare that religion is a personal thing in which private and individual interests alone are concerned.

VI

The system of a " Free Church in a Free State " is founded on abstract principles and hypotheses. It embodies not the principle of belief, but the principle of religious indifferentism, and it is associated with doctrines which inculcate, not tolerance and respect, but a manifest or tacit contempt for religion, as an outworn factor of the psychical

development of individual and national life.   In
the abstract conception of this system, which is the
product of the latest rationalism, the Church appears
as a political institution of abstract construction, with
a definite aim ; or as a private corporation established
likewise with a definite aim, as other corporations
recognised by the State.   The conception of this
aim is abstract also, for on it are reflected the diverse
shades associated with one or the other conception
of religion, from abstract respect for religion, as the
highest element of psychical life, to fanatical contempt for it as the basest factor, and as an element
of danger and disintegration.   Thus, in the construction of this system we see at the first glance the
ambiguity and indistinctness of its fundamental
principles and propositions.

What the consequence of this system in practice
will be must be proved by the experience of ages
and generations.   Hitherto our experience has been
insignificant compared with the experience of the
many centuries through which the ancient system
acted and acts.   But it is easy to foresee that the
new system cannot be durable, for it does not
correspond with the essential needs and conditions of
human nature.   However logically we may affirm
the proposition, that "all Churches and all religions
are equal, and all the same," this proposition will
not be admitted unreservedly by a single man
who preserves religion in his soul, and feels the
need of it.   Such a man will answer, "Yes, all faiths
are equal ; but for me mine is best."   Were the
State to establish to-day the severest and most precise
equalisation of all Churches and religions before the

law, to-morrow signs would appear that the relative powers of the various religions were no longer equal ; in thirty or fifty years from the time of legal equalisation, we should find that one enjoyed a preponderating influence, dominated minds, and determined judgments ; and this, either because it approximated more closely to canonical truth, or because its doctrine and ritual corresponded better to the character of the people, or because its organisation and discipline were more perfect and increased its opportunities for systematic activity, or because it counted more devoted adherents and workers. Of this there are many instances. In Ireland British legislation has established equality of the rival Churches. But it does not, therefore, result that the Churches are equal. In reality, the Roman Catholic Church, at the moment of its legal enfranchisement, received full power to extend and consolidate throughout the country its predominant influence, not only on individual minds, but on all the political institutions of the country—on the courts of justice, the administration, and the schools.

The constitution of the United States requires the non-interference of the State in religion. The consequence is that the Roman Catholic is rapidly becoming the dominant Church in America. In North America it enjoys a greater liberty of action than in any European state. Restricted by no relation to the State, submitting to no control, the Pope distributes dioceses, appoints bishops, founds spiritual orders and convents in vast numbers, and weaves over the whole territory a close network of ecclesiastical agents and institutions. The Papacy controls the great mass of Catholics, yearly increasing with the arrival of fresh immigrants, and counts already as its own a fourth of the total population, while the remaining three quarters is divided into a multitude of sects. Taking advantage of all opportunities to evade the law, the Catholic Church has increased its power to immense proportions. The administration of whole states is in its hand or under its influence. In many large towns the municipal government depends exclusively from the Catholics. The Catholic Church disposes of millions of votes in a country where from numbers alone depends the whole administration of domestic and foreign affairs. From the height of the principle of religious equality, the State regards its dominion with indifference. But the future will show how long this favourite theory will obtain in the United States.

Meanwhile, its defenders ask what concern has the State with inequalities which arise, not by virtue of privileges or legal limitations, but in consequence of the internal strength or internal weakness of private corporations? The law cannot prevent such inequality.

But this is an evasion of the question, or a solution only in theory. On paper any absurdity may be justified, and raised to the dignity of a harmonious system. On paper it is easy to establish a clear boundary between the domain of politics and the domain of religion and morals. In reality, it is not so. Men must not be regarded as intelligent machines to be disposed as the general disposes his troops when he forms a line of battle. Every man embodies a world of moral and spiritual life, from which proceed the impulses which determine his activity in all the spheres of life ; but the chief, the central impulse springs from faith and from the conviction of truth. The theorist only, reasoning independently of actuality, or ignoring it, will be satisfied by the ironical question : What is truth ? In the souls of men this question lives as the gravest question of life ; a question, requiring not a negative, but a positive answer.

Thus the free State may decree that the free Church concerns it not ; but the free Church, if it be truly founded on faith, will not accept this proposition, and will not endure indifferent relations to the free State. The Church cannot abdicate its influence on civil and social life, and the greater its activity—the stronger its consciousness of internal working forces, the less is it possible for it to tolerate indifferent relations to the State ; nor can such relations be tolerated if the Church is not to abjure its duties and abandon its divine mission. On the Church lies the duty of teaching and direction. To the Church pertains the administration of the sacraments, and the performance of ceremonies associated with the gravest acts of civil life. In this activity the Church of necessity is brought into constant contact with public and civil life : of this, marriage and education are sufficient instances. Thus, as the State, denying the Church, assumes control exclusively of the civil part of such affairs and renounces all authority in the spiritual-religious part, the Church assumes the functions surrendered by the State, and, in separation from it, takes possession, little by little but fully and exclusively, of those moral and religious influences which constitute for the State an indispensable element of strength. The State remains master alone of material and, it may be, of intellectual forces, but both one and the other are vain when unsupported by the forces of faith. Little by little, therefore, instead of the imagined equality of influence of the State and Church in a political alliance, inequality and an-tagonism appear. The position in any case is an abnormal one, which must lead either to the pre-dominance of the Church over the apparently dominant State, or to revolution.

Such are the hidden dangers of the system, so lauded by Liberal theorists, of severance of Church and State. The system of State or Established Churches has many defects, many inconven-iences, and many difficulties ; it does not preclude the possibility of antagonism or conflict. But it is absurd to suppose that it has outlived its time, and that the formula of Cavour is the only key to the solution of all the difficulties of the most difficult of questions. The formula of Cavour is the fruit of that political doctrinarianism which regards all questions of faith merely as political questions of the equalisation of rights. It lacks spiritual insight, as lacked it another famous political formula, Liberty, Equality, and Fraternity, which to the present day weighs upon superficial minds with a fatal burden. In both cases the passionate apostles of freedom mistake in assuming freedom in equality. Bitter experience has proven a hundred times that freedom does not depend from equality, and that equality is in no wise freedom. It is equally absurd to believe that the equalisation of Churches and religions before the State must result in freedom of belief. The history of modern times demonstrates that freedom and equality are not identical, and that freedom in no way depends from equality.

THE NEW DEMOCRACY

WHAT is this freedom by which so many minds are agitated, which inspires so many insensate actions, so many wild speeches, which leads the people so often to misfortune? In the democratic sense of the word, freedom is the right of political power, or, to express it otherwise, the right to participate in the government of the State. This universal aspiration for a share in government has no constant limitations, and seeks no definite issue, but incessantly extends, so that we might apply to it the words of the ancient poet about dropsy: *crescit indulgens sibi.* For ever extending its base, the new Democracy now aspires to universal suffrage—a fatal error, and one of the most remarkable in the history of mankind. By this means, the political power so passionately demanded by Democracy would be shattered into a number of infinitesimal bits, of which each citizen acquires a single one. What will he do with it, then? how will he employ it? In the result it has undoubtedly been shown that in the attainment of this aim Democracy violates its sacred formula of "Freedom indissolubly joined with Equality." It is shown that this apparently equal distribution of "freedom" among all involves the total destruction of equality. Each vote, representing an inconsiderable fragment of power, by itself signifies nothing;

26

an aggregation of votes alone has a relative value. The result may be likened to the general meetings of shareholders in public companies. By themselves individuals are ineffective, but he who controls a number of these fragmentary forces is master of all power, and directs all decisions and dispositions. We may well ask in what consists the superiority of Democracy. Everywhere the strongest man becomes master of the State; sometimes a fortunate and resolute general, sometimes a monarch or administrator with knowledge, dexterity, a clear plan of action, and a determined will. In a Democracy, the real rulers are the dexterous manipulators of votes, with their placemen, the mechanics who so skilfully operate the hidden springs which move the puppets in the arena of democratic elections. Men of this kind are ever ready with loud speeches lauding equality; in reality, they rule the people as any despot or military dictator might rule it. The extension of the right to participate in elections is regarded as progress and as the conquest of freedom by democratic theorists, who hold that the more numerous the participants in political rights, the greater is the probability that all will employ this right in the interests of the public welfare, and for the increase of the freedom of the people. Experience proves a very different thing. The history of mankind bears witness that the most necessary and fruitful reforms—the most durable measures—emanated from the supreme will of statesmen, or from a minority enlightened by lofty ideas and deep knowledge, and that, on the contrary, the extension of the representative principle is accom-

panied by an abasement of political ideas and the
vulgarisation of opinions in the mass of the electors.
It shows also that this extension—in great States—
was inspired by secret aims to the centralisation of
power, or led directly to dictatorship. In France,
universal suffrage was suppressed with the end of
the Terror, and was re-established twice merely to
affirm the autocracy of the two Napoleons.   In
Germany, the establishment of universal suffrage
served merely to strengthen the high authority of a
famous statesman who had acquired popularity by
the success of his policy. What its ultimate consequences will be, Heaven only knows!

The manipulation of votes in the game of
Democracy is of the commonest occurrence in most
European states, and its falsehood, it would seem,
has been exposed to all ; yet few dare openly
to rebel against it. The unhappy people must bear
the burden, while the Press, herald of a supposititious
public opinion, stifles the cry of the people with
its shibboleth, " Great is Diana of the Ephcsians."
But to an impartial mind, all this is nothing better
than a struggle of parties, and a shuffling with
numbers and names. The voters, by themselves
inconsiderable unities, acquire a value in the hands
of dexterous agents.   This value is realised by
many means — mainly, by bribery in innumerable forms, from gifts of money and trifling
articles, to the distribution of places in the services,
the financial departments, and the administration.
Little by little a class of electors has been formed
which lives by the sale of votes to one or another

of the political organisations. So far has this gone in France, for instance, that serious, intelligent, and industrious citizens in immense numbers abstain from voting, through the difficulty of contending with the cliques of political agents. With bribery go violence and threats, and reigns of terror are organised at elections, by the help of which the respective cliques advance their candidates; hence the stormy scenes at electoral demonstrations, in which arms have been used, and the field of battle strewn with the bodies of the killed and wounded.

Organisation and bribery — these are the two mighty instruments which are employed with such success for the manipulation of the mass of electors. Such methods are in no way new. Thucydides depicts in vivid colours their employment in the ancient republics of Greece. The history of the Roman Republic presents monstrous examples of corruption as the chief instrument of factions at elections. But in our times a new means has been found of working the masses for political aims, and joining them in adventitious alliances by provoking a fictitious community of views. This is the art of rapid and dexterous generalisation of ideas, the composition of phrase and formulas, disseminated with the confidence of burning conviction as the last word of science, as dogmas of politicology, as infallible appreciations of events, of men, and of institutions. At one time it was believed that the faculty of analysing facts, and deducing general principles was the privilege of a few enlightened minds and deep thinkers; now it is considered an

universal attainment, and, under the name of convictions, the generalities of political science have become a sort of current money, coined by newspapers
and rhetoricians.

The faculty of seizing and assimilating on faith
these abstract ideas has spread among the mass, and
become infectious, more especially to men insuffi-
ciently or superficially educated, who constitute the
great majority everywhere. This tendency of the
people is exploited with success by politicians who
seek power; the art of creating generalities serves
for them as a most convenient instrument. All
deduction proceeds by the path of abstraction;
from a number of facts the immaterial are eliminated, the essential elements collated, classified, and
general formulas deduced. It is plain that the
justice and value of these formulas depend upon how
many of the premisses are essential, and how many
of those eliminated are irrelevant. The speed and
ease with which abstract conclusions are arrived at
are explained by the unceremonious methods observed
in this process of selection of relevant facts and in
their treatment. Hence the great success of orators,
and the extraordinary effect of the abstractions
which they cast to the people. The crowd is easily
attracted by commonplaces and generalities invested
in sonorous phrases; it cares nothing for proof which
is inaccessible to it; thus is formed unanimity of
thought, an unanimity fictitious and visionary, but
in its consequences actual enough. This is called
the "voice of the people," with the pendant, the

"voice of God." It is a deplorable error. The ease with which men are drawn by commonplaces leads everywhere to extreme demoralisation of public thought, and to the weakening of the political sense of the people. Of this, France to-day presents a striking example, and England also has not escaped the infection.

THE GREAT FALSEHOOD OF
OUR TIME

I

THAT which is founded on falsehood cannot be right. Institutions founded on false principles cannot be other than false themselves. This truth has been demonstrated by the bitter experience of ages and generations.

Among the falsest of political principles is the principle of the sovereignty of the people, the principle that all power issues from the people, and is based upon the national will—a principle which has unhappily become more firmly established since the time of the French Revolution. Thence proceeds the theory of Parliamentarism, which, up to the present day, has deluded much of the so-called "intelligence," and unhappily infatuated certain foolish Russians. It continues to maintain its hold on many minds with the obstinacy of a narrow fanaticism, although every day its falsehood is exposed more clearly to the world.

In what does the theory of Parliamentarism consist? It is supposed that the people in its assemblies makes its own laws, and elects responsible officers to execute its will. Such is the ideal conception. Its immediate realisation is impossible. The historical development of society necessitates that local communities increase in numbers and complexity;

that separate races be assimilated, or, retaining their polities and languages, unite under a single flag, that territory extend indefinitely: under such conditions direct government by the people is impracticable. The people must, therefore, delegate its right of power to its representatives, and invest them with administrative autonomy. These representatives in turn cannot govern immediately, but are compelled to elect a still smaller number of trustworthy persons—ministers—to whom they entrust the preparation and execution of the laws, the apportionment and collection of taxes, the appointment of subordinate officials, and the disposition of the militant forces.

In the abstract this mechanism is quite symmetrical: for its proper operation many conditions are essential. The working of the political machine is based on impersonal forces constantly acting and completely balanced. It may act successfully only when the delegates of the people abdicate their personalities; when on the benches of Parliament sit mechanical fulfillers of the people's behests; when the ministers of State remain impersonal, absolute executors of the will of the majority; when the elected representatives of the people are capable of understanding precisely, and executing conscientiously, the programme of activity, mathematically expressed, which has been delivered to them. Given such conditions the machine would work exactly, and would accomplish its purpose. The law would actually embody the will of the people; administrative measures would actually emanate from Parliament; the pillars of the State would rest actually on the

C

elective assemblies, and each citizen would directly
and consciously participate in the management of
public affairs.

Such is the theory. Let us look at the practice.
Even in the classic countries of Parliamentarism it
would satisfy not one of the conditions enumerated.
The elections in no way express the will of the
electors. The popular representatives are in no way
restricted by the opinions of their constituents, but
are guided by their own views and considerations,
modified by the tactics of their opponents. In reality,
ministers are autocratic, and they rule, rather than
are ruled by, Parliament. They attain power, and
lose power, not by virtue of the will of the people,
but through immense personal influence, or the influence of a strong party which places them in power,
or drives them from it. They dispose of the force
and resources of the nation at will, they grant
immunities and favours, they maintain a multitude
of idlers at the expense of the people, and they fear
no censure while they enjoy the support in Parliament of a majority which they maintain by the
distribution of bounties from the rich tables which
the State has put at their disposal. In reality, the
ministers are as irresponsible as the representatives
of the people. Mistakes, abuse of power, and arbitrary
acts, are of daily occurrence, yet how often do we
hear of the grave responsibility of a minister? It may
be once in fifty years a minister is tried for his crimes,
with a result contemptible when compared with the
celebrity gained by the solemn procedure.

Were we to attempt a true definition of Parliament,
we should say that Parliament is an institution serving

for the satisfaction of the personal ambition, vanity, and self-interest of its members. The institution of Parliament is indeed one of the greatest illustrations of human delusion. Enduring in the course of centuries the tyranny of autocratic and oligarchical governments, and ignoring that the evils of autocracy are the evils of society itself, men of intellect and knowledge have laid the responsibility for their misfortunes on their rulers and on their systems of government, and imagined that by substituting for these systems government by the will of the people, or representative government, society would be delivered from all the evils and violence which it endured. What is the result? The result is that, *mutato nomine*, all has remained essentially as before, and men, retaining the weaknesses and failings of their nature, have transfused in the new institutions their former impulses and tendencies. As before, they are ruled by personal will, and in the interests of privileged persons, but this personal will is no longer embodied in the person of the sovereign, but in the person of the leader of a party ; and privilege no longer belongs to an aristocracy of birth, but to a majority ruling in Parliament and controlling the State.

On the pediment of this edifice is inscribed : " All for the Public Good." This is no more than a lying formula : Parliamentarism is the triumph of egoism— its highest expression. All here is calculated to the service of the ego. In the Parliamentary fiction, the representative, as such, surrenders his personality, and serves as the embodiment of the will and opinions of his constituents ; in reality, the constituents in the

very act of election surrender all their rights in favour
of their representative.   In his addresses and speeches
the candidate for election lays constant emphasis
upon this fiction ; he reiterates his phrases about
the public welfare ; he is nothing but a servant of the
people ; he will forget himself and his interests for
its sake.   But these are words, words, words alone
— temporary steps of the staircase by which he
climbs to the height he aspires to, and which he
casts away when he needs them no longer.   Then,
so far from beginning to work for society, society
becomes the instrument of his aims.   To him his
constituents are a herd, an aggregation of votes,
and he, as their possessor, resembles those rich
nomads whose flocks constitute their whole capital
—the foundation of their power and eminence in
society.   Thus is developed to perfection the art of
playing on the instincts and passions of the mass,
in order to attain the personal ends of ambition
and power.   The people loses all importance for its
representative, until the time arrives when it is to
be played upon again ; then false and flattering and
lying phrases are lavished as before ; some are
suborned by bribery, others terrified by threats —
the long chain of manœuvres spun which forms an
invariable factor of Parliamentarism.   Yet this electoral farce continues to deceive humanity, and to be
regarded as an institution which crowns the edifice
of State.   Poor humanity !   In truth may it be
said : *mundus vult decipi, decipiatur.*

Thus the representative principle works in practice.
The ambitious man comes before his fellow-citizens,
and strives by every means to convince them that he

more than any other is worthy of their confidence. What motives impel him to this quest? It is hard to believe that he is impelled by disinterested zeal for the public good.

In our time, nothing is so rare as men imbued with a feeling of solidarity with the people, ready for labour and self-sacrifice for the public good ; this is the ideal nature, but such natures are little inclined to come into contact with the baseness of the world. He who, in the consciousness of duty, is capable of disinterested service of the community does not descend to the soliciting of votes, or the crying of his own praise at election meetings in loud and vulgar phrases. Such men manifest their strength in their own work, in a small circle of congenial friends, and scorn to seek popularity in the noisy market-place. If they approach the crowd, it is not to flatter it, or to pander to its basest instincts and tendencies, but to condemn its follies and expose its depravity. To men of duty and honour the procedure of elections is repellent ; the only men who regard it without abhorrence are selfish, egoistic natures, which wish thereby to attain their personal ends. To acquire popularity such men have little scruple in assuming the mask of ardour for the public good. They cannot and must not be modest, for with modesty they would not be noticed or spoken of. By their positions, and by the parts which they have chosen, they are forced to be hypocrites and liars ; they must cultivate, fraternise with, and be amiable to their opponents to gain their suffrages ; they must lavish promises, knowing that they cannot fulfil them ; and they must pander to the basest tendencies and prejudices of the masses to acquire majorities for themselves. What honourable nature would accept such a rôle? Describe it in a novel, the reader would be repelled, but in elections the same reader gives his vote to the living *artiste* in the same rôle.

Parliamentary elections are a matter of art, having, as the military art, their strategy and tactics. The candidate is not brought into direct relations with his constituents. As intermediary stands the committee, a self-constituted institution, the chief weapon of which is impudence. The candidate, if he is unknown, begins by assembling a number of friends and patrons. Then all together organise a hunt among the rich and weak-minded aristocrats of the neighbourhood, whom they convince that it is their duty, their prerogative, and their privilege to stand at the head as leaders of public opinion. There is little difficulty in finding stupid or idle people who are taken in by this trickery; and then, above their signatures, appear manifestoes in the newspapers and on the walls and pillars, which seduce the mass, eager always in the pursuit of names, titles, and wealth. Thus are formed the committees which direct and control the elections. They resemble in much public companies. The composition of the committee is carefully elaborated: it contains some effective forces — energetic men who pursue at all costs material ends; while simple and frivolous idlers constitute the ballast. The committees organise meetings, where speeches are delivered, where he who possesses a powerful voice, and can quickly and skilfully string phrases together, produces always an impression on the mass, and acquires notoriety—thus comes out the candidate for future election, who, with favouring conditions, may even supersede him whom he came to help. Phrases, and nothing but phrases, dominate these meetings. The crowd hears only him who cries the loudest, and who with impudence and with flattery conforms most artfully to the impulses and tendencies of the mob.

On the day of polling few give their votes intelligently : these are the individual, influential electors whom it has been worth while to convince in private. The mass of the electors, after the practice of the herd, votes for one of the candidates nominated by the committees. Not one exactly knows the man, or considers his character, his capacity, his convictions ; all vote merely because they have heard his name so often. It would be vain to struggle against this herd. If a level-headed elector wished to act intelligently in such a grave affair, and not to give way to the violence of the committee, he would have to abstain altogether, or to give his vote for his candidate according to his conviction. However he might act, he could not prevent the election of the candidate favoured by the mass of frivolous, indifferent, and prejudiced electors.

In theory, the elected candidate must be the favourite of the majority ; in fact, he is the favourite of a minority, sometimes very small, but representing an organised force, while the majority, like sand, has no coherence, and is therefore incapable of resisting the clique and the faction. In theory, the election

favours the intelligent and capable; in reality, it
favours the pushing and impudent.   It might be
thought that education, experience, conscientiousness
in work, and wisdom in affairs, would be essential
requirements in the candidate; in reality, whether
these qualities exist or not, they are in no way
needed in the struggle of the election, where the
essential qualities are audacity, a combination of
impudence and oratory, and even some vulgarity,
which invariably acts on the masses; modesty, in
union with delicacy of feeling and thought, is
worth nothing.

Thus comes forth the representative of the people,
thus he acquires his power.   How does he employ it,
how will he turn it to advantage?   If energetic by
nature he will attempt to form a party; if he is of an
ordinary nature, then he joins himself to one party
or another.   The leader of a party above all things
requires a resolute will.   This is an organic quality,
like physical strength, and does not by any means
inevitably accompany moral excellence.   With
limited intellect, with infinite egoism, and even
wickedness, with base and dishonest tendencies,
a man with a strong will may become a leader in
Parliament, and may control the decisions of a party
which contains men far surpassing him in moral
and intellectual worth.   Such may be the character
of a ruling force in Parliament.   To this should be
joined another decisive force — eloquence.   This
also is a natural faculty, involving neither moral
character, nor high intellectual culture.   A man may
be a deep thinker, a poet, a skilful general, a subtle
jurist, an experienced legislator, and at the same

time may not enjoy the gift of fluent speech, while, on the contrary, one with ordinary intellectual capacity and knowledge may possess a special gift of eloquence. The union of this gift with a plenitude of intellectual power is a rare and exceptional phenomenon in Parliamentary life. The most brilliant improvisations, which have given glory to orators, and determined grave decisions, when read are as colourless and contemptible as descriptions of scenes enacted in former times by celebrated actors and singers. Experience shows that in great assemblies the decision does not belong to reason, but to daring and brilliancy; that the arguments most effective on the mass are not the most symmetrical—the most truly taken from the nature of things, but those expressed in sounding words and phrases, artfully selected, constantly reiterated, and calculated on the instinct of baseness always dominant in the people. The masses are easily drawn by outbursts of empty declamation, and under such influences often form sudden decisions, which they regret on cold-blooded consideration of the affair.

Therefore, when the leader of a party combines with a strong will the gift of eloquence, he assumes his first rôle on an open stage before the whole world. If he does not possess this gift he stands like a stage manager behind the scenes and directs thence all the movements of the Parliamentary spectacle, allotting the parts to others, appointing orators to speak for him, employing in his work all the rich but irresolute intellects of his party to do his thinking for him.

What is a Parliamentary party? In theory,

it is an alliance of men with common convictions, joining forces for the realisation of their views in legislation and administration. But this description applies only to small parties; the large party, which alone is an effective force in Parliament, is formed under the influence only of personal ambition, and centres itself around one commanding personality. By nature, men are divided into two classes—those who tolerate no power above them, and therefore of necessity strive to rule others; and those who by their nature dread the responsibility inseparable from independent action, and who shrink from any resolute exercise of will. These were born for submission, and together constitute a herd, which follows the men of will and resolution, who form the minority. Thus the most talented persons submit willingly, and gladly entrust to stronger hands the control of affairs and the moral responsibility for their direction. Instinctively they seek a leader, and become his obedient instruments, inspired by the conviction that he will lead them to victory —and, often, to spoil. Thus all the important actions of Parliament are controlled by the leaders of the party, who inspire all decisions, who lead in combat, and profit by victory. The public sessions are no more than a spectacle for the mass. Speeches are delivered to sustain the fiction of Parliamentarism, but seldom a speech by itself affects the decision of Parliament in a grave affair. Speech-making serves for the glory of orators, for the increase of their popularity, and the making of their careers; only on rare occasions does it affect the distribution of votes. Majorities and minorities are usually decided before the session begins.

Such is the complicated mechanism of the Parliamentary farce; such is the great political lie which dominates our age. By the theory of Parliamentarism, the rational majority must rule; in practice, the party is ruled by five or six of its leaders who exercise all power. In theory, decisions are controlled by clear arguments in the course of Parliamentary debates; in practice, they in no wise depend from debates, but are determined by the wills of the leaders and the promptings of personal interest. In theory, the representatives of the people consider only the public welfare; in practice, their first consideration is their own advancement, and the interests of their friends. In theory, they must be the best citizens; in practice, they are the most ambitious and impudent. In theory, the elector gives his vote for his candidate because he knows him and trusts him; in practice, the elector gives his vote for a man whom he seldom knows, but who has been forced on him by the speeches of an interested party. In theory, Parliamentary business is directed by experience, good sense, and unselfishness; in practice, the chief motive powers are a firm will, egoism, and eloquence.

Such is the Parliamentary institution, exalted as the summit and crown of the edifice of State. It is sad to think that even in Russia there are men who aspire to the establishment of this falsehood among us; that our professors glorify to their young pupils representative government as the ideal of political science; that our newspapers pursue it in their articles and feuilletons, under the name of justice and order, without troubling to examine without prejudice the working of the parliamentary machine. Yet even where centuries have sanctified its existence, faith already decays; the Liberal intelligence exalts it, but the people groans under its despotism, and recognises its falsehood. We may not see, but our children and grandchildren assuredly will see, the overthrow of this idol, which contemporary thought in its vanity continues still to worship.

II

The philosophy of the school of Rousseau has done much evil to humanity. This philosophy took possession of many minds; but at the same time it was all based on one false idea of human perfectibility, and on the assumption in every individual of capacity to comprehend and appreciate those principles of social organisation which it proclaimed.

The prevalent doctrine of the perfection of Democracy and of democratic government, stands on the same delusive foundation. This doctrine presupposes the capacity of the people to understand subtleties of political science which have a clear and substantial existence in the minds of its apostles only. Precision of knowledge is attainable only by the few minds which constitute the aristocracy of intellect; the mass, always and everywhere, is *vulgus*, and its conceptions of necessity are vulgar.

Democracy is the most complicated and the most burdensome system of government recorded in the history of humanity. For this reason it has never appeared save as a transitory manifestation, with few exceptions giving place before long to other systems. It is in no way surprising. The duty of the State is to act and to ordain: its dispositions are manifestations of a single will; without this government is inconceivable. But how can a multitude of men, or a popular assembly act with a single will? The upholder of Democracy takes little trouble over the decision of this question, but evades it by means of those favourite phrases and formulas:—"The will of the people," "public opinion," "the supreme decision of the nation," "the voice of the people is the voice of God," and others of a like nature. All these phrases signify that a multitude of men on a multitude of questions may form a common conclusion, and, conformably with their conclusion, arrive at a common decision. This may be possible sometimes, but only on the simplest questions. Where questions present the slightest complexity their decision by a numerous assembly is possible only through the medium of men capable of judging them in all their details, and of persuading the people to accept their judgment. In the number of complex questions may be counted all political questions requiring great concentration of the intellectual forces of the most capable and experienced statesmen; on such questions it would be absurd to rely upon unanimity of thought and will in a numerous assembly; the decision of the people could only be ruinous to the State. The enthusiasts

of Democracy contend that the people may manifest its will in affairs of State: this is a shallow
theory. In reality, we find that popular assemblies
are capable only of accepting—through enthusiasm
—the opinion expressed by individuals or by a
small minority — the opinion, for instance, of the
recognised leader of their party, of some local
worker of repute, of some organised association, or
the impersonal opinion of an influential journal.
Thus the discussions which precede decision become
an absurd comedy played on a vast stage by a multitude of heads and voices, the greater the multitude
the more unintelligible is the comedy, and the more
the *dénouement* depends upon fortuitous and disorderly
impulses.

To evade all these difficulties, the system of government by representation has been devised, a system
first established, and first justified by success, in
England. Thence, through the influence of fashion,
it spread to other European countries, but proved
successful only in the United States of America,
and there by tradition and by right. Yet even in
England, the land of their origin, representative
institutions are in a critical epoch of their history.
The very essence of the idea of representation has
submitted already to modifications which have
changed its primitive significance. In the beginning,
the assemblies of electors, on a strictly limited
franchise, sent to Parliament a certain number of
persons whose duty it was to represent the opinions
of the country, but who were not bound by any
definite instructions from the mass of their constituents. It was assumed that these elected repre-

sentatives were men who understood the real needs
of their country, and who were capable of justly
controlling the politics of the State. The problem
was resolved simply and plainly : it was required to
lessen, as far as possible, the difficulties of government by the people, by limiting in number the members of the assemblies summoned for the decision of
questions of State. These men appeared in the
capacity of free representatives of the people, and
not as instruments of the opinions of factions ; they
were bound by no instructions. But in the course
of time this system changed under the influence of
that fatal delusion about the great value of public
opinion, as enlightened by the periodical Press
which gave to the people the capacity to participate
directly in the decision of political questions. The
idea of representation altogether lost its form, and
reappeared as the idea of a *mandate*; or of specific
commission. From this point of view each representative is accounted a representative of the
dominant opinions of his constituency, or of the
party under the banner of which his victory was
gained. Thus he is no longer a representative of
the country, or of the people, but a delegate bound
by the instructions of his party. This change in
the very essence of the idea of representation was
the germ of the disease which has since devoured the
whole system of representative government. With
the disintegration of parties, elections have taken
the character of personal struggles restricted by
local interests and opinions, but independent of their
primary purpose of subserving the advantage of the
State. With the great increase of the numbers

in Parliament, most of the members, apart from the interests of party strife, are characterised by indifference to public affairs ; they neglect their duty of attendance at all sessions, and of direct participation in the consideration of business. Thus the work of legislation, and the direction of the gravest political affairs, become a play composed of formality, compromise, and fiction. The system of representation has falsified itself in practice.

These deplorable results are all the more manifest where the population of a country is of heterogeneous composition, comprising nationalities of many different races. The principle of nationality may be considered the touchstone which reveals the falseness and impracticability of parliamentary government. It is worthy of note that nationality first appeared as an active and irritant force in the government of the world when it came into contact with the new forms of Democracy. It is not easy to apprehend the nature of this new force, and the ends which it pursues ; but it is unquestionable that it contains the source of a grave and complex struggle, impending in the history of humanity, and it is vain to predict to what issues this struggle will lead. To-day we see the various races of composite States animated by passionate feelings of intolerance to the political institution which unites them in a single body, and by an equally passionate aspiration to independent government with their generally fictitious culture. We see this not only among those races which have had a history and a separate political life and culture, but, to an equal extent, among races which have never known inde-

pendence. Autocracy succeeded in evading or con-
ciliating such demands and outbreaks, not alone by
means of force, but by the equalisation of rights and
relations under the unifying power. But Democracy
has failed to settle these questions, and the instinct of
nationality serves as a disintegrating element. To
the supreme Parliament each race sends representatives, not of common political interests, but of racial
instincts, of racial exasperation, and of racial hatred,
both to the dominant race, to the sister races, and to
the political institution which unites them all. Such
is the unharmonious consequence of parliamentary
government in composite States, as Austria, in
our day, so vividly illustrates. Providence has
preserved our Russia, with its heterogeneous
racial composition, from like misfortunes. It is
terrible to think of our condition if destiny had
sent us the fatal gift—an All-Russian Parliament!
But that will never be.

III

The advocates of representative institutions point
to England as an illustration of their argument, but
to this reference we might apply the proverb, "They
hear a sound and know not where it is." Social
science in our day has begun to investigate the historic
and economic sources whence flow the peculiar institutions of the Anglo-Saxon, and to some extent
of the Scandinavian races, in comparison with the
institutions of the other European peoples. The
Anglo-Saxon race, from the time it appeared on the

D

stage of history up to the present day, has been distinguished by a strongly developed independent personality ; and in the political and economic sphere this attribute of the Anglo-Saxon race has been bound indissolubly with the steadfastness of its ancient institutions, with the firm organisation of its family life, with its local self-government, with those incomparable successes which it has attained by its energetic action, and with the influence which it enjoys in both hemispheres. By means of this personal energy, it was able in the beginning of its history to overthrow the strange Norman customs of its conquerors, and to consolidate its polity on those principles which it preserves unchanged to the present day. The essential characteristic of this polity lies in the relation of the citizen to the State. From early youth all are accustomed to independence, to fashion their own careers, and to earn their daily bread. Parents are not burdened with the duty of providing for the careers of their children, or of leaving to them inheritances. Landlords maintain their own properties, and encourage husbandry and handicraft. Local government is carried on by the personal participation of the people, inspired by sentiments of duty. The administrative institutions work without an army of officials maintained by the State, and looking to it for affluence and advancement. On these bases developed the representative institutions of free England, and for these reasons its Parliament is actually composed of representatives of local interests in close association with the land ; for these reasons its voice may be considered to a large extent as the voice of the people, and as the organ of national interests.

The other European communities were organised upon a different foundation — the foundation of common interest. Individuals were characterised less by an independent life than by their solidarity with the social alliance to which they belonged. Thence, in the course of social and political development, sprang the personal dependence of individuals from some social alliance; and in the end of ends from the State. These alliances, being in the beginning firm institutions—family, political, religious, social — strongly supported men in life and action, and men in turn strongly upheld the social and political edifice. In the course of time, these alliances either were dissolved, or lost their ancient political significance, yet men continued as before to seek assistance in the making of their careers from their families, their corporations, and finally from the State, whether monarchical or republican, and to lay on it the responsibility for misfortunes when these supports gave way. To put it shortly, each citizen looks to one of these powers to determine his career. Such a state of society is commonly found deficient in independent and self-reliant men, men who stand upon their own feet and master their fates, thus constituting an element of support to the State; while on the other hand, there exists a great multitude of men who seek support from the State, nourish themselves on its sap, and take from it much more than they give. Thence in such societies springs the immense increase on the one hand of the official class, and on the other hand of the so-called liberal professions. Thence, through decay of independent action, the extreme complexity of the administrative and legislative power which is obliged to provide for many, where each should be sufficient for himself. Society, in such a condition, gradually prepares for the advent of Socialistic doctrines ; and general reliance upon the State to provide for the prosperity of all gives birth to the idiotic theory of State Socialism. With such conditions of social development the Continental states established among themselves representative institutions on the Anglo-Saxon pattern, some with universal suffrage. It is plain that in the condition of society described above, with its light relation to social work, the people cannot elect true representatives of the land and of its immediate interests. The result of this we see in the deplorable fate of representative assemblies of Europe ; in the burdensome and hopeless position of the governing power which is indissolubly bound with them and of the people whose fate upon them depends.

What, then, shall we say of Slavonic races, peoples distinguished as they are by their peculiar polity and by the extreme youth of their culture—of Roumania, of unhappy Greece? Representative institutions established a disintegrating principle in the life of the Slavonic peoples resembling in some cases a bitter caricature of the West, which reminds us of Kruiloff's fable " Martuishko and the Spectacles."

IV

The greatest evil of constitutional government lies in the formation of ministries on parliamentary or party principles. Each political party aspires to seize the reins of government at any cost. The chief of the State must submit to the party which commands a majority in Parliament; a ministry is formed from the members of this party, and to maintain itself in power, enters upon a contest with the Opposition, which, in its turn, puts forth its whole strength to overthrow its rivals and take their places. If the chief of the State were to favour the minority and nominate his own ministry from its ranks, the new ministry would dissolve Parliament, and direct all its strength towards gaining a majority at the general election—with the support of this majority being enabled to withstand the Opposition. The place-men of the ministerial party vote always for the Government, not for the sake of upholding authority, not from intimate community of opinions, but because this Government in its turn supports the members of its party in power, and in its concomitant privileges, advantages, and emoluments. The natural instinct of all parties is to support their own in all circumstances, either on account of common interests, or simply by virtue of that gregarious instinct which impels mankind to unite in societies and to march into battle side by side.

It is evident, then, that unanimity of opinion has little influence, and that the pretended solicitude for the public welfare serves as the concealment of motives and instincts in no way related to it. This is the ideal of parliamentary government! It is a gross delusion to regard it as a guarantee of freedom. The absolute power of the sovereign is replaced by the absolute power of Parliament, with this difference only, that the person of the sovereign may embody

a rational will, while in Parliament all depends upon
accident, as the decisions of Parliament are brought
about by the majority. But as, by the side of the
majority constituted under the influence of party
gambling, a powerful minority exists, the will of the
majority is in no way the will of Parliament. Still
less can it be regarded as the will of the people,
the healthy mass of which abstains from participation in the comedy of parties, and turns away from it
with abhorrence. On the other hand, the corrupt
part of the population mingles willingly in politics,
and thereby is driven to a worse corruption, for the
chief motive of this comedy is appetite for power
and plunder. Political freedom becomes a fiction
maintained on paper by the paragraphs and phrases
of the constitution ; the principles of monarchical
power disappear ; the Liberal Democracy triumphs,
bringing into society disorder and violence with the
principles of infidelity and materialism, and proclaiming Liberty, Equality, and Fraternity—where there is
place neither for Liberty nor for Equality. Such
conditions inevitably lead to anarchy, from which
society can be saved alone by dictatorship — that
is, by the rehabilitation of autocracy in the government of the world.

The first example of representative government
by the people was set to modern Europe by
England. Towards the middle of the eighteenth
century French philosophers began to glorify
English institutions as models for universal imitation. But at that time French intelligence was
fascinated less by the principles of political freedom
than by the principle of religious toleration—in

other words, by the principle of unbelief—dissemi
nated by the English philosophers of the day,
Once sanctioned by France, which then gave tone
to the morals and the literature of the West,
the fashion of English institutions spread over
the whole European continent. Meantime, two
great events took place, of which one confirmed
this faith in representative institutions, while the
other shook it to its foundations. The republic
of the United States of America was established,
and its institutions, with the exceptions of monarchy
and aristocracy, modelled on the institutions of
England took root on the new soil steadfastly
and fruitfully. This success infatuated many minds,
above all, in France. On the other hand arose
the French Republic, and horrified the world
with the disorders, and violence of a revolutionary
Government. Everywhere arose a cry of indignation and abhorrence of French and of all democratic institutions. The dread of revolution was
imaged even in the internal politics of the British
Government. In 1815, under the influence of
political events, this feeling began to abate; and
again the intellect of Europe aspired to combine
political freedom with civil order in forms resembling
those of the English constitution; political Anglo-
mania was fashionable once more. Then followed
a series of attempts to realise the British ideal,
first in France, then in Spain and Portugal, then
in Holland and Belgium, and finally, in later times,
in Germany, in Italy, and in Austria. A faint
echo of this movement reached even Russia in
1825, in the insensate attempts of aristocratic

the people in the days of the great war of deliverance.   But, with a few trifling exceptions, representative institutions did not exist in Germany before
1847, when the King of Prussia established a peculiar
form of constitutional government which lasted no
longer than a year.   But it needed only the success
of the Paris mobs in destroying the French charter,
and dethroning their constitutional king, to revive
in Germany the popular movement with the co-
operation of the army.   In Berlin, in Vienna, in
Frankfort, national assemblies were established on
the model of the French.   Hardly a year had passed
when the Government overthrew them by military
violence.   The modern constitutions of Germany
and Austria emanated from the will of the sovereign,
and still await the judgment of history.

TRIAL BY JURY

THE following is the judgment of a famous English writer,* a profound student of history, on the jury system of his country :—

"Popular Government and Popular Justice were originally the same thing. The ancient democracies devoted much more time and attention to the exercise of civil and criminal jurisdiction than to the administration of their public affairs ; and, as a matter of fact, popular justice has lasted longer, has had a more continuous history, and has received much more observation and cultivation, than popular Government. . . . We have in England a relic of the ancient Popular Justice in the functions of the Jury. The Jury—technically known as the 'country'—is the old adjudicating Democracy, limited, modified, and improved, in accordance with the principles suggested by the experience of centuries, so as to bring it into harmony with modern ideas of judicial efficiency. The change which has had to be made in it is in the highest degree instructive. The Jurors are twelve, instead of a multitude. Their main business is to say 'Aye' or 'No' on questions which are doubtless important, but which turn on facts arising in the transactions of everyday life. In order that they may reach a conclusion, they are assisted by a system of contrivances and rules of the highest artificiality and elaboration. An expert presides over their investigations—the Judge, the representative of the rival and royal justice—and an entire literature is concerned with the conditions under which evidence on the facts in dispute may be laid before them. There is a rigid exclusion of all testimony which has a tendency to bias them unfairly. They are addressed, as of old, by the litigants or their advocates, but their inquiry concludes with a security unknown to antiquity, the summing-up of the expert President, who is bound by all the rules of his profession to the sternest impartiality. If he errs, or if they

* Sir Henry Maine.

59

flagrantly err, the proceedings may be quashed by a superior Court of experts. Such is Popular Justice, after ages of cultivation. Now it happens that the oldest Greek poet has left us a picture, certainly copied from reality, of what Popular Justice was in its infancy. The primitive Court is sitting; the question is ' guilty ' or ' not guilty.' The old men of the community give their opinions in turn; the adjudicating Democracy, the Commons, standing round about, applaud the opinion which strikes them most, and the applause determines the decision. The Popular Justice of the ancient republics was essentially of the same character. The adjudicating Democracy simply followed the opinion which most impressed them in the speech of the advocate or litigant. Nor is it in the least doubtful that, but for the sternly repressive authority of the presiding Judge, the modern English Jury would, in the majority of cases, blindly surrender its verdict to the persuasiveness of one or other of the counsel who have been retained to address it."—" Popular Government," pp. 89-91. London 1885.

These are the words of an Englishman, a profound student of his country's history, and a deep thinker. We involuntarily remember the fate of this unhappy institution in countries where the historical and economic conditions from which in England it sprang do not exist. To those who introduced this institution into Continental countries we might apply the Russian proverb, " They hear a sound, but know not where it is." It was at once reckless and irrational to entrust to the justice of the people the decision as to the guilt of an accused person without devising practical measures of discipline, and without preparatory study of this alien institution in the land of its origin and with all its complex surroundings.

The consequences are apparent. After tests extending over many years, in every country where trial by jury modelled upon the English system has been established, the question has arisen by what it is to be replaced to avoid the inconsequence of the judgments of which it has been the cause. Such difficulties multiply daily, and have permeated even those States where there is a strong judicial system, the product of centuries of experience and of rigorous discipline in science and practice.

It is not hard to understand the consequences of popular justice in those younger States which lack these saving elements—where, instead, we find an innumerable host of advocates who, impelled by ambition and selfishness, quickly attain that remarkable skill in the arts of casuistry and verbal subtlety needed to influence a jury of incongruous constitution, chosen at random, or with ulterior design, by whom the elements of justice are inaccessible, and the necessity for subjecting to analysis the mass of facts requiring consideration ignored. Behind these comes the motley crowd, attracted as to a play, to dissipate the monotony begotten of idleness—the mob, in the phraseology of idealists, denominated "the people." It is not to be wondered at that with such conditions the consequence so often corresponds with the judgment which I have taken from Sir Henry Maine, that "the modern jury, in the majority of cases, surrenders its verdict to the persuasiveness of one or other of the counsel who have been retained to address it."

THE PRESS

I

FROM the day that man first fell falsehood has ruled the world—ruled it in human speech, in the practical business of life, in all its relations and institutions. But never did the Father of Lies spin such webs of falsehood of every kind, as in this restless age when we hear so many falsehoods uttered everywhere on Truth. With the growing complexity of social problems increases the number of relations and institutions pervaded with falsehood through and through. At every step appears some splendid edifice bearing the legend, "Here is Truth." Do you enter—you tread on falsehoods at every step. Would you expose the falsehoods which have angered you, the world will turn on you with anger greater still, and bid you trust and preach that this is truth, and truth unassailable.

Thus we are bidden to believe that the judgments of newspapers and periodicals, the judgments of the so-called Press, are the expression of public opinion. This, too, is a falsehood. The Press is one of the falsest institutions of our time.

But who will dare to stand against the forces of *opinion*—the opinion of the world on men and institutions? Such is the nature of man that each one of us, whatever his words or actions may be, takes care that he shall conform with the opinions of the people. The man is yet unborn who can truly boast himself free from this servility.

In our age the judgment of others has assumed an organised form, and calls itself Public Opinion. Its organ and representative is the Press. In truth, the importance of the Press is immense, and may be regarded as the most characteristic fact of our time—more characteristic even than our remarkable discoveries and inventions in the realm of technical science. No government, no law, no custom can withstand its destructive activity when, from day to day, through the course of years, the Press repeats and disseminates among the people its condemnations of institutions or of men.

What is the secret of this strength ? Certainly not the novelties and sensations with which the news-paper is filled, but its declared policy—the political and philosophical ideas propagated in its articles, the selection and classification of its news and rumours, and the peculiar illumination which it casts upon them. The newspaper has usurped the position of judicial observer of the events of the day ; it judges not only the actions and words of men, but affects a knowledge of their unexpressed opinions, their intentions, and their enterprises ; it praises and condemns at discretion ; it incites some, threatens others ; drags to the pillory one, and others exalts as idols to be adored and examples worthy of the emulation of all. In the name of Public Opinion it bestows rewards on some, and punishes others with the severity of excommunication. The question naturally occurs : Who are these repre-

sentatives of this terrible power, Public Opinion?
Whence is derived their right and authority to rule
in the name of the community, to demolish existing
institutions, and to proclaim new ideals of ethics and
legislation?

But no one attempts to answer this question;
all talk loudly of the liberty of the Press as the
first and essential element of social well-being.
Even in Russia, so libelled by the lying Press of
Europe, such words are heard. Our so-called Slavo-
philes, with amazing inconsistency, share the same
delusion, although their avowed object is to reform
and renovate the institutions of their country upon
a historic basis. Having joined the chorus of
Liberals, in alliance with the propagandists of
revolution, they proclaim exactly in the manner of
the West: "Public Opinion—that is, the collective
thought, guided by the natural love of right in all—
is the final judge in all matters of public interest;
therefore no restriction upon freedom of speech can
be allowed, for such restriction can only express the
tyranny of the minority over the will of the mass."

Such is a current proposition of the newest
Liberalism. It is accepted by many in good faith,
and there are few who, having troubled to analyse
it, have discerned how it is based upon falsehood
and self-deception.

It conflicts with the first principles of logic, for
it is based on the fallacious premiss that the
opinions of the public and of the Press are identical.

To test the validity of this claim, it is only
needful to consider the origin of newspapers, and
the characters of their makers.

Any vagabond babbler or unacknowledged genius, any enterprising tradesman, with his own money or with the money of others, may found a newspaper, even a great newspaper. He may attract a host of writers and feuilletonists, ready to deliver judgment on any subject at a moment's notice; he may hire illiterate reporters to keep him supplied with rumours and scandals. His staff is then complete. From that day he sits in judgment on all the world, on ministers and administrators, on literature and art, on finance and industry. It is true that the new journal becomes a power only when it is sold in the market—that is, when it circulates among the public. For this talent is needed, and the matter published must be attractive and congenial for the readers. Here, we might think, was some guarantee of the moral value of the undertaking—men of talent will not serve a feeble or contemptible editor or publisher; the public will not support a newspaper which is not a faithful echo of public opinion. This guarantee is fictitious. Experience proves that money will attract talent under any conditions, and that talent is ready to write as its paymaster requires. Experience proves that the most contemptible persons — retired money-lenders, Jewish factors, newsvendors, and bankrupt gamblers—may found newspapers, secure the services of talented writers, and place their editions on the market as organs of public opinion. The healthy taste of the public is not to be relied upon. The great mass of readers, idlers for the most part, is ruled less by a few healthy instincts than by a base and despicable

E

hankering for idle amusement; and the support of
the people may be secured by any editor who
provides for the satisfaction of these hankerings,
for the love of scandal, and for intellectual pruriency
of the basest kind. Of this we meet with evidence
daily: even in our own capital no search is necessary
to find it; it is enough to note the supply and
demand at the newsvendors' shops, and at the
railway stations. All of us have observed the
triviality of conversation in society; in provincial
towns, in the government capitals, the recrea-
tions of the people are well known—gambling,
scandal, and anecdotes are the chief. Even
conversation on the so-called social and political
questions takes in a great measure the form of
censure and aphorisms, plentifully supplemented
with scandal and anecdote. This is a rich and
fruitful soil for the tradesmen of literature, and
there, as poisonous fungi, spring up organs of
calumny, ephemeral and permanent, impudently
extolling themselves as organs of public opinion.
The great part which in the idle life of government towns is played by anonymous letters and
lampoons, which, unhappily, are so common among
us, is played in the newspaper by "correspondence,"
sent from various quarters or composed in the
editorial offices, by the reports and rumours invented
by ignorant reporters, and by the atrocious practice
of blackmailing, often the strongest weapon of the
newspaper press. Such a paper may flourish, attain
consideration as an organ of public opinion, and
be immensely remunerative to its owners, while no
paper conducted upon firm moral principles, or

founded to meet the healthier instincts of the people could compete with it for a moment.

This phenomenon is worthy of close inspection, for we find in it the most incongruous product of modern culture, the more incongruous where the principles of the new Liberalism have taken root, where the sanction of election, the authority of the popular will, is needed for every institution, where the ruling power is vested in the hands of individuals, and derived from the suffrages of the majority in the representative assemblies. For the journalist with a power comprehending all things, requires no sanction. He derives his authority from no election, he receives support from no one. His newspaper becomes an authority in the State, and for this authority no endorsement is required. The man in the street may establish such an organ, and exercise the concomitant authority with an irresponsibility enjoyed by no other power in the world. That this is in no way exaggeration there are innumerable proofs. How often have superficial and unscrupulous journalists paved the way for revolution, fomented irritation into enmity, and brought about desolating wars! For conduct such as this a monarch would lose his throne, a minister would be disgraced, impeached, and punished; but the journalist stands dry above the waters he has disturbed, from the ruin he has caused he rises triumphant, and briskly continues his destructive work.

This is by no means the worst. When a judge has power to dishonour us, to deprive us of our property and of our freedom, he receives his power from the hands of the State only after such prolonged labour and experience as qualify him for his calling. His power is restricted by rigorous laws, his judgments are subject to revision by higher powers, and his sentence may be altered or commuted. The journalist has the fullest power to defame and dishonour me, to injure my material interests, even to restrict my liberty by attacks which force me to leave my place of abode. These judicial powers he has usurped ; no higher authority has conferred them upon him ; he has never proven by examination his fitness to exercise them ; he has in no way shown his trustworthiness or his impartiality ; his court is ruled by no formal procedure ; and from his judgment there lies no appeal. Its defenders assure us that the Press itself heals the wounds it has inflicted ; but any thinking mind can see that these are mere idle words. The attacks of the Press on individuals may cause irreparable injury. Retractions and explanations can in no way give them full satisfaction. Not half of those who read the denunciatory article will read the apology or the explanation, and in the minds of the mass of frivolous readers insulting or calumnious suggestions leave behind an ineffaceable stain. Criminal prosecution for defamation is but the feeblest defence, and civil action seldom succeeds in exposing the offender, while it subjects the offended to fresh attack. The journalist, moreover, has a thousand means of wounding and terrifying individuals without furnishing them with sufficient grounds for legal prosecution.

It is hard to imagine a despotism more irrespon-

sible and violent than the despotism of printed words.
Is it not strange and irrational, then, that those who
struggle most for the preservation of this despotism are
the impassioned champions of freedom, the ferocious
enemies of legal restrictions and of all interference by
the established authority. We cannot help remem-
bering those wise men who went mad because they
knew of their wisdom.

II

There is nothing more remarkable in this century
of advancement than the development of journalism
to its present state as a terribly active social force.
The importance of the Press first began to increase
after the Revolution of July 1830, it doubled its
influence after the Revolution of 1848; since then
it has grown in power not only year by year but
day by day. Already Governments have begun
to measure their strength against this new force,
and it has become impossible to imagine not only
public but even individual life without the newspaper; so that the suppression of newspapers, if
it were possible, would mean as much to daily
life as the cessation of railway communications. Without doubt, the newspaper serves
the world as a powerful instrument of culture.
But while we acknowledge the convenience
and profit derived from the dissemination of
knowledge among the people, and from the
interchange of thought and opinion, we cannot
ignore the dangers imminent from the unbounded

growth of the Press; we cannot refuse to recognise with a feeling of terror, the fatal, mysterious, and disintegrating force which threatens the future of humanity.

Every day the newspaper brings us a mass of varied news. How much of this is of real use to our lives, and to our educational development? How much is fit to feed in our souls the sacred flame of aspiration unto good? How much is there not to flatter our baser instincts and impulses? We are told that the newspaper gives what the taste of readers demands, that its level reaches the level of the reader's taste. But to this we may reply that the demand would not be so great were the supply less energetically pushed.

If news alone were published the case would be different; but no, it is offered in a special form, embellished with personal opinions, and accompanied by anonymous but very decided commentaries. Papers controlled by serious persons of course exist, but such are few, while to the making of newspapers there is no end; and no morning passes without some writer, unknown to me, whom, perhaps, I should not care to know, obtruding upon me his views, expressed with all the authority of public opinion. What is graver still, however, is that this newspaper addresses not only a single class, but all men, some of whom can barely spell out a page of print, and offers to each a ready-made judgment upon everything, in such a seductive form that, little by little, by force of habit, the reader loses all wish for, and feels absolved from the duty of, forming his own opinions. Some

have no ability for forming opinions, and accept
mechanically the opinions of their newspapers;
while others, born with a capacity for original
thought, in the trials and anxieties of daily life
have not the time to think, and welcome the newspaper which does their thinking for them.   The harm
that results from this is too visible, especially in
our time when powerful currents of thought are
everywhere in action, wearing down the corners
and distinctions of individual thought, reducing to
uniformity the so-called public opinion, and weakening all independent development of thought, of
will, and of character.   Moreover, for many of the
people the newspaper is the only source of education
—a contemptible, pretended education—the varied
mass of news and information found in the newspaper being taken by its readers as real knowledge, with which he proceeds to arm himself
complacently.   This we may take as one of the
reasons why our age brings forth so few *complete*
individuals, so few men of character.   The modern
Press is like the fabled hero who, having inscribed
upon his visor some mysterious characters, the
symbols of divine truth, struck all his enemies with
terror, till one intrepid warrior rubbed from his
helm the mysterious letters.   On the visor of our
Press to-day is written the legend " Public Opinion,"
and its influence is irresistible.

III

In the present constitution of society the Press has

become an *institution* which cannot be ignored, but
which must be considered side by side with the existing institutions which constitute the State and are
subject to control and responsibility, for there is
no institution which may be accounted uncontrolled
and irresponsible. The greater the growth of the
Press, the more clearly appear, side by side with
the apparent advantages of rational and conscientious publicity, those social dangers which it creates.
One of these dangers is the production and multi-
plication of a class of journalists, adventurers, and
writers, who feed and grow fat upon the pen.
The more serious workers on the serious Press
never cease to complain bitterly of the multipli-
cation of these fellows, with whom they are
ashamed to be associated, even in name. In all
the great States, in all the great markets, out of
this rabble of scribbling brethren springs a class
of men whom it is no exaggeration to describe as
parasites on society.

In fact, these men stand on a special footing in
relation to the general welfare, which should unite
and inspire all institutions. They are in no way
directly interested in the preservation of social
order, in the reconciliation of opposing minds and
contending parties. This is in the nature of things.
The newspaper lives and is nourished by daily
events and news. In troubled times its circulation
increases ; then its energies are expended in the
dissemination of rumours and sensations which
alarm and irritate the minds of the people ; while
on the other hand in times of quietude its circulation
is sensibly diminished. Hardly has trouble begun

when the streets are flooded with new publications which discord nourishes till peace returns, when they vanish as quickly as they appeared. But even in quiet times some must live, and for that end, new agitations are fomented, new interests developed, and sensations invented or exaggerated.

Those journals which pretend to seriousness find matter in the consideration of political questions, and in the frothy polemics which daily appear. The journalist is ready at a moment's notice to decide any imaginable political question; and by his position he is bound to consider and decide it immediately, for he is a servant not of thought, or of reason, but a servant of the actual day. No sooner does the thought occur than it flies to paper, thence to the printing press; there must be no delay, no time is allowed for the ripening of his thought. You ask these men are they ashamed. Not at all. They would laugh in your face at such a question, they are persuaded that they render great services to society. They resemble in this the ancient augurs who made merry both over themselves and over their dupes.

If the journalist is to attract attention, he must raise his voice to a scream. This his trade requires, and exaggeration capable of passing into pathos becomes for him his second nature. When he enters upon a controversy he is ready to denounce his adversary as a fool, a rascal, or a dunce, to heap upon him unimaginable insults—this costs his conscience nothing; it is required by journalistic etiquette. His cries resemble the protestations of a trader in the market-place when he cheats his customers.

These are the practices and qualities which un-happily flourish in the Press and among its workers. It would be very laughable were it not so harmful. It is harmful because the Press now occupies an arena in which are discussed and decided the gravest questions of internal and external policy—questions of economy and administration indissolubly bound with the vital interests of peoples. For all this passion is but a weak equipment; sage reasoning and maturity and sanity of thought are also needed; needed, too, is knowledge of the history of peoples, and of practical life. Yet in Europe things have gone so far that from the ranks of journalism rise orators and states-men who, together with the advocates with whom they share the capacity for abusive language, con-stitute in Parliament an overwhelming force. In the French Chamber there are but twenty-two repre-sentatives of large and fifty of small property, while all the talking strength belongs to journalists, of whom there are fifty-nine, and to advocates, of whom there are a hundred and seven.

And these are the representatives of their country, and the judges of the lives and requirements of the people ! The people groans at this confusion of legislators. But it cannot deliver itself.

PUBLIC INSTRUCTION

I

WHEN reason is severed from life it becomes at once artificial, formal, and, in consequence, sterile. Problems are then regarded and solved from the point of view of abstract propositions and principles taken on faith ; and thought glides along the surface of things, never seeking to penetrate its object, and ignoring the facts of actual life. Of such abstractions and generalities the number has multiplied incredibly, especially since the end of the last century ; they have filled our lives, they have made our legislation independent of the facts of existence, and have set up science itself in opposition to life and its phenomena. In the wake of the doctrinaires of science, whose doctrinarianism often approaches infatuation, in the wake of the adepts of scholasticism, marches the great herd of intellect. Abstract propositions attain the rank of indisputable axioms, which to oppose would be a heavy and often impossible task. It is difficult to estimate the damage which legislation has suffered from such abstractions, and how they have fettered, hand and foot, the living organism of social life with artificial formulas imposed by force. In the van of this movement marched the French, who first gave the sanction of fashion to the movement for the equalisation of the national life by means of

abstract principles deduced from hypothetical premisses. The example of France has been followed
by all, even by those States in which the conditions
of life, and the ethnical, geographical, and climatic
conditions are infinitely varied. How much even
our own country has suffered from such experiments
there is no need to remark.

Take, for instance, the phrases, repeated unto
weariness among us, and everywhere : Free Education, Obligatory Attendance, the Restriction of
Child - Labour During the Years of Obligatory
Attendance. There can be no question that learning
is light, and that ignorance is darkness, but in the
application of this rule we must take care to be ruled
by common-sense, and to abstain from violating
that freedom, of which we hear so much, and which
our legislators so ruthlessly restrict. Inspired by
an idle saying that the schoolmaster won the battle
of Sadowa, we multiply our model schools and
schoolmasters, ignoring the requirements both of
children and of parents, of climate, and of nature
itself. We refuse to recognise, what experience has
shown, that the school is a deceptive formality where
its roots have taken no hold among the people,
where it fails to meet the people's necessities, and to
accord with the economy of its life. That school alone
is suited to the people which pleases them, and the
enlightening influence of which they see and feel ;
but all schools are repugnant to them to which
they are driven by force, under threats of punishment, or which are organised, in ignorance of the
people's tastes and necessities, on the fantasies
of doctrinaires. In such schools the work becomes

mechanical; the school resembles an office with all the formality and weariness which office life involves. The legislator is satisfied when he has founded and organised in certain localities a certain number of similar institutions adorned with the inscription—School. For these establishments money must be raised; attendance is secured under penalty; a great staff of inspectors is organised whose duty is to see that parents and poor and working men send their children to school at the established age. Already all Governments have transgressed the line at which public instruction begins to show its reverse side. Everywhere official education flourishes at the expense of that real education in the sphere of domestic, professional, and social life which is a vital element of success.

But infinite evil has been wrought by the prevalent confusion of knowledge and power. Seduced by the fantasy of universal enlightenment, we misname education a certain sum of knowledge acquired by completing the courses of schools, skilfully elaborated in the studies of pedagogues. Having organised our school thus, we isolate it from life, and secure by force the attendance of children whom we subject to a process of intellectual training in accordance with our programme. But we ignore or forget that the mass of the children whom we educate must earn their daily bread, a labour for which the abstract notions on which our programmes are constructed will be vain; while in the interests of some imaginary knowledge we withhold that training in productive labour which alone will bear fruit. Such are the results of our complex educational system, and such are the causes of the aversion with which the masses regard our schools, for which they can find no use.

The vulgar conception of education is true enough, but unhappily it is disregarded in the organisation of the modern school. In the popular mind the function of a school is to teach the elements of reading, writing, and arithmetic, and, in union with these, the duty of knowing, loving, and fearing God, of loving our native land, and of honouring our parents. These are the elements of knowledge, and the sentiments which together form the basis of conscience in man, and give to him the moral strength needed for the preservation of his equilibrium in life, for the maintenance of struggle with the evil impulses of his nature and with the evil sentiments and temptations of the mind. It is an unhappy day when education tears the child from the surroundings in which he first acquired the elements of his future calling, those exercises of his early years through which he acquires, almost unconsciously, the taste and capacity for work. The boy who wishes to become a bachelor or a master of arts must begin his studies at a certain age, and in due time pass through a given course of knowledge ; but the vast majority of children must learn to live by the work of their hands. For such work physical training is needed from the earliest age. To close the door to such preparation, that time may be saved for the teaching of schools, is to place a burden upon the lives of the masses who have to struggle for their daily bread, and to shackle in the family the natural development of those economic forces which together constitute the capital of the commonwealth. The sailor qualifies for his calling by spending his boyhood on the sea; the miner prepares for his work by early years spent in the subterranean passages of mines. To the agriculturist it is even more essential that he shall become accustomed to his future work, that he may learn to love it in childhood, in the presence of nature, beside his herds and his plough, in the midst of his fields and his meadows.

Yet we waste our time discussing courses for elementary schools and obligatory programmes which are to be the bases of a finished education. One would include an encyclopædic instruction under the barbarous term *Rodinovyedenie* (knowledge of the fatherland); another insists on the necessity for the agriculturist to know physics, chemistry, agricultural economy, and medicine; while a third demands a course of political economy and jurisprudence. But few reflect that by tearing the child from the domestic hearth for such a lofty destiny, they deprive his parents of a productive force which is essential to the maintenance of the home, while by raising before his eyes the mirage of illusory learning they corrupt his mind, and subject it to the temptations of vanity and conceit.

II

The new school of civilisers has but one receipt for the improvement of humanity—war with the prejudices and ignorance of the people. In the

opinion of the writers of this school all the misfortunes of humanity have had their origin in a few
irrational sentiments and convictions which the
masses have adhered to through the course of
centuries, and which it is necessary to uproot and
destroy. Among such dangerous sentiments and
convictions they classify all the things that do not
admit of logical demonstration. " Were all men," say
these philosophers, " to develop their minds, and to
train their judgments, instead of thinking, feeling,
and living by convictions taken on faith, the golden
age of humanity would soon begin. The world in
one generation would move as far as it has moved
in the course of centuries. If the intellectual faculties
of man could be raised but one degree the results
would be inestimable. Almost every one of us has
one syllogism which has become rooted in the
mind through immediate impressions received in
infancy. If to this syllogism we could add another,
and acquire the faculty for uniting both in one chain
of speculation, the face of the universe would be
transformed, and the destiny of humanity changed."
Such is the end to which we are to be led, and such
the problem of progress and enlightenment as stated
by the philosophers of the nineteenth century.

Why quarrel with this? we are asked. But to
this problem there is another, a reverse and threatening side, which is too often ignored.

Humanity is endowed with another very effective
force — inertia. As the ballast in a ship, inertia
sustains humanity in the crises of its history,
and so indispensable has it become that without
it all measured progress would be impossible. This

force, which the superficial thinkers of the new
school confound with ignorance and stupidity, is
absolutely essential to the prosperity of society.
Destroy it, and you deprive the world of that
stability which serves as the fulcrum of progress.
Contempt or ignorance of this force is the great
failing of modern progressives.

What, let us ask, is a prejudice? A prejudice,
we are told, is an opinion without a rational base,
an opinion which admits of no logical demonstration.
All such opinions must be eradicated. But how?
By awakening in every man the faculty of thought,
and by placing the opinions of every man in
dependence upon logical deduction. Very true; but
true, unhappily, only as an abstract theory. In
actual life we find that we can seldom trust the
operations of the logical faculty in man; that in
practical affairs we rely more upon the man who
holds, stubbornly and unreservedly, opinions which
he has taken directly—opinions which satisfy the
instincts and necessities of his nature—than on him
who is ready at a moment's notice to change his
opinions at the guidance of logic because it appeals
to him as the unanswerable voice of reason. Such
men soon become the slaves of every argument
which they cannot answer at a moment's notice;
they surrender unreservedly themselves and all their
experience to every onslaught of logical argument
on every imaginable subject. They are defenceless
against theories and deductions unless they possess
an arsenal of logical weapons with which, at a
moment's notice, to confound their adversaries. Let
us once grant that the syllogism is the highest and

F

the infallible form of truth, and practical life becomes the slave of speculation; common-sense surrenders to folly and stupidity parading in the armour of formulas; and wisdom, tried by life, must yield to the first youth it meets skilled in the alphabet of formal reasoning.   It is easy to foresee the fate of the masses if our reformers succeeded in converting them to unreserved faith in the infallibility of formal logic.   The precious virtue of steadfastness, which has hitherto sustained society, would vanish in a day.

Further, we would ask, must it be admitted that obstinacy in convictions accepted on faith stands of necessity in opposition to logic, that the so-called prejudice indicates always slowness or inactivity of thought?   This has not been proved.   We have no reason to suppose that a man who is willing to surrender his opinions and beliefs at the bidding of demonstrative logic is necessarily more logical and rational than he who, admitting no argument, stubbornly holds to his beliefs.   On the contrary, the obstinacy of the simple man in opinions which he holds on faith proceeds, although for the most part without recognition by himself, from instinctive but in the highest degree logical impulses.   The simple man instinctively feels that the change of opinion which is thrust upon him by arguments apparently irrefutable, would involve the modification of his whole system of outlook upon life, a system for which, perhaps, he has no conscious justification, but which is indissolubly bound up with his being, and constitutes his spiritual life.   This is the chain which with subtle dialectics contemporary educators seek to break, and, unhappily, too often succeed in breaking. But the simple, common-sense man knows that, surrendering unresistingly to the first assault of logical argument, he must surrender to all, and that the great world of his spiritual conceptions cannot be abandoned merely because he is not in a position logically to overthrow the arguments directed against one of its facts. In vain the cunning adversary seeks to ridicule him, to convict him of absurdity; he is in no way absurd, but far abler than his opponent; he may not indeed analyse in all their relations the phenomena of his spiritual life, he may not dispose of the dialectical skill of his adversary, but, relying on his own good sense, he shows thereby that he cherishes his opinions, guards them, and values the truth of his convictions, not in the view of rational formalities, but in all their completeness.

Such are the methods employed by those who wish to enlighten the people. Such methods may be classified under the title of "subtle." At night when men are sleeping the subtle one appears, disguised in the mask of benevolence and charity, and sows his tares. For him neither knowledge nor ability is needed, subtlety only is required. Little intellect is needed, for instance, to approach a simple man at an opportune moment, and sow distrust in his soul: "Why dost thou pray to thy Saint Nicholas? Hast thou ever seen Saint Nicholas helping those who pray to him?" Or to seek some young girl of humble family, and say: "Who has proven to thee that it is thy lot to depend upon others for ever, to be the slave of thy husband?

Reason tells thee that thou art his equal in all things, that thou hast equal rights with him in all." Or to steal between a young man and his parents with such words as these : " By what logic art thou bound to obey thy parents? Who told thee to respect them, when thy reason tells thee they are unworthy of respect? What are the bonds between you but an accident of nature? Thou art a free man, the equal of the best." Armed with speeches such as these the *subtle* wander among the *simple* and the *weak* throughout the four quarters of our land, under the pretext of guidance stealing the sheep from the flock, and leading or driving them into the wilderness.

THE LAW

HOW many ancient ideas have become obscured and confused in our time! How many ancient terms have changed, or change before our eyes to-day, their original significance!

Thus has changed, and changed by no means for the better, the conception of the law. From one side regarded, law is a regulation, from the other a commandment, and on this conception of a commandment is based its moral acceptation. The prototype of all law remains the decalogue, "Honour thy father and thy mother . . . Thou shalt do no murder . . . Thou shalt not steal . . . Thou shalt not covet." Independently of what in modern phrase we denominate "sanction," independently of punishment for its violation, the commandments have the power of affecting the consciences of men by establishing, with the authority of supreme power, the distinction between light and darkness, between equity and iniquity. And not in the material punishment for its violation is the fundamental, invincible sanction of the law, but in the conscience of man, rebuking his iniquity. Material punishment he may flee, the imperfection of human justice may cast it on the innocent, but from this internal chastisement he can in no way be delivered.

This deep significance of the law is entirely overlooked in the new theories and new practices of

85

legislators.   For them the law has but one significance, as the regulation of external action, the
preserver of mechanical equilibrium of the diverse
operations of human activity in their juridical
relations.   In the preparation of the law great
labour is expended on analysis and technicality.
The importance of technicality and analysis cannot
be gainsaid ; but is it wise in providing for these
to forget the essential significance of the law? Yet
this significance is often not only forgotten, but
actually abjured.

Thus we encumber beyond measure the immense
edifice of the law, and live incessantly devising rules
and forms and formulas of every kind.   In the name
of freedom and the rights of man we do this, yet we
have gone so far that no man can move in freedom
from the network of rules and ordinances extending
everywhere, threatening everyone—all in the name of
freedom.   We seek to define, to measure, and to weigh
all things by formulas, formulas human—therefore
imperfect, and often delusive.   We strive to emanci-
pate the individual, but everywhere we dig pitfalls
about his feet, the victims of which more often are
the innocent than the guilty.   When we consider
the infinite multitude of laws and regulations, and
the bewilderment of legislators and judges, the fiction
that ignorance of the law is in no way justification
assumes an appalling significance.   The simple man
cannot know the law, or vindicate his rights, or
defend himself against attacks and accusations ; he
falls then into the hands of attorneys, the sworn
mechanics of the machine of justice, whom he pays
for every step which his case advances in the courts.

Meantime the immense network multiplies its meshes around him. It was not without cause, even in the sixteenth century, that the famous Bacon condemned this network in the words of ancient prophecy.

In the land of Bacon, since the sixteenth century, this network, which even then seemed intolerable, has multiplied its meshes daily until it has attained monstrous dimensions. A mass of enactments, ordinances, and precedents are mingled in grotesque and inexplicable chaos. No mind can penetrate and reduce it to order, or separate the accidental from the permanent, the obsolete from the active, the essential from the unessential. The roll of statutes resembles a great warehouse, through which only those who know it can find their way, and satisfy their needs. Yet on such conditions is justice based : from this depends the working of all public institutions and of all departments of State. If the voice of right has not been stifled in the conscience of the people this must be ascribed to the experience, dexterity, and knowledge to rule and to judge, and the preservation through tradition from immemorial time of ancient authorities and institutions. For there exist, in addition to the law, a rational force and a rational will which powerfully aid its administration, and to which all submit. Thus, when we speak of respect for the law in England, the word law is not to be taken in its most limited signification : the power of the law is supported, in reality, by respect for the authority which is armed with the law, and by confidence in its equity, skill, and learning. In England the chief indispensable condition for the support of law and order is the clear definition of the

jurisdiction and authority of the judges, so that they
may not doubt the steadfastness or vacillate through
consciousness of the limits of their authority.   The
judges, therefore, are not armed alone with the letter
of the law, or slavishly subservient to it through fear
of responsibility, but armed with the law as a whole,
and charged with its rational interpretation as a
moral force proceeding from the State.

Where this essential element of strength is absent,
where ancient institutions do not exist to serve as
the sanctuary of reason and skill in the application
of the law, the increasing number and complexity
of statutes create a labyrinth in which all those who
enter are lost, for there is no deliverance from the
net which is cast around them.   The law becomes
a snare not only to the people, but what is graver
still, to the very authorities engaged in its administration, restricting by a number of limitary and con-
tradictory interpretations that freedom of judgment
which is essential for the intelligent exercise of their
power.   When wickedness and violence have to be
exposed, the injured to be justified, order to be
restored, and his due to be given to each, most
necessary of all things is a powerful exercise of will,
inspired by ardour for justice and for the welfare of
the people.   But if at every step the executor of the
law finds in the law itself restrictive prescriptions and
artificial formulas, if at every step he fears to trans-
gress the limits by law established, if in addition the
jurisdiction of co-ordinate institutions is obscured by
detailed limitations, then all authority is lost in doubt,
weakened by the laws which ought to be the source
of its strength, and crushed by the fear of responsi-

bility in that moment when not fear but the consciousness of duty and right should be the only guide and impulse. The moral influence of the law is sapped by a multitude of provisions and definitions, accumulated in the incessant activity of the legislative machine ; and, as result, the law in the popular conception assumes the aspect of a mysterious power, existing for a purpose inexplicable, and everywhere restricting and paralysing the operations of life.

THE MALADY OF OUR TIME

I

IN our time discontent is universal. With many this discontent has developed into chronic irritability. By what is it caused? By their lots, their rulers, social order, other men, by all and everything except themselves.

Men grow discontented when their expectations are deceived; this is the discontent of disenchantment, borne for a day, atoned for often by the next. It is a passing malady, not to be confused with the present complaint, a permanent and epidemic disease which has tainted all the younger generation. We grow up with infinite expectations, begotten of immeasurable vanity and innumerable artificial needs. In ancient times the number of restful and contented persons was greater, for men expected less of life, were satisfied with less, and did not hasten to extend their sphere of life. Each was held to his place and to his work by a sentiment of duty associated with them. The humble watched the lives of the rich and idle, and thinking, "This is not for us," resigned themselves to the impossible. Now this impossibility has become possible and attainable in the imaginations of all. The private soldier aspires to the dignity of a general, and seeks to attain it, not with hard service, with duty performed, or distinction gained, but by accident and sudden acquisition. Success is now believed to be the result of accident or good fortune, and by this belief all are incited, as the gambler by the hope of gain.

In business transactions the credit system rules. Credit has become the most powerful instrument for the creation of new values, and this instrument is accessible to all; and, owing to the comparative facility with which it is employed, by no means all the values created are real or subserve the purposes of production, while many are fictitious and ephemeral, for the satisfaction of adventitious and temporary interests created for the purpose of sudden enrichment. As a consequence, the success of an enterprise is no longer proportionate to the personal activity, the energy, aptitude, and knowledge of its promoter. In the economic sphere, towards every undertaking are drawn a multitude of unseen currents and intangible eventualities, which cannot be foreseen or provided for. The worker has no longer to strive merely with definite obstacles but also with a complex network of difficulties which surrounds him on every side. Calculations fail, because circumstances essential to their accuracy have escaped consideration. Hence the condition of uncertainty, alarm, and weariness from which so many suffer. All activity is paralysed by mental conditions in which the worker feels that he lacks the strength to conquer circumstances, that his will and intellect are feeble before the obstacles which confront him. His energies are weakened, the man of action becomes a fatalist, and relies for success no longer upon foresight and sagacity, but upon blind accident and good fortune. This is the prime cause of the pessimism which infects so many of our generation ; and, to some extent, also the cause of another prevalent ailment, practical material-ism—the craving for sensual pleasures. The sensual instincts awaken with peculiar strength in a life spent in anxious and feverish activity, and founded upon infidelity and accident.

The same phenomena appear in other spheres of social work. Everywhere credit is the strongest instrument, everywhere we see created with aston-ishing ease swollen and fictitious values, which, under favouring circumstances, bring fortunes to some, while in the hands of others, at the first contact with the actualities of life, they crumble into dust. Reputations are gained with amazing speed. The required training once obtained or evaded, appointment to responsible positions may be obtained with commensurate emolument and authority. The illiterate journalist becomes the celebrated littérateur and publicist ; the mediocre lawyer wins the glory of a great orator ; the char-latan of science appears a learned professor ; the ignorant, inexperienced youth becomes a procurator, a judge, an administrator, the draughtsman of im-portant laws ; and a young slip, yesterday breaking through the earth, stands to-day in the place of a great tree. All these values are swollen and fictitious, but they multiply daily in the market of life, and their possessors traffic with them as brokers traffic with worthless shares. Many maintain their false values throughout life, remaining, nevertheless, shallow, feeble, frivolous, and unproductive. But the honours of most are quickly dissipated in dust, and the worthlessness of their owners exposed. Meantime their vanity has swollen to unnatural limits, their pretensions and needs have grown beyond measure, their desires have been inflamed, and in the moment of trial when action is needed their resources fail them, in strength, in reason, in character, in knowledge. Thence comes the number of moral bankruptcies, which spring from causes identical with the causes of bankruptcies in the economic world. It is hard to estimate the amount of energy wasted in our time through its irregular, abortive, and thoughtless application, and through the irregular circulation of capital of all kinds in our markets. As a result, we see around us young people broken, ruined, and mutilated for life. Some cannot bear their own burdens, and, as overheated vessels, burst asunder: in exasperation, they end by suicide lives which thenceforth are worthless to those who have been accustomed to consider themselves the centre of life, and to measure all things by a purely material standard, which the moment it slips from their hands sends all their calculations astray. Others shuffle through the world, multiplying the number of the discontented and the irritated against life and society. It will be a sad day when their number shall so increase as to give occasion for satisfying their vengeance and desire.

II

The ancients, we are told, were accustomed to place a skeleton or a skull in the midst of their banquet halls that they might be reminded of the proximity of death. This custom has decayed : we feast and make merry and strive to banish all thoughts of death. Nevertheless, at the back of each stands death, and his threatening face at any moment may appear before us.

Every morning brings news of suicides, those suicides unexplained and inexplicable, which threaten to become a familiar feature of our lives. It is terrible to think that some day we may become accustomed to this feature. Never has there been a time when the human soul was valued at so low a price, when there reigned such indifference to the fate of men created in the image of God and redeemed by the blood of Christ. Rich and poor, learned and ignorant, age and youth which has hardly begun life, nay, the very tottering infant, throw away their lives with inconceivable reckless-ness ; some without a word, others in their last moments extolling to the world themselves and their deed.

What is the cause? That life has become de-formed, false, and meaningless beyond belief, that order has disappeared, that all rational sequence in human development has vanished, that all discipline of thought, of sentiment, and of morals has disappeared. Corruption and disintegration have destroyed the simple, organic relations of public and family life ; their place has been usurped by institutions and abstract

principles for the most part false in themselves, or
in false relations to life and actuality. The simple
needs of the soul and body have been expelled by
a multitude of artificial requirements, and the
simplest sentiments have given way to sentiments
complex and artificial, which seduce and irritate the
soul. Vanity, which once grew commensurately with
our environment and conditions, has suddenly been
magnified to the immensity of the human ego,
which violates all discipline and usurps an absolute
dominion over life, liberty, and happiness, claiming
to rule alike over circumstance and fate. The minds
of men, strong and weak, high and low, great and
small, all alike have lost the faculty of recognising
their own ignorance, and the capacity to learn—
that is, *to submit to the law of life ;* while men exalt
themselves to that visionary height, from which each,
great or small, holds himself as judge of life and
of the universe.

Thus has accumulated an infinite mass of falsehoods, pervading all relations, poisoning the atmos-
phere which we breathe, the medium in which we
live and move, the thought that controls the
will, the word with which the thought is expressed.
Among such falsehoods what can we seek but
a feeble growth, a feeble existence, and feeble
deeds? The very conception of life and of its
aims becomes falsified, our relations are disordered,
and life has lost the harmony essential to tranquil
development and normal activity. Is it strange,
then, that so many cannot bear the burden, and
lose the balance of moral and intellectual forces
essential to life? A crystal vessel heated equably

will bear a high temperature, while heated suddenly
or inequably it bursts asunder.   Is it not thus with
those unhappy suicides of whom daily we hear?
Some perish from the inherent falsehood of their
conceptions of life, which reality shatters in the
dust.   The miserable man who knows no support
in life other than himself, who seeks outside himself no moral principle to sustain him in the
struggle, flees from the field, and seeks oblivion
in effacement.   Others perish from inability to
reconcile their exalted ideals of life and action
with the falsehoods around them, the falseness of
men and the falseness of institutions; these lose
faith in their ideals, and having no true faith to
console them, they lose their balance, and, as
cowards, cast away their lives.   Many are ruined
by sudden and unmerited success, victims of the
power which they coveted so madly, but the burden
of which they are unable to bear.   For ours is a
time of fictitious, artificial greatness and celebrity
for the mutual deception of men, and real merit
finds it hard to arise and justify itself from
obscurity, because in the market of human vanity
only glittering money is gold.   Men recklessly
undertake responsibilities, imagining themselves
capable of all things, and with little ability, without
great effort, attain the highest positions.   The
prospect of power is seductive to human vanity: it
brings a vision of honours and privileges, of power
to bestow favours, and to create other powers.   Yet,
whatever be the vulgar conception, the moral principle of power is simple and immutable, "Whosoever
of you will be the chiefest shall be servant of all."

Were this not forgotten, who would seek to bear the unbearable burden ? Nevertheless, all men are eager to accept power, and the burden has crushed and ruined many, for in our time the exercise of power is more arduous and complicated than ever. Great is the number of those for whom power, recklessly conferred, and recklessly accepted, becomes a sphinx, and asks its fatal riddle. He who cannot solve it must perish.

III

If we would reason aright, we must regard the object of our reasoning from the proper point of view ; all depends upon this, and all human error proceeds from failure to observe this rule. We are accustomed to trust to our impressions, but impressions are received merely from the surfaces of the objects along which we glide with such remarkable speed and agility. Delighted with our first impression, with human impatience and vanity we hasten to impart it to others. By transmission of our impressions to receptive natures, error is formed, develops, and matures, percolates to the masses, and too often is accepted as the opinion of the public.

This holds true in great matters as well as in small. Whole systems of astronomy obtained acceptance through the course of centuries, were considered indisputable, yet in the end were proven to be false, being formed from a wrong point of view. Such was the Ptolemaic system. For centuries astronomers persisted in looking at the universe from the earth

G

as the central point of view—the earth seemed so infinitely vast that no other centre could be conceived. The system was full of contradictions and inconsistencies, for the removal of which men of science had recourse to an artificial system of cycles and epicycles. Centuries passed before Copernicus appeared and drew the false centre out of the system. All was plain when once it was shown that the universe did not revolve about the earth, that the earth held no ruling position among the heavenly bodies at all, but was merely one of many planets, controlled by forces in power and importance immensely exceeding its own.

The system of Ptolemy has long outlived its day, yet in our time its errors obtain in a new sphere of ideas and conceptions. For does not modern philosophy, which deals with man as the centre of the universe, assuming that all existence revolves around him as science once made the sun revolve around the earth, fall into a similar pit? It is plain indeed that there is nothing new under the sun. This outworn creed is offered us as a novelty, as the last word of science. Then follow, one after another, contradictions, rejection of accepted propositions, new theses categorically expressed, their categorical refutation, then wondrous discoveries, no sooner made than forgotten. All this is termed progress, and "the onward march of science." But in truth are these not the cycles and epicycles of the Ptolemaic system? When will the new Copernicus appear to break the spell, and prove that the centre is not in man, but outside him, and infinitely higher than he, than the earth, than the universe itself?

The same phenomena appear in the history of all sects, from the Gnostics and the Arians to the Nihilists of to-day, the disciples of Pashkoff, of Sutayeff, of Tolstoi. Man, pursuing impressions, regards all things from the false point of view which he finds in himself, vainly imagining that the universe revolves around him; he looks for truth in all things and everywhere, and is wrathful with all whom he convicts, save himself, of passion and sin. It is a fatal error.

IV

Obstinacy and dogmatism in belief will always, it seems, be the attributes to our poor and narrow humanity, while men of deep and liberal thought must always be few. Faith gives place to faith, dogma hastens after dogma, the objects of fanaticism change for ever. In our day enlightened intelligence is ruled by generalisation, and seeks for a logical constitution of life and society on abstract principles. These are the new fetishes that have taken the place of the old idols, for we, as our forefathers, set up graven images, and bow down before them. Our modern idols are phrases and generalities, such as Liberty, Equality, and Fraternity, with all their variations and extensions. And are not as idols, also, the abstract propositions propounded by scholars, and raised to the rank of dogmas, as, for instance, the "Origin of Species," and "The Struggle for Existence"?

Faith in abstract principles is the prevailing

error of our time. This error consists in the dogmatic and absolute faith by which we disregard the facts of life with all its conditions and needs, ignoring distinctions of time and place, the characteristics of individuals, and the peculiarities of history.

Life is not a science, or a philosophy, but a living organism. Neither science nor philosophy, as external forces, can rule our lives ; both have their origin in life, for they are built upon the observation, analysis, and classification of its phenomena : but it would be vain to think that they can exhaust and comprehend life in all its infinite manifestations, endow it with new elements, or reconstruct it upon new foundations. In their application to life, the propositions of science and philosophy have the value of hypotheses, and in all cases must be tested by common-sense, by clear reasoning, and by the facts and phenomena to which they are applied ; other application would lead to violence and falsehood. The fact that there exist so few indisputable propositions in science and philosophy ought to be a warning to us. Most of the theses of science are the subjects of contention between schools and parties ; many are shaken by fresh experiment and research. Not a single practical science may be likened to a seamless garment : all are stitched from rags, more or less skilfully, the shape following the fashion, often with fragments hanging down in tatters, torn by the polemics of the different schools. Nevertheless, the representatives of the schools maintain their propositions absolutely, and demand their unconditional application to life. As an example, Political Economy is enough : political economists have earned the reputation of dogmatic and intolerable

pedants for wishing to apply to legislation and
industry their abstract laws of production and of
division of labour and capital, while they forget
more or less the living forces and phenomena which
in practice controvert these laws and destroy their
operation. Their formulas have been deduced from
a multitude of facts and phenomena, the infinite
variety of which they cannot exhaust in all the
combinations which present themselves. These
formulas have been of great advantage to science,
which, thanks to them, has gained simplicity and
advancement, yet not one of them is the unalterable,
absolute law of life; each serves only to show the path
to those who follow, each expresses only a certain
movement, a certain direction of forces which in a
given case must balance or contend with other forces
acting in opposite directions. To calculate mathematically the action of these forces is impossible;
only the just instincts of common - sense may
estimate it; thus the general conclusions of
political economists, although deduced from indisputable premises, have only a contingent, hypothetical value, and not the value of absolute and
unalterable laws. As such are they regarded by
every true scholar uninfected with the pedantry of
the schools. But this cannot be said even of all
scholars. What, then, shall we say about the mass
of superficial readers, whose knowledge, as a rule,
is derived from a few pages of a text-book or from
contemporary newspapers, and who expect, at a
moment's notice, without any research, to find an
answer to all questions by turning to the pages
indicated in the contents table. For them every

generality serves as the supreme authority of science, as an easy means to the decision of the gravest questions, and as a convenient arm with which to resist the impulses of common-sense, and to overthrow all the teachings of history and experience. Thanks to these abstract propositions and principles, it is easy for the emptiest and most superficial men, the idlest intriguers, to pass as profound philosophers, statesmen, and administrators, and to gain a cheap victory over common-sense and experience. Such scholars, in the vulgar phrase, leap at once to "the height of contemporary science and thought." Once on this height, who shall have strength to withstand them ?

The minds of the people are quite incapable of understanding general propositions in their true, conditional significance ; all formulas, all phenomena, are embodied by them in living, concrete images and forms. There is no more deplorable error than that through which we, inspired by a baseless faith in abstract propositions, would inspire the people with it also. This new play with the abstract conceptions circulated by the idealist educators of the masses is only too dangerous, for it involves the demoralisation of the public conscience. Too often, unhappily, it is indulged in by our schools, but most of all it has been practised by democratic Governments; and many Governments have dearly paid for it by the sacrifice of sincerity in their moral relations to the people. One falsehood brings forth another ; once false conceptions, false expectations, and false beliefs have taken root in the minds of the people, it is difficult for a Government, itself corrupted by falsehood, to extirpate them : it becomes necessary for the Government to accept such falsehoods, to play with them anew, and to maintain its power artificially by a fresh network of subterfuges in its institutions, its language, and its actions—a network inevitably woven from its earliest compromise with untruth.

The example of France is a clear demonstration of this. In the last century the fantasy of idealist philosophers fashioned a new evangel for humanity— an evangel constructed wholly upon ideals and abstractions. The disciples of Rousseau had painted in a rosy colour the natural man, predicting through return to Nature universal content and felicity upon earth : they had revealed to all the newly-solved mysteries of social and political life, and fabricated a fictitious social contract between the people and its rulers. The celebrated *programme* of popular happiness was revealed as the secret of peace and concord and content for peoples and Governments. The revelation was constructed upon monstrous generalities in no way related to actual life, on the wildest, most extravagant fantasies ; yet this falsehood which, it would seem, must have vanished at the faintest touch of actuality, infected the minds of men with a passionate desire to realise it in practice, and to construct upon its basis a new society and a new government. But one step more, and the theories of Rousseau gave birth to the celebrated formula : Liberty, Equality, Fraternity. These ideas, *in indissoluble union with the ideas of duty and sacrifice*, on which is set, as the living head upon the body, the whole organism of the moral universe, contain in themselves the eternal truth of the ideal moral law. But when it was sought to turn this

formula into a law binding upon society—when it was
sought to embody it in a formal law defining the relations of the people to its rulers—when it was to become
the basis of a new religion for the nations, its fatal
falseness was betrayed, and the perfect seed of love
and peace and tolerance sown in the soil of formal
legislation sprang up as violence and discord and
fanaticism.   For these maxims were proclaimed, not
as the evangelic commandment of love, not as a
summons to duty in the name of an ethical ideal, but
as a covenant between the people and its rulers—as
the annunciation of a new era of natural happiness,
a promise of perpetual felicity.   *In no other way could
the people accept or understand.*   The masses are not
philosophers ; Liberty, Equality, and Fraternity they
accept as their right, as privileges they have won.
How then can they be reconciled to all the evils that
afflict mankind, the poverty, the lowliness, the depriva-
tion, the self-denial, the subjection.   Tolerate these
they cannot, they murmur, they are exasperated,
they protest, they rise and overthrow institutions and
Governments which have not kept their word and
have disappointed expectations.   Misled by fantastic
delusions they build up new institutions again to
destroy them, they rush into the arms of new rulers
whose flattering words have seduced them, to overthrow them in turn upon fresh disillusion.   To rule
the people by the direct exercise of authority becomes
impossible without the aid of flattering words and
false institutions, and Governments are driven to dis-
honesty that they may evade destruction.   Terrible
indeed is this chaos in our institutions.   Tumultuously
the waves of passion roll on every side, tranquillised

only for a moment by the magic sounds of Liberty, Equality, Publicity, the Sovereignty of the People : and he who best can play with these words becomes the master of the people.

V

In ancient Rome an abyss appeared which threatened to engulf the whole city. All efforts to remedy the disaster were vain. The people appealed to the oracle, which answered that the abyss would be closed when Rome gave up in sacrifice its greatest treasure. We know the sequel. Curtius, the first citizen of Rome, the bravest of the brave, flung himself into the gulf, which closed for ever.

Among us, also, in the modern world a terrible chasm has appeared, the chasm of pauperism, which separates the poor from the rich by an impassable gulf. What have we not sacrificed to fill it up? Mountains of gold, and wealth of every kind, masses of sermons and instructive works, floods of enthusiasm, a hundred social institutions organised expressly, all are swallowed up, yet the gulf yawns open as before. We, too, have invoked the oracle to reveal to us a certain remedy. The word of this oracle has long been spoken, and is well known to all. "A new commandment I give unto you, That ye love one another : as I have loved you that ye also love one another." Could we find the true meaning of this precept, could we rise to its height, could we cast into the gulf all that is most precious to us— the theories, the prejudices, the practices which are

bound with our respective callings, and confirmed in
the hearts of each, we should sacrifice ourselves
to the abyss and close it for ever.

VI

The justest sentiments of the human soul remain
true only while they preserve their independence and
simplicity, for there is nothing simple which is not also
right.   The danger for every simple sentiment is its
image in the consciousness—its reflex action.   Sentiment acquires a new force when confirmed by reason
and sanctioned by ideas ; but at the same time it
meets with the new danger of absorption by the
reflective faculty, and of consequent loss of simplicity.
It may happen that sentiment, leaning upon thought
for support, partakes of its nature, and re-issues as
a conscious formula, from which the element of
sentiment has disappeared.   The form, as the letter,
may kill the living spirit; the form deceives, for
beneath it insensibly develop hypocrisy and the
seductions of human vanity.   Is there one thing
more splendid, more precious, more fruitful than the
sentiment of love in the human soul?   Yet, from the
moment it unites with reason, a danger threatens it
from this reflex action.   It may create itself a form,
divide itself into classes, doctrines, categories, orders,
and schools.   At last the time must come when it is
no longer a simple sentiment, filling and enlivening
the soul, but our poor human vanity imagines that
it masters the sentiment, and makes it its bonds-
man and instrument.   Here simplicity disappears,

decomposition begins, and, with but little more, hypocrisy may end it. The works of love, it may be, will multiply, order will replace impulse, but simplicity of feeling has flown, the perfume has departed.

These thoughts are inspired by consideration of our organised philanthropic institutions and benevolent societies, with their regulations, their committees, their honorary members and their honorary rewards. In principle, all institutions are devoted to charity and beneficence. But in view of their proceedings we are forced to ask, Where is there room here for active, sympathetic love? We watch the meetings of boards, where speeches are delivered, and the committees where men and women sit wearied and indifferent, ignorant of affairs, discussing regulations and paragraphs; we read reports prepared by paid officials; we hear the magniloquent verdicts of self-appointed pedagogues on systems of instruction; we attend, O height of hypocrisy! the charity bazaar, where the lady stall-keepers, who have sacrificed not a penny, are dressed in costumes costing double the profit on their sales. And these we call the works of Christian charity!

Such is love as a social institution. There is still justice on which the world is based, justice without which life would become the nightmare of a wild imagination: how stands justice in its modern artificial European dress of a judicial institution? We find a machine for the artificial execution of justice, but justice itself is dumb in the triumphant turmoil of mechanical production, its voice is stifled in the tumult of the wheels of the great machine. We

seek here a moral force—alas, the only force is con-
sumed in the turning of the wheels which keep the
machine in incessant motion, the only moral strength
of the workers is spent in the greasing of these
wheels and their connections. There sit the judges
in proud consciousness of their priestly dignity, and,
like the ancient augurs, listen with more or less
attention while lawyers bring forth magniloquent and
sonorous phrases from the narrow byeways of the
pettifogging mind, carefully estimating first the
money value of their long periods. Thus pass away
the wearying hours of trials, while the chief victim
of the sacrifice to unhappy Justice must reach the
promised land by the thin hair of Mahomet's bridge,
and woe unto him who relies for safety upon his own
strength. He only finds justice who, having studied
the arts of the acrobat, on his pathway neither
stumbles nor trips.

VII

All human life is a search for happiness. The
unquenchable thirst for happiness burns in man from
the awakening of consciousness, and is sated never
at his latest breath. The hope of happiness has no
limits; it is infinite as the universe; it knows no ultimate aim, for its beginning and its end are in eternity. The Mongol fabulist symbolises this incessant
chase of joy in the story of a mother who has lost
her dearly-loved daughter—her only child. The rude
imaginations of the dwellers on the steppes conceive
this mother as an old woman, with one eye on the top

of her head. With bitter sobs she wanders through
the world, seeking her lost child, and stopping time
after time at some object in which she thinks she sees
its face. She takes it up, bears it away, and then
lifts it high above her head to satisfy herself that she
has really found her treasure. Scarcely has she
looked at it when she sees that she has been mistaken, and in despair throws it to the earth, dashing
it to pieces, and starts again on her unfruitful quest.
The happiness sought by man determines his fate,
and brings forth too often unhappiness as its fruit.
The wretchedness of man, says Carlyle, comes from
his greatness; he is wretched because of the infinite
within him, and with all his art he cannot imprison
this infinite within the limits of the finite.

Therefore is unhappiness, being infinite, unattainable. Why, then, does man, conscious of this, so
gaily hasten on his fruitless journey? Why, abandoning the present, and turning aside in despair from
the future, does he look to the past and find the
possibility there? There are few men who have not
in their past some time of which they may say,
" Happiness was possible then—so near."

But happiness forsook man at that moment when
first he sought to master the infinite, to make it
his own domain, to *know* it.   "And ye shall be as
gods, knowing good and evil." This knowledge he
has not attained, only a dual nature has been given
to him. From that day one-half of his spiritual being
has sought the other, to establish an unity and in-
tegrity in life.

If there is one thing on this earth which may rightly
be called happiness, it is the state of the few in that

period of simple existence and simple consciousness when the soul feels life in itself, and finds in that feeling rest, seeking not to know at all, but imaging in itself eternity, as a drop of pure water on a twig reflects the splendour of the sun. Where such a state exists Heaven grant that it may endure; that its subject by his will may strive not to escape from the limits of his destiny! The door of such happiness opens not towards the inside; push it from the inside it will shut no more. It opens from the inside, and he who wishes that it remain closed must not even touch it.

We condemn our past, because we seek there vainly those principles which constitute for us the standard of truth and happiness. From this material of principles, of which the chief is equality, we wish to reconstruct life, to divert those ancient springs which nourished former generations, to reconstitute our lives upon our newest plans, and to delineate these plans by the rules of science, while forced often to admit our ignorance of science itself. At every step life reveals records of injustice instead of the justice with which we promised to enrich it; egoism, interest, and violence instead of love and peace; the sores of poverty and wretchedness instead of wealth and growing prosperity; tears and complaints instead of the joy which we foretold. Never mind! we repeat, each time louder and louder, to still the questionings, doubts, and objections—"At least the *principles* of our century are preserved and upheld. Does it matter if the generations of to-day suffer, if, in place of the strong, a weak people appears about us?—evil may reign to-day, to-morrow all will be well. A new generation will arise on the ruins of the old;

our principles will be justified in a new world by posterity in futurity. The dreams which fill our lives and inspire our labours will be realised some day." Alas, they will be realised as realised were the dreams of Swift! In youth he built an asylum for the mad ; in old age he found a refuge there.

VIII

How seldom do we find simplicity and directness in social intercourse. How seldom do we meet with men with whom conversation is the simple and natural interchange of thought! When we mix in society we find ourselves daily brought into communication with men with whom we have nothing in common but humanity. We find no time to rest, none to observe, none to await in silence ; if one should wish to act so, his partner would not allow it. Relationship must at once be established, and etiquette demands that this relationship appear natural. Conversation must begin, and once begun upon the barren soil of trivialities, it becomes a mere exchange of phrases on subjects touching upon ordinary life. Men approach one another on the basis of triviality, in which all are liberal, and at later meetings the conversation thus begun seldom leaves the footing on which it was established first. Or it may be worse. At the first meeting men strike attitudes, and pose to one another. This happens most often between persons of different positions, when one of the parties is in some way remarkable or distinguished, and the other wishes

to place himself upon an equal social footing. For
who does not imagine in himself some remarkable
gift? Thus begins a duel between two insignificant
personalities.   Each strives to display his good
qualities, to concede nothing, to awaken the interest
and admiration of the other.   To shine in conversation commonly implies intelligence, and who,
nowadays, does not lay claim to intelligence, to
wit, or to that knowledge of the world which often
surpasses intelligence itself?   What a vast field, what
an infinite career for vanity and self-love!

To this is joined the affectation of amiability.
Every social virtue has its reverse of baseness,
which is most openly revealed where the virtue
assumes the aspect of propriety, and is changed
into social small coin of a familiar stamp.   What
quantities of this coin have we not in circulation
among us!   How dulled has it become in passing
through so many hands—and such hands!   The
noblest words have lost their primitive significance
in ceasing to be the expression of sincere thought;
the deepest truths have become degraded by association with vulgar words ; the most precious sentiments
have become outworn and defiled by exhibition to all.

The affectations of cleverness and amiability, these
are the two great stimulants to conversation in
society.   We excuse the baseness of the first
motive by the apparent respectability of the second.
Conscience may convict us of folly, of pretence, of
playing with words.   We have an answer ready: "I
tried to be agreeable ; I had to keep the conversation
alive to aid my host and hostess, and to prevent their
guests being bored."

But conscience judges justly, and amiability in no way covers or justifies baseness. Without the impulse of childish vanity, amiability alone will not induce one who respects himself and his words to play with phrases for hours, to assume, as necessity demands, the accents of love and indignation, to walk perpetually on stilts, to tell imaginary tales, and to give a free course to raillery and to sarcasm at the expense of a neighbour's weaknesses and faults.

IX

The nineteenth century justly boasts itself a century of reform. But these reformatory movements, beneficent in many of their operations, in others constitute the most terrible affliction of our time. The speed with which thoughts of analysis and reform circulate has brought to our veins a fever, to allay which—with rest and diet—the time has long since arrived; but while the paroxysms of disturbed thought continue, one cannot think that reform can be healthy or fruitful. Life has marched so quickly that many ask with terror, "Whither do we go, where shall we stop? If we fly upward we shall not be able to breathe, if downward then we shall fall into the pit."

The idea of reform is passing through the same stages as every new and sound idea after it has attained popularity. At first it is the privilege of a few master spirits, burning with the fire of thought, of long experience, and of sincere feeling, who strive for its realisation. Then, when the idea

H

has become familiar, it becomes the property of the masses, it is accepted on faith, and at last circulates in the market - place and loses its sincerity and worth.   In a moment of enthusiasm the great apostles of the movement raise the standard, and while they bear it this standard is the symbol of a great work, drawing servants to its ministry.   But when it passes into the hands of the people, and little boys find pleasure in bearing it from place to place with meaningless cries, it loses its prestige, and serious persons turn away when they see it approach.

There are periods when reform is the ripe fruit of social evolution, the expression of a necessity felt by all, when it loosens the knots bound by immemorial social relations; then the reformer appears a prophet who speaks with the voice of the public conscience, and realises the thought which all bear in themselves.

His words and his works master all because they bear witness to the truth, and all who are of the truth echo and emulate them.   But when his work is done, sometimes arise after him legions of false prophets.   All men, great and small, wish to be prophets: each bears a new word upon his lips which has never been borne in his soul, or ripened by experience—a catch-word, cheap, and therefore feeble, stolen from the market - place, and therefore base. He who has never done useful work, to whom idleness is the work of life, prepares projects for new legislation, or raises himself a little chair from which to preach reform, demanding that work which he has never done, and knows not how to do, be placed upon a new foundation.   Such are the little. What shall we say of the great, who suffer equally from the fever of reform ?

The prevalent ailment from which our so-called statesmen suffer is ambition, or the thirst for renown. In our time life flows with immeasurable speed, statesmen succeed statesmen, each while in power burning with impatience for celebrity while there is yet time. He will not trouble to collect the threads laid down by his predecessor, he cannot waste his time with the little labours of organisation, the amelioration of established institutions, or current affairs. Each must begin his work from the beginning, clear himself a field, make *tabula rasa* on which to create anew, for all men flatter themselves that they possess creative powers. What he shall create from, what are his materials—this question he seldom troubles to answer from a practical consideration of affairs. It is the act of creation which attracts him : he aspires to create from nothing, and his excited imagination answers all questions with the familiar phrases: "The institution will support itself, it will make its men, they will appear in due time." It is remarkable that the more infatuated the statesman is with this belief, the less is he prepared for his work by knowledge and experience. This desire for creation is the more seductive, as it requires no real knowledge, while it gives a wide field for the activity of the political charlatan, and makes celebrity attainable by the vulgarest means. Where active management, the knowledge of work, and the direction and improvement of existing institutions are required, it is easy to distinguish the man of knowledge and experience

from the charlatan and dunce; but where under-
takings are to be begun by criticism and condemnation of existing institutions, where institutions are
to be organised anew on vaunted lines and principles,
it is easy without immediate knowledge of affairs
to contend in generalities, to show external perfection of construction, and to appeal to precedents
existing, perhaps, beyond mountains and seas.   On
this field it is harder to distinguish the efficient
from the inefficient, and the charlatan from the
man of action.   Here every *great* man, knowing
little of affairs, and troubling less to understand
them, may easily justify any project of reform
fabricated in subordinate offices by petty reformers
themselves incited by a desire for cheap notoriety.

This extraordinary phenomenon must be numbered
among the characteristic elements of our political
life: in different measures it may be observed
everywhere—in administrations, in privy councils, in
committees.   It is seen most plainly, of course, in
those countries where institutions lack the sanction
of historic precedent, where discipline has not
been affirmed by centuries, where society by its
historic development has brought out no defined
classes or ramparts to guard against the gusts of
thought and aspiration.   The wider and freer the
historic and economic field, the greater the room for
the fantasies of reformers.   In such circumstances,
there is no conflict, and little need for reformers to
measure themselves with affirmed ideas, interests,
and parties; then licence reigns without control.

While these appearances are seen on high, analo-
gous action proceeds in the depths and abysses of the

earth. In its nature this movement also is reformatory, but it seeks a more radical reform. Masses
of men dissatisfied with their condition, dissatisfied
with social institutions, blinded by the wildest instincts
of their nature, or infatuated by ideals born of the
fantasies of narrow thought—rejecting all existing
institutions sprung from the historic development of
society, abjuring the Church, the State, the family,
the rights of property,—aspire to the realisation of
their wild ideals on earth. These men demand that
the reforms they extol shall begin at the beginning
upon a clear field, which they desire first to dis-
encumber of the ruins of all existing institutions.

"These are the enemies of civilisation!" cry the
statesmen of Europe; and in the name of civilisation
arm themselves against the mass of improvised
reformers. But the defenders of the existing order
would do well to remember that they themselves
have been the first to raise a daring hand against
existing things, to overthrow the ancient edifices,
and to build others in their places; that often
with reckless confidence they hasten to condemn
that order, and to destroy the traditions and customs
sprung from the genius and history of the people.
By establishing new laws which ignore and cannot correspond with life, they have violated those
same conditions of actuality which the enemies of
civilisation refuse to acknowledge. Victory over such
enemies may be gained only in the name of these
vital principles, and in the domain of sound reality.

The word reform is so often repeated that we have
begun to confound it with improvement. In the
popular opinion the apostles of reform are the apostles

of improvement, or, as we say, progress ; while on the
other hand, those who question the need or utility of
reform upon new principles are enemies of progress,
enemies of advancement, enemies almost of good, of
justice, and of civilisation.   In this opinion, so widely
disseminated by our publicists, there is a great error and
delusion.   With such errors current a common-sense
judgment on any subject finds it hard to make a
path through prejudices ; and concrete, actual, healthy
thought must surrender to abstraction and fantasy.
Men of action and knowledge are forced to give place
to dreamers armed with abstract ideas enveloped in
loud phrases.   On the other hand, he enjoys credit
from the first who poses as the representative of new
ideas, the advocate of reform, who carries plans in his
hands for the construction of new buildings.   The
political profession is crowded with architects, and all
who would be workmen, landlords, or tenants must
needs be architects first.   It is plain that with such
tendencies of thought and taste an infinite field is
open for all manner of charlatanry, for all the dexterity of the hypocrite, and the daring of ignorance ;
while practical work is hampered beyond measure
when accomplished in the midst of a disposition to
analysis and criticism, and subjected to the test of the
general principles and phrases which obtain currency
in the world.   He who ought to concentrate all his
attention and all his strength upon his work, and upon
devising means the better to fulfil it, must constantly
take into account the opinions of others, and the impression it will produce on the world and on superiors,
more especially if those superiors are infected with
the new ideas.   Thus, on criticism and resistance to

criticism, for the most part quite absurd, is wasted much force which might have accomplished great work ; so much time goes in friction, in unfruitful struggle, that but little remains for real, concentrated labour. The worker is surrounded on all sides by illusory work, while the real and needed work slips from his hands and is left undone. Such a position is intolerable by good and earnest men. When concerned with life itself, with facts and living forces, they feel themselves strong ; they trust in their work, and this trust gives them the power to create wonders in the actual world. But they lose heart when they deal with images, symptoms, forms, and phrases ; then they have no faith, and without faith all work is fruitless. Shall we wonder then that the best workers retire, or—what is worse and what more often happens—without leaving their posts, become indifferent to their duties, fulfilling them outwardly only for the sake of influence and emolument?

Such are often the consequences of the fever for reform when it extends too far. Where shall we find a physician to cure the evil? What hero will direct our strength to that actual amelioration which we so much need, for which in reality we thirst so much? "Wait a little," we are told ; "the mysterious veil of reformation will be lifted, and a new and virgin life spring forth in the plenitude of beauty and strength ; a new dawn will appear, revealing a country flowing with milk and honey." We have waited long, but the curtain has not been lifted, the new world has not appeared ; but across the ancient veil another has been drawn.

Meantime it is enough to pass through the streets of cities, great or small, to see at every step the ameliorations we need. Everywhere round lie formless masses of abandoned work, forsaken institutions, and ruined temples. There are schools where the teachers have forsaken the pupils to compose papers on methods of instruction, or wordy discourses for public meetings; colleges where, under the externals of education, nothing is learnt, and the bewildered teachers, in the confusion of orders and instructions, know not what to teach; there are hospitals where the afflicted fear to go because of the cold, the hunger, and the disorder, caused by the indifference of interested managers; there are administrations with large funds at their disposal, where each official neglects all save his interests and ambition; there are libraries where all is disordered or destroyed, where we cannot understand either the employment of the income or the disposition of the books; there are streets which we cannot pass without terror or abhorrence from uncleanliness poisoning the air, and from the houses of drunkenness and disorder which encumber them; there are courts of justice, dedicated to the greatest of all the functions of government, through the incapacity of officials ruled by a chaos of disorder and injustice; there are departments from which the officials are absent; churches, a lamp unto the people, forsaken and closed, without service or song, or from which, through the irregularity of their services, the worshippers bring away nothing save confusion, ignorance, and irritation.

Is there not here a harvest for which gleaners are needed? where all the forces of thought, of love, of indignation might well be directed; where we need, not legislation to divert these forces, but the measures of masters and rulers, concentrating their efforts on a single spot for culture and improvement. There lies the real need of our time, which we sacrifice to abstract questions and sounding words. " Do not trespass beyond the limits of thy destiny," was the advice of the ancient oracle, " Do not undertake a charge beyond thy strength." How excellent the advice! All wisdom is in the concentration of thought and power, all evil is in its dispersion. To work is not to dissipate our strength on a multitude of generalities and aspirations, but to choose a work and a field according to our measure, and to dig, and plant, and cultivate, to spend our living strength thereon, and to raise ourselves from work to knowledge, from knowledge to perfection.

X

Wealth sets in motion a multitude of the basest impulses of human nature. It imposes on men great responsibilities, and binds and restricts their freedom in many things. It becomes the object of exploitation, and is surrounded by a web of falsehoods of every kind. If the feelings of the rich were not benumbed, they would daily feel that their relations to men had changed, that many, even of their nearest friends, behaved no longer with simplicity; and that for a great number of the people with whom they dealt, their personalities did not exist but had been replaced by their external figure, their capital. By men of sensibility such a position is unbearable, and the rich man must possess great simplicity of heart to continue in pure and benevolent relations to the people around him, and to escape the demoralisation and perversion which arise under the influence of his wealth.

To a similar fate is subjected another great human force—intellect, more particularly intellect above the general level, and, above all, the intellect of the ruler. When an able man attains authority, when his name has become celebrated, all the basest impulses of human nature awaken around him. To approach him is an honour: he is no longer approached simply, but with the ulterior motive of appearing clever and awakening his attention. When the clever man is in fashion there is no baseness too low to put on the mask of ability, and to display before him all the affectations of which baseness is capable. The consciousness of this falsehood and affectation would be intolerable, and would force him to avoid his kind if he were not himself the victim of similar weaknesses. Thus, too often we find clever men who, accustomed to the affectation of others, pose before their subordinates with all the absurdities of little minds, and find more pleasure in such society than in the society of their equals. Few minds are free from this weakness.

In one of her caustic letters to her husband Mrs Carlyle says :

"Geraldine came yesterday afternoon. . . . I fancy you would find our talk amusing if you could assist at it in a cloak of darkness, for one of the penalties of being 'the wisest man and profoundest thinker of the age,' is the royal one of never hearing the plain 'unornamented' truth spoken ; everyone striving to be wise and profound *invitâ naturâ* in the presence of such a one, and making himself as much as possible into his likeness. And this is the reason that Arthur Helps and so many others talk very nicely to me, and bore you to distraction. With me they are not afraid to stand on the little 'broad basis' of their own individuality, such as it is. With you they are always balancing themselves like Taglioni, on the point of their moral or intellectual great toe."—"Letters and Memorials of Jane Welsh Carlyle ; Ed. by J. A. Froude," vol. i. p. 321.

XI

In the dark ages of history a condition of society existed in which over all citizens hung a feeling of suspicion and distrust. Contemporary writers speak with terror of cities where men feared to look into each other's eyes, to speak to their neighbours— even to the members of their households—a frank word devoid of artifice, or to give rein to the simplest impulses of their minds, for fear of malevolent interpretation which might lead to persecution in the name of the State or in the interest of public safety. From the dark corners and lowest strata of society appeared a body of prosperous professional informers, actually formed into corporations—a mysterious power before which all prostrated themselves in silent terror, or, when silence could not be, expressed their thoughts in false, flattering, and hypocritical words.

When we read such accounts of the times of Duke Biron in Russia, and of the Terror in France, we rejoice that we live in another age, and that the events of those days are but traditions for us. Yet, if we examine more closely the appearances around us, we shall have to admit that symptoms of similar conditions are not unknown. We might indeed go further, and say that mutual suspicion has driven its roots deeper into our inner life than even in those ages. What strikes us most in recent years is the absence of that simplicity and sincerity in our relations which constitute the chief interest of social life, inspire it with the breath of freshness, and serve as a symptom of healthiness. How seldom do we find simplicity in the conduct of men! How delightful would it be to approach men simply, without those artifices and ulterior motives which bring forth dark shadows confounding our relations to our fellow-creatures! Of such shadows an innumerable multitude has formed in these later times, resembling a host of evil spirits sowing discord in the air. Whence have they come? Did they reflect defined ideas, we might oppose them with similar ideas. But no; for the most part they are engendered by impressions unconsciously inspired with the air we breathe, as atoms of infected matter in a time of pestilence. The air to-day is tainted with the germs of moral and intellectual epidemics of every kind: their name is legion, and other name it would be hard to find.

Observe how men, strangers or friends, behave in society, upon business or pleasure. Hardly have they met, hardly have they exchanged a greeting, when shadows arise between them. With the first word uttered by one, through the mind of the other a reservation has passed: "Ah, these are his opinions, this is his school, these are his *convictions* (the favourite of modern terms, and one of the most deceptive). This man is a Liberal, a Clerical, a Reactionary, a Socialist, an Anarchist, a Free-Trader, a Protectionist—he is a disciple of the *Moscovski Vedomosti*, a supporter of the *Nedel*, of the *Vestnik Yevropui*"— and so on. Observe how, after this first impression, mutual distrust burns more and more fiercely, degenerating at last to irritation, till all rational exchange of thought becomes impossible ; then sharp and caustic phrases relieve intermittently a constrained silence, till at last the new acquaintances part in total ignorance of one another, yet with mutual condemnation. Each at once classified the other in a certain category with which he had before decided he had nothing in common. Whence does this absurd irritation spring? From convictions? In the majority of cases neither one nor the other has any reasoned convictions, or belongs to any recognised party. He has repeated something read in the newspapers a day before, or taken from the conversation of a friend, who himself seeks his opinions at an equally childish source.

How much great strength is lost or sterilised by this childish play with impressions and symptoms of conviction! Men, in reality honest, virtuous, and capable, instead of working as hard as may be at the practical, actual work to which they are called, cross their arms, waste their energy, exhaust themselves in fruitless irritation and anger, because work on certain principles, with certain theories and certain views, is impossible. They have scarcely put their hands to their work before it has repelled them ; they lose

faith in it because it does not correspond with their
conceptions of usefulness.   Everywhere we see the
same absurd failing.   Masters, from fanatical attachment to principles, systems, and methods of education,
neglect their schools, where the unhappy pupils are
sacrificed to stupid or idle teachers, yet each of these
teachers in turn is ready at a moment's notice to
argue on the abstract principles of a work which he
cannot do, and does not understand.   Our courts cry
out for lawyers of experience, devoted to their profession for love of it ; our universities for jurisprudents
who love their work as the work of their lives: but
our jurists, professors and practitioners alike, have
hardly met when, through mutual suspicion, they seek
to tear each other asunder as Reactionaries, Clericals,
or Radicals, or over ideas of punishment, of trial by jury,
of civil marriage, or the administration of prisons on
one system or another.   Go to the meetings of the innumerable commissions for consideration of new projects, observe the wild disorder, listen to the interrup-
tions of members from the various departments across
the green table, see the glances they cast at one another
—what distrust, what suspicion ; what affectation in
the delivery of speeches, what turgid and empty
phrases !   Whence does it spring ?   From the task
appointed, which is seldom performed ?   No ; from
some petty *idea* which the speaker has picked up
elsewhere, and which he brings with himself, rather
on which he brings himself *ad astra*, or from some
theory, on rare occasions taken carefully from a good
book.   In our salons hardly has the conversation
passed from banal phrases and the latest news, when
the same phenomenon is reproduced.   A confusion

of tongues with like confusion of ideas is heard, an inconsistency of thought, from which we shrink with amazement and repulsion. Often we meet men whose speeches and actions protest against their names, their callings, the work which they outwardly perform and by which they live. The heads of schools contemptuously refer to pedagogues who insist upon rigorous discipline; the soldier condemns the old-fashioned persons who maintain the necessity of military discipline; the priest condemns the practice of attending mass on festival days; judges and jurists discuss the ignorance of those who require the punishment of thieves, or the obedience of servants to their masters. All fly asunder over theories, few can unite for action, because from their first steps they differ in their conceptions of work, or rather in those obscure phrases with which they express their conceptions.

Whence does all this proceed? We must seek the cause in the monstrous, immeasurable development of vanity in all and each. This is the same petty self-love as inspires a youth, ignorant of the world of men, on entering the society of strangers, to assume an inimical tone, to lose his self-possession, to affect bitterness, irony, and arrogance. He bears to this unknown exchange his only capital, a high opinion of himself; and the knowledge that others value him below his own estimate irritates him, deprives him of his simplicity, sets him, as it were, perpetually on his tiptoes, and gives him an air of meaningless protest against his surroundings. Conceive a company wholly formed of persons as sickly, as immeasurably vain as he. Taken by itself, such a group would be ludicrous enough, yet, absurd as it appears, it serves as a true image of assemblies of persons met by accident, or for the purpose of some common action.

XII

There are many terms which have been outworn to worthlessness through constant employment by every one without precise application ; terms by use of which the fool in his own mind is made wise, and the most ignorant exalted to the height of know-ledge. Current words may be vulgarised to such an extent that serious men have scruples in employing them. They feel that these terms, bandied every-where, have taken permanently the associations of baseness and triviality inseparable from vulgar use. The time has then come for such words to be laid away in the lumber room of thought : they must rest awhile and be purified in the crucible, before they may again appear in the world as precise and com-prehensible expressions.

With such a fate is threatened that favourite word—evolve or evolution. In books, in pamphlets, in leading articles and feuilletons, in intercourse at table, in sermons at church, in the conversation of salons, in official documents, in lectures, in the lessons of gymnasia and elementary schools — everywhere flies the sound of this magic word, till we feel wearied when it is pronounced. It is indeed time to test the idea which this word expresses. It is time to reflect that this term evolution, in disunion from its comple-

mentary term *involution*, has no definite meaning at all.
It is time to turn to our common mother and teacher,
Nature, for the explanation of the idea. By her we
are taught that all development proceeds from a
centre, and without a centre is inconceivable ; that
no plant can rise from the soil, that no flower can
bear fruit if the centre of creative force, of development and production of sap, is withered. Unhappily
we have forgotten Nature, and so, without regarding
her, we construct our childish schemes of development.
With rude hand we would open the bud mechanically
before the time has come for its opening by the internal action of natural forces. We rejoice, and call this
evolution. We destroy the bud, and its opened petals
wither, without a healthy blossom, or hope of healthy
fruit. Is not this madness ? Is it not like the folly of
the child in the fable, who strove to dry up the sea
with a spoon ?

How many of such foolish children have we in our
self-appointed developers and teachers ! In them the
passion for evolution becomes fanaticism, and there
is no blockhead or dunce who does not consider himself capable of evolving something. Yet, were these
the sole victims of the infatuation it would be well.
What is most remarkable is that, beside them,
and sometimes behind them, stand men of apparent
ability, serious thinkers, enchanted by the magic
word, bought with the current money of the market-
place, who repeat it, affirm it, and on this shibboleth
and the vague conceptions it expresses, organise
whole systems of educational training.

And all these fantasies arise, all these plans are
composed for the purpose of operating *in anima*

I

vili on the mass of the so-called uncultivated classes,
on the body of the people. A campaign is planned,
but there are neither leaders nor soldiers ; no one
will trouble to mingle with the masses, to live their
lives, to examine their psychic nature, their soul, for
the masses have a soul, with which those who would
understand them must enter into communion. No,
our reformers and educators see in them only a certain
mass, an aggregation of intellectual forces on which
to try their experiments. And what astonishing
audacity ! They demand in the name of some
supreme and absolute aim that submission to these
experiments be obligatory, and by force. How they
are to be conducted—on this our teachers are at
variance, but there are as many systems and methods
as there are heads. In one thing only all agree—in
a determination to act on the *thought* and *develop* it.
In vain our weak voices protest that the simple
man is not mind alone, but soul also ; that, like all
other men, he has in his heart a base on which he
builds his whole life, by which the *edifice of the church*
is supported. No, our educators will address themselves to the mind alone, and strive to incite in it an
idle activity on those questions which the enlighteners
have themselves so cheaply and cheerfully solved.
What a ludicrous error ! If, abandoning their baseless
assurance—their exaggerated conception of their own
intelligence—these men were to descend to the dark
masses beneath, and enter into communion with them,
they would find that while those who live in darkness seek and cry for light, and thirst for enlightenment, yet they will let it enter only from that side
from which they feel that it will truly enlighten

them, leaving their souls untroubled and their lives undestroyed. They feel that of all things dear to them their spiritual nature is the dearest, and through their hearts alone will they let in the light. When the light of reason dawns from this side it does not blind them, or ruin their lives, or disturb the equilibrium of existence. But when the operations of development are directed exclusively to the mind, when they are begun with the imparting of generalities and the so-called knowledge of text-books, our educators act as men who would stand a cone upon its apex.

XIII

All life is movement. Never, it seems, has the movement been so swift as in our time ; but this movement is intermittent, feverish, sickly, not a natural succession, but an involuntary course of sensations ; not a constant aspiration to a single aim, but a sequence of diverse desires affected by every wind.

"Can this be life ? " we ask ourselves as we watch a crowd devouring and devoured by life, in thought and anxiety for ever.

"The highest gift of God and of Nature," said Goethe, "is life, the revolution of the monad about itself, a movement which knows no stoppage or repose ; while to each is given a congenital impulse which incites him to sustain and develop it, although its nature remains a mystery for all men living." To live—what a simple matter it seems. "*Quel est*

mon meҍtier ? " asked Montaigne, and answered himself, " *Mon méstier c'est vivre.*"

But how complex are the lives created by men,
above all by men of modern times, when each day
they meditate more deeply upon life, its purpose
and its aim, concentrating upon one object all
their thoughts. Life without thought would be the
life of animals, but thought should be a living thing,
turned to the practical purposes of life. Yet
in our day men live for thought—and life, the
simple and precious gift of God, is swallowed up
by it. Life is the free movement of all the powers
and impulses of human nature. In this movement
itself is its end, and therefore, to state the aim of
life as a movement of intellect only, of heart only,
of passion only, is to restrict and deform it. Life
has been artificially deformed by these thoughts upon
itself. Goethe in his time cried with disgust, " Poor
men to whom the head is everything" (*Armer
Mensch, an dem der Kopf alles ist*). " Do we live? "
he continues. " We have worked ourselves out of life
by its analysis (*herausstudirt aus dem Leben*), and
must attempt to enter it again." Goethe's words
were inspired by thought of the professors, the
scholars, and the young students of his time. Since
his time how much farther has this analysis gone,
and how much of life has been devoured by it. In
Goethe's time, in the latter half of the eighteenth
century, thinkers were struck by the growing discord between thought and life, by the prevalence
of that of weariness of life (*Weltschmerz*), then in
fashion among the younger generation. This complaint is no longer common, but its place has been

taken by the theory of pessimism, a new conception of life, which rules men's minds with a hopeless and intolerable dominion. This is no simple disillusion sprung from the contradiction between actuality and the highest ideals of the soul, it is a set negation of the world in which we move; not a simple weariness of life awakened by struggle with the ills of humanity, but a wicked, hopeless, and destroying denial, which admits of but one issue from the gulf of despair—to pluck from the soul itself the very desire to live.

To this extent have we perverted life. We trusted that thought alone would serve for the direction of life, for the better ordering of its movements; we believed that it would help us to live; yet we find that life has been annihilated by thought, till neither life nor thought remains. Such is the fashionable theory of life, greedily seized by the readers of its illustrious apostle; a theory which has made life more illusive—illusive enough before; for the partisans and supporters of this theory continue to satisfy freely all their animal impulses, in themselves proving the contradiction between life and their artificial theory of life, a theory in which there is no room for faith, or justice, or energy of will striving to embody itself in activity. What then remains? There remains a negation of life stolen from books, without experience of life, a sterile scheme of truth taken from books also, a dead effigy of Nature in the dress of a chemical formula, and a feeble will, inclined to renunciation of a life which from the material point of view has been a failure.

KNOWLEDGE AND WORK

SINCE the first awakening of thought, and its first manifestation in our society, the value and necessity of knowledge have been preached on every side, until the very idea of enlightenment in the minds of the most intelligent has been confounded with extent of learning. Everywhere we see an extension of programmes in the higher, intermediate, and even elementary schools; everywhere we find incompetent masters hastily appointed merely to fill vacancies; everywhere the formalism of examinations and inspecting commissions; everywhere a host of journals treating *de omni re scibili et quibusdam aliis*, which swell the heads of their readers with a mass of confused and disordered information. The deplorable result is the increase of a pretended intelligence with a high opinion of itself, which lacks that for which all true knowledge is meant, that is, the ability to accomplish work, to accomplish it with conscience and skill, and to make it the interest of life.

To every man a task is appointed, which, to understand, he must make a part of himself, and concentrate his powers upon. " Do not go beyond the limits of thy destiny," said the ancient oracle; "do not go beyond the limits of thy work." He who dissipates his powers in many directions distracts his thoughts, enfeebles his will, and loses the power of concentration upon work. Distracted by the

134

impulse of curiosity and the desire to know, men cannot amass and concentrate the reserve of vital force necessary for the free transition from knowledge to action. However great the knowledge acquired by the trifler, all is unfruitful if he cannot concentrate his powers and direct them to work.

By itself, knowledge educates neither the understanding nor the will. Of this we see examples daily. Daily we meet clever men, gifted with strong memories and imaginations, cultivated and learned, yet resourceless in the decisive moment when a judgment is required for work, or a firm word in council. Our life, both private and public, through the complexity of its relations, and the confusion of its ideas and tastes, demands continually a quick and firm decision. Yet, when such decisions are required, we find men approaching questions, not with firm steps, but by roundabout paths. In these moments a man of clear conscience and will, capable of apprehending all the relations of the subject, is more valuable for practical work than a multitude of feeble and vacillating minds.

From such causes spring the formalism and unfruitfulness of the many councils and conferences which are held among us: men deliver judgments without troubling to concentrate their minds upon the subject of speech. The best orator is not he who searches for means to confound his adversary with the little arm of casuistry or with torrents of splendid imprecation, but he who, inspired by a clear apprehension of the affair he deals with, expresses his thoughts clearly and firmly — not he who, confusing light and shade, can prove that white is black and that black is white, but he who straightly and firmly says that white is white and that black is black. The best judge is not he who analyses by the standard of a hair every claim and defence, and delivers judgment conformably to the formalities of jurisprudence, but he who, looking only to essential rights, with clear thought penetrates to the essence of the relations between the litigants. The best general is not he who has studied in detail the history of all battles and of all strategy, but he who, in the critical moment, realises his condition, his locality, and his strength, and with a strong exertion of will decides the fate of battle.

FAITH

I

ON earth we walk by faith and not by sight; and
he is mistaken greatly who thinks that having extinguished faith in himself, he can walk thenceforth by
sight alone. However high the human mind has
risen above the world, it cannot rid itself of the soul,
which aspires to belief—and to unconditional belief
—for without belief man cannot live. And is not
that a pitiable delusion which, rejecting faith in that
which exists—in that which is revealed to the soul
as real truth, accepts the theory and the formula as
objects of faith, of honour, and of adoration, as idols
to which men sacrifice themselves, the whole world
in their souls, their freedom and that of their neighbours. Theories and formulas cannot in themselves embrace the absolute, and each is of necessity
incomplete, questionable, conditional, and false. That
which is infinitely above me, which from ages was and
is, which is infinite and immutable, which I cannot
comprehend, but which comprehends and sustains me:
in that I wish to believe as absolute truth — not in
the work of my hands, the creations of my mind, or
the logical formulas of my thought. The infinity of the
universe and the principle of life cannot be expressed
by any logical formula. The unhappy man who relies
on such a formula to cross the chaos of existence will,

with his wretched formula, be swallowed up by the chaos he defies.   The recognition of an immortal self, faith in the only God, the consciousness of sin, the yearning for perfection, the sacrifice of love, the feeling of duty : these are the truths in which the soul may trust—not in the idols of formula and theory.

II

What a mystery is the religious life of a people such as ours, uncultivated and left to itself!   We ask, whence does it come? and strive to reach the source, yet find nothing.   Our clergy teach little, and seldom ; they celebrate the service in the churches, and direct the administration of the parishes.   To the illiterate the Scriptures are unknown ; there remain the church service and a few prayers, which, transmitted from parents to children, serve as the only link between the Church and its flock.   It is known that in some remote districts the congregation understands nothing of the words of the service, or even of the Lord's Prayer, which is repeated often with omissions and additions which deprive it of all meaning.

Nevertheless, in all these untutored minds has been raised, as in Athens, one knows not by whom, an altar to the Unknown God ; to all, the intervention of Providence in human affairs is a fact so indisputable, so firmly rooted in conscience, that when death arrives these men, to whom none ever spoke of God, open their doors to Him as a well-known and long-awaited guest.   Thus, in the literal sense, *they give their souls to God.*

"In the beginning was the Word." Thus proclaims the Evangel. . . . The great German poet
wished to improve the thought of the Evangelist
by passing it through the mind of Faust. "No,"
said Faust; "In the beginning was the Deed." Had
Goethe written his "Faust" in our age, he certainly
would have said: "In the beginning was the Fact."
This Fact is the favourite idea of contemporary
materialists, the alveole from which they develop an
universe, the base and fundament of all that they
call truth.

How false is it all! Truth is absolute, and only
the absolute may be the foundation of human life.
Things not absolute are unstable; all else vanishes
in the midst of images, which cannot serve as a
base. A fact is something by its nature indissolubly
bound with the conditions of the material world,
and only conceivable thus. But hardly have we
tried to detach this fact from its material surroundings, to determine its spiritual principle, to ascertain
its true nature, than we are entangled in the network of propositions, hypotheses, and doubts which
arise in the mind of every individual thinker, till we
feel our utter incapacity to discern the truth. Hence
history presents such confusion of judgment on
events when we try to analyse their spiritual significance. The most conscientious student can do
no more than paint a faithful picture of events in
their relations to contemporary conditions of life and
action, recounting them with their material surround-

ings, analysing the causes, effects, and motive principles of historic activity. Here, it is plain, science must seek refuge in art: thus, all true historians are artists of necessity. For art an ideal is needed ; consequently, the writers of history in their appreciation of events and men must ceaselessly aspire to an ideal, the form of which will be peculiar to each. All historians are inclined to be carried away by their ideals —that is, by the conceptions which they form of perfection in human motives, acts, and institutions. To events taken together the historian stands in the position of a critic, and the character of the critic is determined by his general philosophy of life. For this reason, the judgments of historical critics on celebrated persons and events are so various and irreconcilable. Whom one to-day has exalted the other to-morrow degrades ; while in him whom yesterday history depicted as a monster to-morrow she finds a pattern of moral excellence. It is unlikely that the differences of historical critics will ever be settled, for the very ideal of their criticism is mutable, and changes with every generation of historians.

Long before the dawn of pragmatic history, tradition sprang from the depths of the popular imagination, and to the present day continues to develop side by side with history. It serves as a source of history, and as one of the objects of its criticism ; but, in addition, it remains the precious heritage of the people, preserving in itself the freshness of immediate impressions. The masses understand and love tradition, and continue to create it, not merely because they incline to the marvellous, but because they in-

stinctively see there a profound truth, an absolute
truth of idea and sentiment—a truth which they
cannot discern in the subtlest and most artistic
analysis of facts. Those heroes of popular song
whom history condemns are worshipped still by the
people; in them it sees the embodiment of its
ideals—the ideals of strength, beneficence, and piety,
in which, and not in persons, or in the passing
images of life, it finds an absolute truth. The
learned do not understand that the masses see
with their souls—that this absolute truth cannot be
seized materially, displayed visibly, determined by
numbers and weights, but that it may yet be seen
and trusted in, for absolute truth is accessible through
faith and only through faith. There is nothing perfect,
nothing complete, nothing unique in the actions, the
sentiments, or the impulses of men; all things human
are of dual nature, and men aspiring to unity totter
and fall at every step. To those who analyse every
exploit, every event, every historic figure, not one
hero will remain. All great deeds are preceded by
chains of moral vacillation, surrounded by a network
of diverse sensations, impulses, and adventitious circumstances, which direct, modify, and counteract one
another so that investigation leaves not a single deed
as the complete expression of a free will directed to
an ideal. In the conception of the people, all exploits
appear as the complete and living manifestation
of strength. Thus the masses judge; without this
faith they cannot live; on faith the life of man
sustains itself in the midst of the tears, the regrets,
the misfortunes and falsehoods with which it is
afflicted.

Hence the error of those who would deprive the people of their faith, under the pretext of reverence for a pretended historical truth. All men feel the need of faith in some ideal of truth and virtue, but how shall this faith be satisfied if it be not embodied in a living image? To destroy these images is to destroy the faith of which they are the expression—the faith in an absolute truth, in an ultimate perfection. And this faith explains why the favourite reading of the Russian people is those Lives of the Saints which are composed of living pictures of heroic deeds, of beneficence, of moral perfection. Each of these hero-saints was a man, with all the weaknesses of human nature, the vacillation of thought, of impulse, and of will, with all the baseness of fallen humanity; and if we could analyse his soul we should see the mystery of original sin, and all the impotence of the man in his struggle with himself. But out of this conflict he issued conqueror, and this conflict was carried on in the name of that high ideal of perfection, the measure of which is not on earth but in heaven, in the domain of the absolute. The heroic deeds of the conflict are painted in living colours by the sympathetic pens of pious chroniclers inspired to their work by a living love of the same truth, a living aspiration to the same ideal. In such works the masses instinctively discern the truth, and accept it without question, while the sceptical philosophy of the learned agnostic examines facts, thinks to extract from them the material truth, and abjuring the spiritual truth which echoes through every faithful soul, asks the ironical question, "What is truth?"

IV

In the classic myth of Prometheus nailed by Zeus to the Caucasian cliff, we may easily recognise the idea of modern scepticism in contradistinction with the idea of an Almighty God, the Creator of the universe. It is the protest of the proud soul against the general belief in the existence of God, the negation of that feeling of reverence for Godhead which pride cannot bear; the revolt against submission and adoration of the divinity. It matters little that from Godhead was stolen the sacred fire, which animates, warms, and fructifies mankind. The sceptic cares nothing for this— while enjoying the fire of divinity, he strives to live separate from divinity, as his own master.

The Sphinx of ancient fable sat at the cross-roads, and put a riddle to every passer-by. He who could not solve it was the Sphinx's prey, and disappeared into the pit; only the wise man who found a solution overcame the monster.

What is the sphinx in our life? Our whole life is an endless chain, a mechanical sequence of phenomena and facts. One succeeding another, one with another uniting, all on their flight bear questions to the human soul, and every instant in the course of time they bring to us the questions of the day. What wisdom do we need to solve them! He who does not possess that wisdom remains the *slave* of facts and phenomena—*the slave of his time*—of which he boasts himself the master. On all sides he is crushed by facts; they rule over him, till he becomes a man of vulgar routine, going so far in his blind submission to facts, that at last he loses the last gleam of that light which enlightens every being worthy of the calling of humanity. But when he remains faithful to the highest spiritual impulses of his nature; when he learns to appreciate the fundamental principles of spiritual life; when he firmly takes his stand in the domain of the soul, submitting to no facts, but ruling over them—then facts range themselves around him, each in its appointed place; they have not conquered him, for he has conquered them.

The sphinx of ancient Egypt differs from the sphinx of Greece, although both may be taken to symbolise the mystery of the human soul.

The sphinx of Egypt was a peaceful being, half human, half animal. Passing the long line of sphinxes before the temples and the royal sepulchres, man feels the proximity of God and the mystery of death. The sphinx is the symbol of mysterious contemplation absorbed in itself and in the idea of divinity. The ancient Egyptians personified in it the divinity of the sunlight.

Not such was the sphinx of the new world, the creation of Grecian fantasy. This sphinx was of demoniacal origin, the offspring of the monstrous Typhon and Echidna, the personification, not of the bright divinity, but of the dark powers of Tartarus, a being ferocious, predatory, and destroying. In it also is expressed a mystery, not the mystery of inspired contemplation, but the mystery of passionate, denying, violent, and destructive thought.

To the present day this sphinx has never ceased

to set to humanity riddles, terrible, mysterious, and insoluble. Thousands of minds have sought to find a solution of the riddle of life and of religion, but have failed. Each failure to find a solution but precipitates the thought and sentiment into new abysms, and each enigma brings forth hundreds and thousands insoluble as itself. Meanwhile, before our poor humanity gapes the monstrous pit of destruction, wherein each must fall if he does not stand on the rock of simple unshakeable faith and calm contemplation.

V

A great question which never ceases to trouble the conscience of humanity is the absence in human relations of the love and justice preached by Christ, and proclaimed by the Christian Church as the foundations of its doctrine. No human mind has yet found a key to this contradiction, yet no human conscience has escaped disturbance by it. When we consider the endless tale of sanguinary warfare, dissension, violence, injustice, ignorance, and superstition in public as in private life, with terror we ask ourselves, Where is the fulfilment of the law of Christ in the hell in which we live and move? How can we escape this tyranny where religion itself appears but as a mirror of falsehood and hypocrisy—a symbol of the contradiction that exists between conscience and action, a curtain of rites and formalities concealing an ensnared conscience, and a pretended justification of injustice? There are, indeed, the elect, men of justice, the humble

K

in spirit; there are works of charity and of reason, on which our minds may rest for a time. But consider life as a whole. We see authority abusing its mission; the unjust distribution of honour and glory; wealth acquired by rapine overmastering power itself and possessing the earth; insolent lawlessness veiled in external piety; thousands and millions borne in sacrifice to the god of war, to the idol of violence and enmity; finally, we see the innumerable multitude vegetate in insensibility, racked by privation, living and dying in wretchedness. Where is the kingdom of Christ, the kingdom of love and justice? where is the effective strength of religion? what is the aim and object of our miserable human life?

How often have we heard in the past, as we hear to-day, the proclamation of a golden age for humanity, ending in disillusionment if not in hopelessness—for the Christian may not abandon hope. The prophets of the Old Testament foretold a future condition of peace and prosperity for the world. Christ bore to the earth a commandment of love and peace, but not the realisation of His commandment, which would have left no freedom to men; this same commandment brought not peace but a sword, and lit a fire in the hearts of humanity. When, on His resurrection, from hearts inflamed with hope for the regeneration of the world the timid question rose, "Lord, wilt thou at this time restore again the kingdom to Israel?" His answer was: "It is not for you to know the times or the seasons which the Father has put in his own power." Time, measured by little periods among men, is infinite to God. To Him a thousand years are as a day, and a day is as a thousand years.

The young Christian Church of the first centuries through persecution and calamity was sustained by hope for the re-establishment of the kingdom of Israel : this hope for justice on earth was a new force which was borne by Christianity to the joyless pagan world. Then terrible times came when this force seemed to fail, and hope changed into despair. The destruction of Rome by Alaric struck the Christian world with inexpressible terror, and many trusting souls were darkened by doubt. Where was the Christian strength, where was its salvation? The pagan world cried out, "Behold the calamities which this new religion of Christ has brought!" Then Saint Augustine calmed the troubled conscience and revived the hopes of Christendom by his inspired book, "The City of God," in which he explained the ways of Providence in the history of the world, and the infallibility of the Christian teachings on the kingdom which is not of this world.

Since then in times of public calamity, in outbreaks of violence and social depravity, how many times has the same question been asked in the Christian world? We live in a time when the dead Paganism comes to life again, and, raising its head, strives to overcome Christianity, denying its dogmas, its ordinances, even the principles of its moral teaching. Like the pagan philosophers of the past, new prophets, with malicious irony, turn to the remnant of the faithful with the bitter reproach, "See to what a pass your Christianity has brought the world! What is the worth of a religion which has mutilated human nature, stealing from it that freedom in the satisfaction of its desires which alone constitutes happiness?" Can it be possible that that "victory which has vanquished the world" is to perish at the onslaught of Paganism?

No, for faith remains; the Holy Church, of which its Creator has said, "And the gates of hell shall not prevail against it," still holds the key of truth, and to-day, as in the past, those who are of the truth shall hear its voice. Through the medium of symbols and images it maintains the truth, and the power to collect that which is dispersed and to renovate the face of the earth. But He alone who holds the times and seasons in His hand knows when that day will come.

Meantime, from the day of its foundation, the proud and impatient have not ceased to seek outside the Church, and in opposition to it, new gospels to regenerate humanity, to fulfil the law of love and justice, to realise the ideal of peace and prosperity upon earth. Struck by the monstrous inconsistencies between the teachings of Christ and the lives of Christians, they impeach the Church and its works; abjuring an institution established since the foundation of Christianity, they aspire to replace it by a Church of Christ, in their opinion purified, severed from the universal Church, and based on their own interpretation of single precepts of the Gospel.

It is a strange error. Here are men subject to the passion and the sin to which all their fellow-creatures are given — men, in common with all the world, afflicted with a dual nature—condemned to will what they cannot do and to do what they do not will, priding themselves on unity of spirit, and taking up the unappointed work of the teacher and the prophet. While all the world, and they together with it, turn around, they delude themselves that they stand upon an immovable point. They begin with the destruction of the law, yet they are unable to establish a new law from the scraps and fragments of the teaching which they reject. They deny the Church, yet they must needs build a Church for themselves, with their own preachers and ministers, repeating among themselves that which they condemned and rebelled against, with the added faults of falsehood and hypocrisy, and an insensate pride which lifts them above the world. The pride of intellect and contempt for men of their own flesh and blood impel them to destroy the old law and to establish a new. They forget that the Divine Master whose name they invoke, being meek and humble of heart, would not change a single word of the law, but inspired each with the spirit of love and charity which He found concealed there.

While condemning dogma and ceremony, they themselves end as narrow and masterful dogmatics ; revolting against fanaticism and intolerance, they become the fiercest fanatics and persecutors. Unconsciously they themselves are corrupted by malice and passion. Blinded by pride they know not the scandal they bear to the faith, destroying its simplicity and completeness in the souls of those simple ones whom the Church has not yet enlightened and taught to know it well.

It is easy—but how mad, how iniquitous it is—to seduce a simple soul in which there is a pure, clear field of religious feeling, a soul uncultured and virgin to the influence of belief. It is sad to think that such souls are approached with confident denial of the

Church, and persuaded that the Church, with its doctrine and mysteries, its symbols, its ceremonies, and its traditions, with its poetry which has inspired from generation to generation a multitude of Christians, is a false and execrable institution. These souls in themselves are humble, sectarianism leads them to the heights of pride, while faith decays in the narrow prison of sectarian formulas. There is no soul, however virgin, which cannot be imbued with this insensate pride, this confidence in its own justice. And this before the whole people which constitutes the Church, living in humble consciousness of its sinfulness before God, with the humble hope of forgiveness, and salvation through the prayers of the Church! The fruits of this pride in its ultimate development are known. They are, first, *hypocrisy* in the pretence of righteousness; then malice and intolerance of all other faiths; and, lastly, a passionate desire to lead astray from the Church its scattered flock, to attain which end all means are allowable.

The Church is truly a lifeboat for inquiring minds, tortured by questions of what and how to believe. To start laden with these questions on the shoreless sea of research, doubt, and logical deduction, is perilous equally to the narrow mind of man, to his capricious imagination, and to his vanity seeking for a new path. Affirmed in a faith created by himself, abjuring the dominion of the Church, he may end by regarding himself as the prophet of a new faith; he may become intolerant and fanatical; a terrible delusion may ensnare him to make faith alone the necessary element of salvation, independent of life and work.

Christ, in His terrible denunciation of the scribes and pharisees of His time, not to them alone uttered a stern word of warning and condemnation. His words should be remembered by all the brainless fanatics of our time, the self-appointed teachers of new religions. "Neither be ye called masters, for one is your master, even Christ, and woe unto you, . . . for ye compass sea and land to make one proselyte!" The Christian Church has its teachers, appointed by Christ Himself as head of the Church. But who has appointed and sent these teachers of new religions? The spirit of vanity and pride has sent them, the spirit of the discord and hatred which they disseminate in men by their teachings. They fancy that by destroying the fence which guards the doctrine of Christ they will draw the people to the new teaching which they alone can understand. They speak of love, while, in seducing their fellow-man from communion with the Church, they instil in his heart feelings of pride, of malice, and hatred to his fellows who remain behind; and, using an instrument which they themselves have fashioned and name truth, they base their truth on negation of what has been accepted as truth by the Church which they have forsaken.

"Truth," these prophets tell us, "is the most precious attainment of the human soul. And if we be convinced that we possess the truth, shall we remain in inaction, when we may communicate it to our neighbours who have fallen away and know it not?" But who can assure these self-appointed teachers that this truth is not affirmed merely on personal conceptions and experience? where is their testimony? Can they maintain that it bears the

stamp of divine revelation? Have they a right to
proclaim it in the words of the ancient prophets,
" Thus spake the Lord." Their pretended authenticity
is nothing better than personal conviction, sincere
it may be : if for them this is enough, to their neighbours it is nothing. Have they received commands
from above to go into the world with a gospel and
teach humanity an inspired religion? Can they
show such commands, and prove their authenticity?
No. So each prophet of a new religion, however
irresistible his convictions, must show respect to the
convictions of his fellow-men.

But the fanatic of the new religion will not
admit the necessity for this respect, he casts it
away as something unworthy of him. He begins
his operations, advancing against the stronghold
of his neighbour's faith with intent to destroy all
its defences, bringing to bear at once the whole
religious system with which he would replace it.
The ancient faith, consecrated by centuries, for
those who hold it is the main support of life ;
and the deeper and sincerer, the firmer its foundations the more provocative is his attack, the
more he is inflamed by desire to destroy it,
and on its ruins to raise the religion devised
by himself. His aim, in appearance, is construc-
tive, but all his actions are destroying. Having
overthrown the ancient edifice, our architect wishes
to raise it anew, but he has never reflected how
easy it is to destroy and how difficult to rebuild.
The ruined building stood on foundations rooted
in the depths : the new building must have new
foundations in a new soil. With a daring hand

he strives to surpass the immemorial work of the human soul. Who gave strength and authority for this to the destroyer? He has taken his victim, and led him—whither? Into the wilderness, where a hundred sinuous paths diverge, but no straight road is found. Whatever the aim, such is the end of the fanatical religious reformer—the wilderness.

VI

The founders of religion recognising from the heights of contemplation the idea of Godhead and its relations to man, evolved in conformity therewith an order of rites and ceremonials inspired by that idea. But the mass of the people remains in the valley, and the light of pure contemplation shining above the hills does not reach it at once. To the people religious sentiments are expressed by a number of ceremonies and traditions which from the austerest standpoint may seem superstition and idolatry. Zealous defenders of the faith, alarmed and indignant, sometimes attempt with violent hand to destroy these external expressions of the vulgar faith, as Moses destroyed the golden calf raised by Aaron at the demand of the people, when the prophet was lost in high contemplation on the summit of Mount Sinai. Thence springs the Puritan zeal of the leaders of religion, passing often to fanaticism.

But in this envelope of the popular religion, often rude, are hidden elements of faith susceptible of development and sublimation, the germs of eternal truth. In tradition and in ceremonial, in symbolism and in custom, the people sees the actual incarnation of that which expressed in abstract formula would be neither real nor effective. What if destroying the husk we deaden the kernel of truth ; if pulling up the tares we pull up also the wheat ? What if in striving to purify the faith of the people under the pretext of enmity to superstition we destroy the faith itself? If the forms by which simple men express their faith in the living God repel us, let us remember that it is to us, perhaps, the command of our Divine Master was given : " Take heed that ye despise not one of these little ones that believe in Me."

In an Arabic poem we find the instructive parable of the celebrated teacher Djelalledin. Once Moses, while wandering in the wilderness, came upon a shepherd who was praying fervently to God. This was the shepherd's prayer :—" How shall I know where to find thee, and how to be thy servant ? How I should wish to put on thy sandals, to comb thy hair, to wash thy garments, to kiss thy feet, to care for thy dwelling, to give thee milk from my herd ; for such is the desire of my heart." Moses, when he heard the words of the shepherd, was angered, and reproached him. " Thou blasphemest! The Most High God has no body, he wants neither clothing, nor dwelling, nor service. What dost thou mean, unbeliever ? " The heart of the shepherd was saddened, because he could not conceive a being without bodily form and corporeal needs : he was taken by despair and ceased to serve the Lord. But God spoke to Moses and said : "Why hast thou driven away from me my servant ? Every

man has taken from me the form of his being and
the manner of his speech. What to thee is evil, to
another is good, to thee it is poison, to another it is
sweet honey. To me words are nothing. I look into
the heart of man."

VII

The Persian poet, Mohammed Roumi, who lived in
the thirteenth century, is the author of the celebrated
poem " Masnava." It contains some remarkable
verses on prayer which are worthy of a trusting
soul :—

" A certain man cried out in the silence of the
night, ' Oh, Allah ! ' But Satan answered, ' Be
silent, thou fool, thou hast babbled enough already!
Thou wilt never hear an answer from the height of
the throne, however much thou mayst cry " Allah ! "
and look disheartened.'

" The man's heart was troubled, and he hung his
head. Then appeared to him the prophet Kisr, and
asked : ' Why hast thou ceased to call on God, and
repented of thy prayers ? ' The man answered, ' I
got no answer from Allah ; I heard no voice saying,
" I am here," and I fear that the gates of salvation are
shut against me.' Kisr answered, ' Thus has Allah
commanded me, " Go thou to him and say, ' Oh,
man, tried by much, have I not commanded thee
to serve me ; have I not commanded thee to call on
me. And my reply, " Here am I " is the same as
thine " Oh, Allah ! " Thy suffering, thy ardour, and
thy zeal, all these are my messengers to thee : when

thou strugglest with thyself and cryest for help, by this struggle and cry I draw thee to myself, and answer thy prayer. Thy fear and thy love are the signs of my forgiveness, and in thy words, "O Allah!" is a multitude of answers, "I am with thee."' "

THE IDEALS OF UNBELIEF

I

THE ancient words, " The fool hath said in his heart, there is no God," apply with especial force to-day. Their truth is plainer than the sun, although now all " progressive minds " are possessed by a passionate desire to live without God, to conceal Him, to deny His presence. Even men at heart benevolent and honourable ask themselves how they may realise benevolence, honour, and conscience without God.

The Government of France, in the last stage of political disintegration, has organised its national schools without God. Among us, unhappily, certain representatives of intelligence have rivalled the Moscow princess, who said, " Ah, France, no better country in the world ! "—for not long ago a celebrated schoolmaster pointed out the French scholastic system as a model worthy of imitation.

Among the latest books officially prescribed for study in the female schools of France is one entitled, " Instruction Morale et Civique des Jeunes Filles." This is in the nature of a secular catechism of morals, appointed to replace the study of the Word of God.

This book is worthy of notice. It is divided into three sections, each bearing a different title. The first is composed of certain moral precepts on duty, honesty, conscience, and so forth. The second part

157

contains a short description of the State and of the national institutions. The third part treats of woman, her mission, faculties, and virtues. The matter in the book is concise, simple, and clear, written as a text-book ought to be with a multitude of clear examples and illustrations. No exception can be taken to the manner of this book ; it preaches order, good morals, purity of thought and intention, kind deeds ; it approves with emphasis the sentiment and recognition of duty, and carefully sets forth a woman's duties in social and domestic life.

One thing alone is notable. On no single page is mentioned the name of God, nor is there the slightest reference to the religious feeling. The author, after explaining the great importance of the part played in man by conscience, defines it thus : "Conscience is our conception of the opinion which others have about us and our actions" (*considération de l'opinion des autres*). On this treacherous and mutable base, the *opinion of others*, is affirmed the moral foundation of our lives. How excellently this illustrates the ancient proverb, "Who thinks himself too wise becomes a fool."

Unhappily, to this stream of idiotcy flooding France to-day are drawn even from our poor Russia little rills of native intelligence ; and in our newspapers and gazettes, in our leading articles and feuilletons are repeated in chorus the words of the Moscow princess. To the same chorus too often are drawn those well-meaning, but simple and inexperienced men, who fancy newspapers must bring to them some "new word" of civilisation.

Nothing is more deplorable than the reasoning on

the subject of education of our journalist critics, who tell us that while religion and religious training are indispensable, churches and ministers must be abolished. Sometimes they speak more plainly. "We do not reject religious teaching, we even demand it ; we cannot understand education without it ; but we object to Clericalism." By this term we must understand the Church and everything appertaining thereto. This Jesuitical casuistry, which the apostles of popular education have made peculiarly their own, misleads many readers who cannot appreciate subtlety in writing.

These good men do not know that the word religion, as many other words, has changed its signification, and is made by many to imply something from which, if they but understood it, believers in God would recoil with abhorrence. They do not know that in our time religion may exist without God, and that the very word God, in its application by so-called men of science, has a double meaning.

In 1882 appeared a remarkable book which awakened general interest. Therein the negation of God, by the enemies of all religion, was expressed with ferocity, with reckless and malicious irony, with a demand for the exclusive consideration of matter in the universe. The first part of the work expressed, in a tranquil tone, with dignity, with an ideal outlook on life, the whole teaching of the religion without God. This book was entitled "Natural Religion" (London, 1882). Its author, Professor Seeley of Oxford, was he whose former "Ecce Homo," which appeared ten years before, had attracted the attention, not only of men of science, but of religious idealists who sought in it some new word on Christ and the Christian faith. A Russian translation of this latter work has been published by an admirer.

But to the adherents of the Church Mr Seeley's work seemed strange and questionable. Few could look on it without distrust.

This book contained an artistic analysis of the earthly life and character of Jesus Christ, treating exclusively of his human nature. It was written in a spirit of deep piety, in the language of philosophy, with occasional recourse to the terminology of theologians. The object of the work seemed to be to hold up the image of Christ to pious imitation. The author, it seemed, was a Christian, full of religious feeling. But many religious readers took alarm, as if their views and sentiments of Christianity were not in accord with the views and sentiments of the author. The picture of Christ was a picture of supreme holiness, purity, and goodness, but not that picture which we have been taught to venerate from childhood—not the Christ honoured by the Christian Church. Something discordant appeared throughout the book, as if the author had either lost all faith, or was on the point of losing it. Nevertheless, the writer plainly affirmed his faith in the existence of a personal God; in the immortality of the human soul; in the Messianic significance of the appearance of Christ; and even, although with some hesitation, in the reality of His miracles.

Ten years passed; again Mr Seeley appeared as the inspired prophet of religion, this time a new religion, and not the religion of Christ. The ancient revelation, he said, had done its work; instead, a new revelation had come; the naturalists, historians, and philologists of the age had borne us a revelation of which the ancient prophets had never dreamed. The Biblical criticism of German scholars was greater and more perfect than the Bible itself. With uncommon simplicity, turning to the believers and members of the Church, he asks: " Why should we quarrel, why should there be strife between us? We may unite in a single faith. We, men of science, also trust in God. Our God is Nature, which in one sense is a revelation too. Therefore we are not atheists," he repeats, "and the battle between us, men of science, and you, men of faith, is merely a battle of words. Is it not the same? For us God is Nature, and the scientific theory of the universe is a theory of theism also. Nature is a force existing outside of us; its law for us is absolute: there is the divinity which we adore."

Is it not strange that the author, while rejecting the personal existence of God, at the same time protests with energy against the accusation of atheism, which he rejects and condemns? What is atheism, then? This question Mr Seeley answers with a tortuous subtlety which to a simple mind must seem insanity.

"There is an atheism which is a mere speculative crotchet, and there is an atheism which is a great moral disease. . . . The purest form of such real atheism might be called by the general name of *wilfulness*. All human activity is a transaction with Nature. It is the arrangement of a compromise between what we want on the one hand, and what Nature has decreed on the other. Not to recognise anything but your own will, to fancy anything within your reach if you only will strongly

L

enough, to acknowledge no superior power outside yourself which must be considered, and in some way propitiated, if you would succeed in any undertaking : this is complete wilfulness, or, in other words, pure atheism."—Seeley, " Natural Religion," p. 27.

To illustrate this obscure and disorderly argument, our author takes as example a country in its fate a symbol of pure atheism, and points to Poland.

" *Sedet æternumque sedebit*," says he, " that unhappy Poland, not indeed extinguished, but partitioned, and every thirty years decimated anew, expiates the crime of atheistic wilfulness, the fatal pleasure of unbounded individual liberty, which rose up against the very nature of things."—*Ibid.* p. 29.

Having disclosed this theory of religion, he describes in detail how the religious feeling is born from science, and, passing through the prism of imagination, is refracted in the moral nature of man into a religious trinity : the religion of Nature, the religion of Humanity, and the religion of Beauty.

In this book, written with talent and spirit, is a doctrine by no means new, although for the first time expressed with such completeness. The reader finds there the well-known features of the Positivism so fashionable in our time—features familiar through the writings of Kant, George Eliot, and Herbert Spencer—the well-beloved of Russian translators. Not one of these writers exposes so clearly the internal weakness of this fashionable theory as the author of " Natural Religion." To what idiotcy must the mind have sunken when, drawn by the pride of self-adoration, it rejects the supernatural in life and nature, and strives to build a theory of life in relation to the universe. This theory is condemned to turn in an enchanted circle, and to contradict itself for ever. Denying a personal God, in vain it would sustain religion and establish an object of religious feeling; for, except the living God, there can be no object of religion. Rejecting the invisible world, the immortality of the soul, and the future life, it proclaims that the end of life is happiness, and would confine humanity within the limits of matter and of its earthly nature. Condemning revelation as invention or fantasy, and every dogma as falsehood, it seeks to support itself by a new dogma, proclaiming as an indisputable axiom the constant and endless progress of humanity.

This theory, in a flash, reflects that *wilfulness* and that obduracy of thought which our author combines in his conception of atheism. It shows no sign of that clear and simple confidence which serves as a symptom of the truth and durability of doctrines. In their sermons on the happiness of humanity, its prophets all stumble on an actuality which they cannot deny. This actuality is the inevitable presence of evil and of evil works, of violence and of injustice in human life—the argument of pessimism. This argument cannot be lived down, although some of the apostles of Positivism strive to stifle its voice or hypocritically to ignore it, while others, more conscientious, stand by it with grief and questioning. To the number of the last belongs our author. While extolling the new religion of Nature, Humanity, and Beauty, and proving the strength and actuality of the cult it preaches, at the same time he admits that hardly have we found satisfaction in these ideas when pessimism raises its head

and brings us to despair. If it were not for pessimism, he declares, nothing would destroy our religious
beliefs. And at the end of the book, when crowning
his edifice, he makes these remarks :

> "The more our thoughts widen and deepen, as the universe
> grows upon us and we become accustomed to boundless space and
> time, the more petrifying is the contrast of our own insignificance,
> the more contemptible become the pettiness, shortness, fragility of
> the individual life. A moral paralysis creeps upon us. For a while
> we comfort ourselves with the notion of self-sacrifice ; we say, What
> matter if I pass, let me think of others ! But the *other* has become
> contemptible no less than the self ; all human griefs alike seem little
> worth assuaging, human happiness too paltry at the best to be worth
> increasing. The whole moral world is reduced to a point ; the
> spiritual city, 'the goal of all the saints,' dwindles to the 'least of
> little stars' ; good and evil, right and wrong, become infinitesimal,
> ephemeral matters, while eternity and infinity remain attributes of
> that only which is outside the realm of morality. Life becomes
> more intolerable the more we know and discover, so long as every-
> thing widens and deepens, except our own duration, and that remains
> as pitiful as ever. The affections die away in a world where every-
> thing great and enduring is cold ; they die of their own conscious
> feebleness and bloodlessness.
>
> "Supernatural Religion met this want by connecting Love and
> Righteousness with eternity. If it is shaken, how shall its place
> be supplied ? And what would Natural Religion avail then ?"
> *Ibid.* p. 261.

Who would believe that these words were written
by the ardent prophet of Natural Religion? Thus
may a serious mind be entangled in the intellectual
network it weaves.

The essence of this work, with all its moderation
of tone, with all the sincerity of its author, is a joyless
paradox. That the various systems of cosmology,
the scientific, the artistic, and the humanist, contain elements of religious feeling cannot be denied.

But they do not embody the elements of a new faith, of a new church ; they are separate limbs— *disjecta membra*—of the Christian philosophy of life. Religion is impossible without the recognition of axiomatic truths unattainable by the path of induction. To such truths belong the existence of a personal God, and the immaterial nature of the human soul, whence springs supernaturalism, without which religion is inconceivable. With the exception of mathematics, scientific truths are by their nature hypothetical : they exist consciously only for scholars, and only by deception may be imparted to the mass in dogmatic form. This deception obtains among us and progresses—of this we find fresh evidence every day.

II

Intolerance of strange beliefs and strange opinions has never been so sharply expressed as it is nowadays by the apostles of radical and negative beliefs, among whom such intolerance is merciless and bitter, and joined with animosity and contempt. When we consider the relations of these teachers to the new doctrines they proclaim, their intolerance is more abhorrent than the old religious intolerance which expressed itself in sanguinary persecution. Then persecution was based on unqualified faith in a truth which absolutely existed. When men believe that they possess an absolute truth, sprung from the ultimate principle of life and involving happiness for all, as the Moslem believes in the Koran, it is conceivable that they may consider it a duty

not only openly to preach their doctrine, but, if need
be, by violence to enforce it upon others. But when
it is merely an opinion, although it may be that
nothing is more probable for him who formed it,
how can we understand fanaticism so great that its
advocate does not admit not only contradiction but
even compromise, although conditional and temporary, with adverse opinion? Yet such passionate
attachment to their own convictions or to the doctrines
of their schools is an attribute to all the prophets of
negation. Rejecting, as if it were not, the whole
former history of the spiritual development of
humanity, ignoring all ancient faiths and the spiritual
conditions of peoples, denying all rights of independent
existence, repelled not by the sanctity of personal faith,
they claim admittance to every soul, and everywhere
strive to establish their new religion. This they call
the truth of their convictions. One of the representatives of the doctrine of Comte and the Positivists
(John Morley "On Compromise") maintains that
the first duty of every man to himself and to
humanity is to solve in his heart the question, Does
he or does he not believe in the existence of God?
Should he reach the conviction that faith in God is no
better than a blind and unhealthy superstition, it is his
sacred duty to break in with this conviction on every
soul, to take advantage of every occasion to convert,
firstly, his kinsmen and neighbours, and then, if possible,
the people ; to proclaim it everywhere, and in private
and public life wholly to renounce all forms and
ceremonies which, directly or indirectly, express
a faith opposed to his conviction. What is this
but a terrible violence against the conscience of

others—and in the name of what? In the name of a personal opinion.

In this hell of vanity we can find neither love nor faith. But without love and without faith there can be no truth. How different to listen to the voice of the old true teacher! What faith and love, what knowledge of the human soul is there in those words in which the Apostle to the Corinthians enjoins respect for human conscience. He knows the truth, but with his deep spiritual knowledge how cautiously would he approach the human soul! His purpose is that the soul shall accept and embrace the new belief in the spirit of *sincerity and truth* by faith alone, without disunion, without discord with itself. All that comes not from faith is sin. And the Apostle teaches the strong and learned that they must spare the consciences of their weaker brethren even in superstition, when the soul is not ripe to accept the truth with entire faith.

The Apostle, the herald of Christian freedom, acting from conviction, sacrifices freedom itself to the sanctity of conscience, knowing that conscience is dearer than all. You know, says he, that meat commendeth us not to God; for neither if we eat are we the better; neither if we eat not are we the worse. You know that the idol is nothing, that the false God does not exist, therefore with quiet conscience buy meat and eat it, which was brought as sacrifice to the idol.

III

Nothing is more surprising than the fatuity of clever men who have grown up in estrangement from actual life, and who are blinded by confidence in the infallibility of logic. By adoration of reason they are seduced from religion, and at last incited to hatred of every faith in the only living God. But those who at the same time are men of conscience, find that they cannot rid themselves of the aspiration to faith innate in humanity; those whose hearts are unhardened by the severity of logic admit the lawfulness of religious feeling in man, and strive to satisfy it by some religion devised by themselves. We may wonder at the fancifulness of plans contrived by minds apparently striving to drive away everything like fancy out of their reasoning and deliberations. Strauss, in his work on "The Old and the New Faith," while rejecting Christianity, speaks with enthusiasm of the religious sentiment, but as its object and centre replaces the living God with the idea of the World, the so-called *Universum*. After the death of Mill, his occasional thoughts on religion appeared in London under the title, "Three Essays on Religion: Nature, the Utility of Religion, and Theism." The utility of religion he admits without reserve, and, while rejecting Christianity, he speaks of the individual Christ with the greatest enthusiasm.

"The value of religion to the individual, both in the past and present, as a source of personal satisfaction and of elevated feelings, is not to be disputed. But it has still to be considered whether, in order to obtain this good, it is necessary to travel beyond the boundaries of the world which we inhabit; or whether the idealisation of our earthly life, the cultivation of a high conception of what *it* may be made, is not capable of supplying a poetry, and, in the best sense of the word, a religion, equally fitted to exalt the feelings, and (with the same aid from education) still better calculated to ennoble the conduct, than any belief respecting the unseen powers." "Three Essays on Religion" (Utility of Religion), pp. 104-5. London, 1874.

The question is worthy of Mill as we know him by the history of his education. It is interesting to note how in his decision of this question, Mill could not, with Strauss, accept as decisive the idea of the Universe, for Mill, strange to say, did not trust in Nature. In the beginning of the same book, true as ever to his estrangement from reality, he speaks of

"Enquiry into the truth of the doctrines which make Nature a test of right and wrong, good and evil, or which in any mode or degree attach merit or approval to following, imitating, or obeying Nature."—*Ibid.* (Nature), p. 13.

These doctrines Mill rejects, for in Nature he sees blind force and nothing more. Nature inspires desires which it does not satisfy; it builds great edifices, powers, and actions, in a moment to overthrow them; it destroys blindly and indiscriminately all that it has created. For this reason Mill declines to construct on Nature any system of morals or of religion.

What, then, does he think? These are his own words:

"When we consider how ardent a sentiment, in favourable circumstances of education, the love of country has become, we cannot judge it impossible that the love of that larger country, the world, may be nursed into similar strength, both as a source of elevated emotion and as a principle of duty. He who needs any other lesson on this subject than the whole course of ancient history affords, let him read Cicero *De Officiis*. It cannot be said that the standard of morals laid down in that celebrated treatise is a high standard. To our notions, it is on many points unduly lax, and admits capitulations of conscience. But on the subject of duty to our country there is no compromise. That any man, with the smallest pretensions to virtue, could hesitate to sacrifice life, reputation, family, everything valuable to him, to the love of country, is a supposition which this eminent interpreter of Greek and Roman morality cannot entertain for a moment. If, then, persons could be trained, as we see they were, not only to believe in theory that the good of their country was an object to which all others ought to yield, but to feel this practically as the grand duty of life, so also may they be made to feel the same absolute obligation towards the universal good. A morality grounded on large and wise views of the whole, neither sacrificing the individual to the aggregate nor the aggregate to the individual, but giving to duty, on the one hand, and to freedom and spontaneity, on the other, their proper province, would derive its power in the superior natures from sympathy and benevolence and the passion for ideal excellence ; in the inferior, from the same feelings cultivated up to the measure of their capacity, with the superadded force of shame. This exalted morality would not depend for its ascendency on any hope of reward ; but the reward which might be looked for, and the thought of which would be a consolation in suffering, and a support in moments of weakness, would not be a problematical future existence, but the approbation in this of those whom we respect, and ideally of all those, dead or living, whom we admire or venerate. For, the thought that our dead parents or friends would have approved our conduct is a scarcely less powerful motive than the knowledge that our living ones do approve it ; and the idea that Socrates, or Howard or Washington, or Antoninus, or Christ, would have sympathised with us, or that we are attempting to do our part in the spirit in which they did theirs, has operated on the very best minds as a strong incentive to act up to their highest feelings and convictions.

"To call these sentiments by the name of morality, exclusively of any other title, is claiming too little for them. They are a real religion ; of which, as of other religions, outward good works (the utmost meaning usually suggested by the word morality) are only a part, and are indeed rather the fruits of the religion than the religion itself. The essence of religion is the strong and earnest direction of the emotions and desires towards an ideal object, recognised as of the highest excellence, and as rightfully paramount over all selfish objects of desire. This condition is fulfilled by the Religion of Humanity in an eminent degree, and in as high a sense, as by the supernatural religions even in their best manifestations, and far more so than in any of their others." *Ibid.* (Utility of Religion), pp. 107-9.

The foregoing words explain themselves. They show the narrowness, we should say rather the idiotcy, of human wisdom when it seeks an abstract conception of life and of humanity, while ignoring life itself, and rejecting the human soul. Such a religion may indeed be sufficient for thinkers like Mill, secluded from the world in abstract speculation, but how shall the people accept and understand it?—the people, a living organism held in communion only by living sentiment and conscience, and repelled by abstractions and generalities. In the people, such a religion, if it bore fruit at all, would bear fruit in reversion to paganism. The people—which we cannot conceive detached from Nature—if it forgot the faith of its fathers, would again personify the idea, either of the universe, resolving it into separate forces, or of that humanity which stands as a binding spiritual principle, resolving it also into its representative spiritual forces; and there would result so many false gods instead of one true God. It cannot be that we are condemned to suffer this?

THE NEW RELIGION AND THE NEW MARRIAGE

WE are told that our religion is drawing to its end, that a new faith will replace it, the dawn of which is on the point of appearing. God grant that this may be delayed, and that, if it must come, it may not be for long! For it will not be a time of enlightenment, but of darkness.

The ancient faith contains all that human nature has of sincerity—the sincerity of direct sensations and conscience, the sincerity which, from the depths of our spiritual nature, corresponds to the words of divine revelation. This is a living truth, and its roots are sunken in the souls of all. Of it was it said: "Every one that is of the truth heareth my voice."

The ancient faith was founded on the consciousness of every man of a living soul which is immortal and one, a living soul he confounds neither with Nature nor with humanity. By this he knows himself before God and before his fellow-men, by this he wishes to live eternally. By this he enters into the free alliance of love with others, and, as he lives in his soul, so he answers for it himself. Through this the existence of his Creator is revealed as simply as his own life, and by this simple feeling, independently of reason, he maintains his faith.

The prophets of a new religion appear. Some laugh at the ancient faith, and would destroy it,

without the will to create anew. Others appear
more serious ; they seek supreme wisdom, and strive
to impose on us a wisdom of their own. Each offers
us his own conception of truth, his favourite system
of religion, for all apprehend the necessity of religion,
and each would create one himself. How pitiable
are these creations ! They lack the power to draw
the living soul and inspire it with a living idea, for
not one of them sets the living spirit of God in the
centre of his faith.

In recent times many various systems have appeared from the pens of philosophers, each at will
attempting to construct for humanity a faith without
God. Each would constitute his system on the basis
of reason, by its nature an absurdity. For human
reason in a straight path, ignoring and rejecting no
facts of Nature or of the human soul, can never
eliminate the idea of God. The true source of atheism
is not in the mind but in the heart, for, as the prophet
said, "The fool hath said in his heart, there is no God."
In the heart, that is, in the will, is the source of all
error, however reason may seek to explain it. Error
is born by the desire of the heart for full freedom,
by rebellion against the commandments, and against
Him who is the beginning and the end of all commandments. To free oneself of the commandments, there
is no other path than to reject their supreme authority,
and to replace it by the authority of self. The oldest
of human histories is repeated from generation to
generation, " Ye shall be as gods, knowing good and
evil." This has been the source of atheism from
immemorial time.

It is wonderful, indeed, how reason deceives itself.

Without God it seems that there can be no religion, yet such a religion is proclaimed by atheists. They say, "In the place of these outworn tales of God let us put the truth. God is nowhere visible, while Nature and humanity are actual facts. Humanity is not only a fact, it is a force able, by the paths of reason and experience, to attain in the course of centuries unimaginable perfection. This idea of progression contains such internal force and profundity that it is enough to compensate man for religious sentiment, and to bind the race in the universal religion of humanity." Is this not the Biblical, "Ye shall be as gods"? Such are the doctrines of modern Positivist science, and of the so-called Utilitarianism.

From another side appears the celebrated apostle of the Tubingen school, the pillar of Biblical criticism, who lived to an old age in denial of the historic foundation of Christianity. This is Dr Strauss, the author of the "Life of Jesus"; the author of "The Old and the New Religion," in which he himself says he has made his confession, and given to the world the result of all his learned labours and philosophical speculations on God, on Nature, and on humanity. In youth, in the "Life of Jesus," he undertook, with some respect and caution, the analysis of those facts consecrated by the traditional belief of man, touching with tenderness the fundamental ideas of faith. In this work is seen a remnant of respect for God. But later we find a furious irritation against the Godhead, as a false and pernicious fable which has corrupted the minds of mankind.

But while rejecting God, by a strange inconsistency of thought, he does not abandon the religious feeling. In himself he feels the necessity, and affirms the existence, of religious devotion. What is the object of this devotion, which at the same time has power to possess and inspire the soul? Not a personal divinity which exists not, but the world (*Universum*) which constitutes the source of all good and power—which exists by the law of pure reason. We *demand*, he says, for this Universe the same devout feeling as a good man of the ancient faith cherished towards God.

What is this Universe, and what its spiritual element? Answering that question, Strauss reveals himself as a disciple of the Positivist philosophy, and of the new materialism. The doctrine of Kant and of Laplace on the exclusive activity of mechanical forces in the planetary system, he applies absolutely to all the phenomena of animal and spiritual life ; he regards the soul of man as nothing better than the result of the complex interaction of mechanical forces. The soul as a spiritual essence Strauss rejects. As might be expected, he accepts triumphantly the theories of Darwin on the Origin of Species, limiting not their application to the phenomena of the external world, but extending them capriciously to all the manifestations of life. The imperfection and inconsistency of Darwin's reasonings do not alarm him in the least. All doubt is eliminated by his new religion, by faith in his own hypothesis, incompatible, he tells us, with the existence of God. It matters not that such abstract hypotheses as spontaneous generation remain unproven. He cannot say how or when, but without doubt some day they will be proven.   In considering the origin of man, he does not trouble to explain and reconcile the origin of his intellectual powers, his moral ideas, and his æsthetic conceptions.   All is explained by the magic words, "Natural Selection."   Surely, if this capricious infatuation with theory constitutes the new religion, that religion is nothing better than a new superstition.

The doctrine of Darwin could not have appeared at a time more opportune for the prophets of the new religion.   It enlightened them with a new light, it gave them the keystone which they sought to crown the vault of their system.   They seized upon his teaching with eagerness, and then proclaimed that the ancient faith was finally overthrown and annihilated.   From every point they hastened to apply his principles to all the phenomena of social life, deducing conclusions of which, it may be, Darwin never dreamed.   As often happens, the pupils out-distanced the master, and the day is near when they will condemn him as a reactionary. Meantime, the doctrines of Darwin, restricted in application to the facts from which they sprang, hardly justify those apprehensions for the safety of the faith which they awakened in its jealous adherents.   The system of Galileo, the theories of Newton, all new discoveries in geological science, in their day awakened more agitation and fear ; yet the faith of believers has in no way suffered.   So will it be with the teachings of Darwin.   As yet, these are not recognised as confirmed by science, and the first enthusiasm they awakened is beginning to wane.   They are accepted without reserve only by the *dii minorum gentium.* Leading men of science are beginning to learn that these doctrines in reality are hypotheses, more or less in accord with probability, but still unconfirmed by sufficient data ; and that the conclusions drawn by the illustrious scholar from his numerous experiments, in reality are bold and ingenious generalisations, which leave a great field for question and incertitude.

These propositions, exalted to the dignity of absolute truth, are echoed by the masses as *verbum magistri*, they are catch-words on the lips of the base chatterers of Liberalism, and, on the other hand, they lend to many serious minds a basis for new intellectual combinations. Who has not Darwin on his lips to-day? Who does not play with the phrases, Natural Selection, Sexual Selection, the Struggle for Existence? The discoveries of Darwin have forced not only superficial thinkers, but earnest and studious men, to make strange leaps in their reasoning, and to make still stranger speeches, which, to a healthy judgment, seem nothing better than fantasy or madness. This is the more common among those who wish, with the aid of Darwin's teaching, to construct or perfect a system of cosmology independent of God. But above all, the doctrines of Darwin are most useful to the reasoning of modern materialism. Man, in the opinion of Darwin, has wrongly appropriated to himself and to his soul a privileged position in the universe ; of the animal creation he fancies himself alone under the immediate and personal direction of divinity. This, says Darwin, is a " pernicious idea." Like every other animal, man is nothing more than

M

a product of the successive and illimitable evolution of natural forms of animal life. To those who wish to do so, it is easy to conclude from this that there is no God and no immortal soul. It follows, further, from the teaching of Darwin, that all existing forms of life have sprung—as all their successors will spring —from the eternal and unceasing progression of matter, one form evolving another, with fresh developments and proper instruments to supply its needs. To those who are so inclined, it is easy to deduce from this that creative power is constituted by this eternal movement, and is inherent in matter which therefore holds in itself the future of Nature and humanity, being capable of indefinite progress and perfection ; hence there is no need to seek an external ultimate creative power, or a Providence directing the universe and humanity. It may easily be conceived how such reasoning accords with the tastes of those who have rejected God, and put their faith in humanity. But it is incredible that common-sense, rejecting a first cause, can believe in the eternity of matter, and trust that movement alone, although through eternal time, is capable of producing all that may be conceived.

It will be an unhappy time—if ever it should come —when the new cult of humanity shall dominate the world. The personality of man at once would lose its value, and the moral barriers existing against violence and arbitrary power would soon be destroyed. In the name of a doctrine, for the attainment of an imaginary end—the perfection of the race—will be sacrificed without scruple the most sacred privileges of personal freedom. Conscience will not be considered, for the very idea will be denied. Our present-day reformers, trained in a school of conceptions, ideas, and sentiments which they afterwards abjure, are in no state to realise the terrible emptiness which the moral world will present when these ideas shall have been destroyed. Whatever the infatuation of modern lawgivers, modern administrators, and modern authority, over all nevertheless inevitably hangs, though sometimes unconsciously, the conception of a human personality which cannot be crushed as a worm. This conception is rooted in the knowledge that every man has a living soul, one, indivisible and immortal, enjoying, therefore, an absolute existence which cannot be destroyed by any human power. Hence there is no criminal who, in the midst of his crime, does not look on the living soul he injures with terror and respect. Uproot this sentiment, and what will be the fate of our legislation, our government, our social life? The friends of individual freedom strangely deceive themselves when in its name they join the rising cult of humanity.

But happily we may hope that the dawn promised us in the future by the humanist philosophy will never be revealed to mankind, or, at least, will not be revealed to all, or for long. Of the consequence of the new doctrines on religion and life we may judge by some of their political applications indicated from time to time. Here is a specimen of the application of Darwinism to the sphere of practical legislation. A favourite speculation of Darwin treats of the benefit to humanity of restrictions on the liberty of marriage. In the beginning of his treatise Darwin explains that one of the essential elements

of Christianity is the personal responsibility of men
for their souls and their independence in the spiritual
sphere from one another.   In consequence of this
it is assumed that men have a right to dispose, on
their own responsibility, of their bodies also.   This
right, according to Darwin, must give way to the
action of the new law which he has discovered, the
so-called doctrine of evolution.   Man has a right to
dispose of his body and to seek the satisfaction of
his bodily needs only in so far as is compatible
with the normal development of the race.   Thus in
measure as the science of Darwinism, from its observations of material life, makes new generalisations
from the law of evolution, legislation must restrict
the personal freedom of man even in the satisfaction
of his organic needs.

After citing statistics, gathered from two or three
learned works on the physiological influence of
heredity on the human organism, Darwin declares
that in England one in every five hundred is insane,
that this insanity proceeds in many cases from
hereditary disposition, transmitted by marriage and
birth, and that the number of lunatics increases in
geometrical progression.   Thus humanity is threatened
with the infinite spread of an evil against which
measures must be taken.   Our author then proposes
the rigorous restriction of the liberty of the marriage
contract.   It is necessary, he tells us, to improve and
strengthen the physical organism in the human race,
and for this end we must take artificial measures to
compensate for the weakening of the forces of natural
selection.   Only with such conditions, we are assured,
is human progress possible.   *Mens sana in corpore*

sano. The triumphs of the medical art in this matter
are not of general advantage, but a general evil.
Darwin has no doubt that the level of health in
contemporary society has become lowered to an
alarming extent, and that medical art, by sustaining
the weaker organisms, only increases the evil for
future generations. It is necessary, he tells us, to
lessen the number of the weak in conflict with the
strong in the struggle for existence.

The following are the means by which Darwin
proposes that legislation shall attain this end. The
legal obstacles to marriage, which now exist, shall
remain in force. In addition, the law shall, *in the
first place*, recognise the appearance in one of the
parties of certain diseases as cause for obligatory
divorce. What are these diseases? Darwin gives
a long list of ailments transmitted by heredity; we
find there diseases of the lungs, of the stomach,
of the liver, gout, scrofula, rheumatism, and others;
so that every married person who does not enjoy
herculean health must tremble daily for the security
of the marriage contract, with all the more reason
because its dissolution would accord with the
interests of the State, or, we should rather say, with
the interests of mankind. That Darwin had in view
the institution of an inquisitorial process, we must
assume, because, *in the second place*, he proposes to
establish a general system of medical inspection to
search for the diseases mentioned above, *on the
model of the German system of testing the fitness of
recruits.* Darwin proposes to establish the following
rule. No one may contract marriage without producing evidence that he has never suffered from

insanity. But that is not enough. He must produce an untainted pedigree—that is, he must prove that his parents, and even his most distant relations in ascendant and collateral lines, have never suffered from such complaints. All this is necessary, that among the mass the capacity for happiness may be augmented by the extermination of disease—the chief obstacle to happiness.

Is it possible to establish such restrictions? asks Darwin, and answers, Of course. Restrictions of a similar nature already exist in the marriage laws of many countries. As evidence of this, he adduces three pages of examples of the different restrictive laws, mostly from barbarous countries, citing indiscriminately the regulations of Prussia, Siam, China, and Madagascar, even of the Ostiaks and Tunguses. If we may judge by appearance, he is pleased by every restriction of marriage, and every facility for divorce. He ends his dissertation without considering the simple question, What end will be served by legal restrictions on marriage, when it will be impossible to prevent natural unions with the same effect in the birth of children? It may be, indeed, this question has occurred to the author; if so, he has found a reply, which he gives, in the example of Japan, where prostitution is not only tolerated, but even protected by the State, as a means of preventing an undue increase of population.

Thus reasons the herald of Darwinism. It is plain that to him the fundamental law of life is *the preservation of the strong and the extirpation of the weak*. And apparently he would establish this principle as a law of civil society. It is a strange specimen of the infatuation of a scholar with a principle discovered by himself. The legislator of a future society is to accept such ideas as these, and to acknowledge in life and progress no other motives than the interests of physiology—of moral factors he will not even dream. To him all organisms, weak and strong, are numbers, abstract quantities, for the purpose of mathematical calculation. He will not ask himself the question, Will the strong be stronger for having destroyed the weak? He knows not the truth that all strength grows in action, experience, and practice ; that the strong will have no occasion to prove and develop their strength when there shall be no weak who require assistance and protection ; and that the weakest, trained in favourable conditions, may become strong, and be capable of transmitting their strength to future generations. And lastly, will the victors in the struggle of nature be capable of ministering to the perfection of the race, if their strength be sustained by a mechanical process at the expense of the weak?

THE SPIRITUAL LIFE

I

How precious are the old institutions, the old traditions, the old customs! The people guards them as the ark of the covenant of its forefathers. But how often has history shown that popular governments do not value but regard them as an old garment of which they must be rid. Rulers condemn them without mercy, or re-cast them in new forms, and expect a new spirit to animate them at once. Their expectations are seldom fulfilled. The old institutions are precious and indispensable because they have had their origin not in invention but in the life of the past; they are consecrated in the minds of the people by that high authority which history alone can give. This authority cannot be replaced, for its roots rest in that unconscious part of our being where the moral principles are firmly set. It is vain to suppose that the sanction of history can be replaced in the minds of the people by the spirit of an institution newly founded. Few individuals acquire sentiments of reverence through reason, or find in reason the source of inspiration and faith. Such sentiments remain inaccessible to the mass; if we wish to inspire them from without we fail, and awaken false and fantastic ideas. The masses assimilate ideas only through direct sentiment, which is educated and strengthened by history, and transmitted from father to son, from generation to generation. These traditions may be destroyed : to revive them is impossible.

Often in the depths of the old institutions there is embodied some profoundly true idea which springs directly from the spirit of the people. Although such inspiring idea is sometimes hard to recognise through the multitude of forms, excrescences, and veils which have lost to-day their primitive significance, yet the masses apprehend it by instinct, and firmly cling to their institution by its associated forms. They cherish their institution with its excrescences, some- times ugly and often objectless, because their instinct is to guard the hidden germs of truth against shallow attack. These germs are all the more precious because they symbolise the immemorial needs of the soul, protecting the truth hidden in their depths. What if the forms that invest the institutions of the people are rude, the product of rude customs, of a rude temper, these are phenomena temporary and accidental. When manners and customs are softened, the forms themselves also are ennobled and inspired. Purify the mind, elevate the spirit, enlighten the ideas of the people, and the rude forms disappear, making way for others more perfect, until all are simple and pure.

This the reformers of the people ignore when they rave over the rudeness of form, and the abuses of the ancient institutions. Engaged with ceremonies and forms alone, they neglect the spirit of the institution, which they would destroy altogether, seeing there no- thing but rudeness and ceremonial superstition. They know that they have outlived the form, but they forget the millions to whom, by the state of their spiritual development, the spirit is accessible only through rude ceremonial.   Destroy this ceremonial, and the people will think its institution destroyed, and lose, it may be for ever, the occasion of learning aright the ancient ideas it symbolises.   Would it not be well to begin reform from the inside, to enlighten the spirit of the people, to inspire it with thought, to purify and enrich its moral and intellectual life? Then the fundamental idea would be saved, the life of the people would be spared, and the rude forms themselves would be transfigured in the new.

I quote the following passages from Carlyle:

"Great truly is the Actual; is the Thing that has rescued itself from the bottomless deeps of theory and possibility, and stands there as a definite indisputable Fact, whereby men do work and live or once did so.   Wisely shall men cleave to that while it will endure; and quit it with regret, when it gives way under them. Rash enthusiast of Change, beware!   Hast thou well considered all that Habit does in this life of ours; how all Knowledge and all Practice hang wondrous over infinite abysses of the Unknown, Impracticable; and our whole being is an infinite abyss, *overreached* by Habit, as by a thin Earth-rind, laboriously built together?

"Herein too, in this its System of Habits, acquired, retained how you will, lies the true Law-Code and Constitution of a Society; the only Code, though an unwritten one, which it can in no wise *disobey.* The thing we call written Code, Constitution, Form of Government, and the like, what is it but some miniature image, and solemnly expressed summary of this unwritten Code? *Is*—or rather, also, is *not*; but only should be, and always tends to be! In which latter discrepancy lies struggle wthout end?"—"The French Revolution," vol. i. p. 46.

"Where thou findest a Lie that is oppressing thee, extinguish it. Lies exist there only to be extinguished; they wait and cry earnestly

for extinction. Think well, meanwhile, in what spirit thou wilt
do it : not with hatred, with headlong selfish violence ; but in clearness of heart, with holy zeal, gently, almost with pity. Thou
wouldst not *replace* such extinct Lie by a new Lie, which a new
Injustice of thy own were ; the parent of still other Lies ? Whereby the latter end of that business were worse than the beginning."—
Ibid., p. 47.

II

An eternal struggle is waged in the cause of
freedom in the world of human institutions and human
relations. But where shall we find this freedom if
not in the human soul? Everywhere reason arms
against the old authority, seeking to overthrow it,
ostensibly in the name of freedom, in reality to
replace it with new authorities of the minute,
constituted yesterday, and doomed to-morrow to
give way in turn. The modern champion of reason
and liberty looks with contempt on the orthodox
believers who cling to the faith transmitted by their
fathers and forefathers, and remain faithful to tradition, but he himself has evolved what he considers
elemental convictions on the Church, and on the
chief objects of the spiritual life. He laughs at the
pious sentiments of the churchman, and condemns
them as superstition. Yet himself he is filled with
pious terror of the so-called "public opinion": is this
not a superstition still greater? To us our past is
dear : we respect our history. He ridicules this, he
despises the past, and believes only in the present ;
but he cannot explain in what way his adoration
of the present is better than the sentiment which
he reviles. He will say, "Cast away the yoke of the

law, break the immemorial chains of tradition, and you will be free." But what is freedom, when the present is set up as a law, oppressing us with a yoke heavier than before, when instead of the inspired and infallible scriptures of which we are to be deprived, we are bidden to believe in the infallibility of the opinions of the crowd, and to find in the majority of voices the unerring and unanswerable words of truth?

III

Only fools have clear conceptions of everything. The most cherished ideas of the human mind are found in the depths and in twilight: around these confused ideas which we cannot classify revolve clear thoughts, extending, developing, and becoming elevated. If this deeper mental plane were to be taken away, there would remain but geometricians and intelligent animals; even the exact sciences would lose their present grandeur, which depends upon a hidden correlation with eternal truths, of which we catch a glimpse only at rare moments. Mystery is the most precious possession of mankind. Not in vain did Plato teach that all below is but a weak image of the order reigning above. It may be, indeed, that the grandest function of the loveliness we see is the awakening of desire for a higher loveliness we see not; and that the enchantment of great poets springs less from the pictures they paint than from the distant echoes they awaken from the invisible world.

IV

Life, the springtime of youth, of passion, and of aspiration ; life, full of pleasure ; life, in the eternal sunlight, plunges man in dreams which he would never surrender — dreams with enchanting visions and indescribable joy.

But these dreams must be broken by sorrow, anxiety, and disenchantment, the loss of happiness and of justice. The sun must vanish — the night, with all its terrors, draw near.

But in the midst of this night, in the firmament appear to the troubled soul, in all their mysterious beauty, the heavenly stars which it saw not while the sunlight shone. Mystery embraces and calms the troubled soul ; the stars of childhood and youth appear — the simplicity of early sensations, the counsel and caresses of disinterested parental love, the lessons of reverence of God and of duty—all that eternity has made innate in man, all that has nourished, taught, and enlightened him at the beginning of life. It was necessary that the soul should be plunged into the darkness of night for the heavenly stars to be revealed out of the depths of the past.

V

In his celebrated work *Psyche*, Carus says that the key to comprehension of the conscious life lies in the sphere of the unconscious. He traces the correlation of the conscious and unconscious in human life, with many profound reflections. The divine in us—what we call the soul—he says, is not something intermittent or immovable, but incessantly changes form in a steady process of development, destruction, and reformation.   Each phenomenon is an extension or development of the past, and contains the promise of future development.   The conscious life of man is decomposed into separate moments of time ; it has but an indistinct apprehension of its existence in the past and its prospects in the future ; while the present escapes it, for hardly is it born before it mingles with the past.   The reduction of all these moments to unity, the consciousness of the present—that is, the determining of a distinct limit between the past and the future, is feasible only in the domain of unconsciousness, where there is no time, but eternity.   The famous myths of Epimetheus and Prometheus have a profound meaning, and it was not without reason that the Greek wisdom embodied therein its conception of the higher development of humanity.   All organic life recalls to us these conflicting sides of the creative idea in the domain of unconsciousness.   Even in the vegetable and animal worlds each impulse or form reminds us of something related to the past, and foretells to us something to be formed, and to appear in the future.   The more we think on the nature of this phenomenon, the more are we persuaded that all that in the conscious life we denominate memory, foresight, or foreknowledge, serves but as a pale reflection of the exactitude with which they exist in the unconscious life.

Carus examines certain cases where the conscious

life has been suddenly interrupted, and absorbed in the domain of the unconscious. Nothing is more remarkable, he says, than the sudden and involuntary apparition in our souls of images which have long disappeared, yet which are preserved in the depths of the unconscious soul. Ideas of men, of objects, of places, even our peculiar feelings and sensations, which in the course of long years seem to have vanished, suddenly awaken into life, and prove that in reality they were not lost at all. There have been some remarkable instances in which consciousness, in a moment, embraced a whole life with all its events. A case is known of a certain Englishman who was subjected to the strong action of opium : once, in the fierce agitation which precedes the complete prostration of the senses, he suddenly saw a picture of his former life with all its events and sensations. A similar experience was that of a girl who had fallen into the water, the moment before complete loss of consciousness.

Carus gives no details, or references to evidence of the cases cited ; but all have heard such cases in more or less confused forms. The following, however, is the unique, curious, and fully authenticated account of such an occurrence given by the person chiefly concerned.

This happened with the English Admiral Beaufort, who, when a young man, fell out of a boat at Portsmouth, and, not knowing how to swim, sank to the bottom. He was taken from the water, and afterwards, at the request of the well-known Dr Wollaston, recounted the strange history of his experiences. After describing the circumstances of the accident he continues to the following effect :

" What I have told you so far is based on confused memories of my own, and on the testimony of eye-witnesses ; for a drowning man is, of course, entirely absorbed in the consciousness of his own peril and the struggle between hope and despair. For all which happened immediately afterwards, however, I can vouch with a good conscience, for there took place in my mind a revolution so sudden, and so extraordinary, that all the details have remained deeply impressed upon my memory with a freshness and distinctness as complete as if all had happened yesterday. From the moment I ceased to move (which occurred, I suppose, after complete suffocation), the violent sensations were superseded by a feeling of perfect calm and tranquillity, a state which one might perhaps describe as one of apathy, but yet not an attitude of submission to fate. I felt no pain of any kind, nor did I think any longer of either peril or rescue ; on the contrary, the sensation was rather agreeable, resembling the languor which precedes sleep after some fatiguing physical exertion. My senses were paralysed. The opposite, however, was the case as regards my mind, the activity of which increased to an extent which entirely defies description, thought following thought with such rapidity that not only would it be impossible for me to describe what happened, but nobody, unless he should have passed through a similar experience, could form an idea of what I felt.

" I still recall with the greatest distinctness the course of these thoughts, beginning with the accident which had just happened, the awkwardness to which it had been due, the panic that followed (I had seen men jumping into the water immediately after me), the effect which the event would produce upon the mind of my tender father, the announcement of the terrible news to my family, and a thousand other circumstances of my private life. Such was the first sequence of my thoughts. After this the circle of my ideas began to grow wider : first, our last voyage came back to my memory ; then the first of our campaigns, with the shipwreck that occurred on that occasion ; then my school-life, its successes, all its blunders, the follies, the boyish tricks, the little adventures of the time, and so on, always receding further. In this way all the experiences of my life unfolded themselves in my memory in an order opposite to that in which they had occurred, not, however, merely in general outline, as I have given them here, but like living pictures, with their most circumstantial features and details. In one word, the whole history of my life unrolled itself before me as in a panorama, and in recognising each event, I was able even to discern its character, to think of its cause and effect. But what is most remarkable is that almost all the most trivial facts, which I had long forgotten, were revived in my mind with such precision and accuracy, that it seemed as if they had just happened. Does not this prove the infinite power of the memory? Does it not prove, that one day we will awaken in another world in possession of a complete recollection of all that we have passed through in this, and that we shall *have to* contemplate our former life from beginning to end? And, on the other hand, does not all this justify also the belief that death is merely a modification of our being which continues to exist without any real interruption or break in its continuity? However that may be, what is extremely notewothy is the fact that all the thoughts passing before my soul in such great number were turned toward the past. I had been educated in the principles of religion; my ideas regarding our future life and the fears and hopes inseparably connected with those ideas had undergone no modification, and at any other time, therefore, the probability of an imminent peril would have sufficed to produce in me the most terrible emotion; but in that indescribable moment, although fully convinced that I had passed the line separating me from eternity, I had not a single thought for the future: I was entirely absorbed in the past. I am not able at present to estimate exactly the time occupied by the passing of this torrent of ideas before my mind, or, rather, during what fraction of time these recollections occurred, but this much is certain, that less than two minutes intervened between the moment in which suffocation began and the moment in which I was taken from the water.

"When I began to revive, my sensations were of a totally different nature from those that I had experienced before. Instead of the multitude of clear and precise ideas which had passed before my soul, there was now but one confused thought weighing heavily upon it—namely, the danger and the risk which I had

N

undergone. While I was drowning there was not the slightest physical suffering, now the most atrocious pain seemed to rend my entire body; never since have I had to endure such tortures, although I have been wounded on several occasions, and have had to submit more than once to surgical operations. In one instance, a bullet passed through my lungs; I spent the whole night on the bridge of the vessel. Believing that a wound in the lungs must be fatal, I had the fullest apprehension of death. But in that moment I felt nothing like that which I underwent during my drowning experience; and when I came to, after swooning, I recovered immediately full consciousness of my position."

THE CHURCH

I

THE more we consider the distinctive ethnical features of religion the more firmly we are convinced how unattainable is an union of creeds—by a factitious accord in dogma,—on the principle of reciprocal concessions in immaterial things. The essential in religion cannot be expressed on paper, or categorically formulated. The most essential, the most persistent, and the most precious things in all religious creeds are as elusive and as insusceptible of definition as varieties of light and shade—as feelings born of an infinite series of emotions, conceptions, and impressions. The essential elements are so involved with the psychical nature of the race, with the principles of their moral philosophy, that it is futile to separate one from the other. The children of different races and different faiths, in many relations may feel as brethren, and give to one another their hands; but to feel themselves worshippers in the same temple, joined in religious communion, they must have lived together long and closely, they must sympathise with the conditions of each other's existence, they must be bound by the most intimate links in the depths of their souls. A German who has lived long in our country may come unconsciously to believe as Russians believe, and to feel at home in

the Russian Church.   He becomes one of us, and is
in complete spiritual communion with us.   But that
a Protestant community, situated far away, judging
us by report, could, through abstract accord in dogma
and ritual, combine with us in one church in organic
alliance, and become one with us in spirit, is inconceivable.   No reunion of churches based upon
accord in doctrine has ever succeeded ;   the false
principle of such an alliance must sooner or later
manifest itself, its fruit is everywhere an increase
not of love but of mutual estrangement and hatred.

May God forbid that we should condemn one
another because of faith; let each believe as he will!
But each man has a faith which is his refuge, which
satisfies his spiritual needs, which he loves ; and it
is impossible for him when brought into contact with
another faith not to feel that it is not his own, that
it is inhospitable and cold.   Let reason prove, with
abstract arguments, that all men pray to one God.
Sentiment is repelled by reasoning such as this ;
sometimes sentiment feels that in a strange church it
prays to a strange god.

Many will laugh at this sentiment, or condemn it
as superstition and fanaticism.   They will be wrong.
Sentiment is not always delusive, it sometimes expresses truth more directly and justly than reason
itself.

The Protestant Church and the Protestant faith
are cold and inhospitable to Russians.   For us to
recognise this faith would be as bitter as death.
This is a direct sentiment.   But there are many
good reasons to justify it.   The following is one
which especially strikes us by its obviousness.

In the polemics of theologians, in religious dissensions, in the conscience of every man and of every race, one of the greatest questions is that of *works.* Which is the greater, works or faith? We know that on this question the Latin doctrine differs from the Protestant. In his theological compositions, the late M. Khomyakoff well explained how deceptive is the scholastic-absolute treatment of this question. Union of faith with works, like identity of words and thought, of deeds and words, is an ideal unattainable by human nature, as all things absolute are unattainable—an ideal eternally troubling and eternally alluring the faithful soul. Faith without works is sterile. Faith opposed to works offends us with the consciousness of internal falsehood ; but in the infinite world of externals around mankind what can work, what can any possible work signify without faith?

Prove me thy faith by thy deeds,—a terrible command! What can a believer answer when his questioner seeks to recognise the faith by the works. If such a question were put by a Protestant to a member of the Orthodox Church, what would the answer be? He could only hang his head. He would feel that he had nothing to show, that all was imperfect and disorderly. But in a minute he might lift his head and say : "We have nothing to show, sinners as we are, yet neither are you beyond reproach. Come to us, live with us, see our faith, study our sentiments, and you will learn to love us. As for our works, you will see them such as they are." From such an answer ninety-nine out of a hundred would turn with a

contemptuous laugh. The truth is that we do not
know, and dare not show our works.

It is not so with them. They can show
their works, and, to speak the truth, they have
much to show—works and institutions existing,
and preserved for centuries in perfect order. See,
says the Catholic Church, what I mean to the
community which hears me and which serves me ;
which I created, and which I sustain. Here are
works of love, works of faith, apostolic works ;
here are deeds of martyrdom ; here are regiments
of believers, united as one, which I send to the
ends of the earth. Is it not plain that grace is
in me, and has been in me from the beginning
until now ?

See, says the Protestant Church, I do not
tolerate falsehood, deception, or superstition. My
works conform to faith, and reason is reconciled
with it. I have consecrated labour, human relations, and family happiness ; by faith I destroy
all idleness and superstition ; I establish justice,
honesty, and social order. I teach daily, and my
doctrine accords with life. It educates generations
in the performance of honourable work, and in
good manners. My teaching renews humanity in
virtue and justice. My mission is to destroy with
the sword of words and deeds corruption and
hypocrisy everywhere. Is it not plain that the
grace of God is in me, since I see things from
the true standpoint ?

To the present day Protestants and Catholics
contend over the dogmatic signification of works in
relation to faith. But in spite of the total contra-

diction of their theological doctrines, both set works at the head of their religion. In the Latin Church works are the justification, the redemption, and the witness of grace. The Lutherans regard works, and, at the same time, religion itself, from the practical point of view. Works for them are the end of religion ; they are the touchstone which proves religious and canonical truth, and it is on this point more than on any other that our doctrine differs from the doctrine of Protestantism. It is true that these doctrines do not constitute a dogma of the Lutheran Church, but they pervade its teaching. Beyond all dispute they have an important practical value for this world ; and therefore many would set up the Protestant Church as a model and an ideal for us. But the Russian, in the depths of a believing soul, will never accept such a view. " Godliness is profitable unto all things," says the apostle, but utility is hardly one of its natural attributes. The Russians, as others, know that they ought to live by religion, and feel how ill their lives accord with their beliefs ; but the essence, the end of their faith is not the practical life, but the salvation of their souls, and with the love of religion they seek to embrace all, from the just man who lives according to his faith, to the thief, who, his works notwithstanding, would be pardoned in an instant.

This practical basis of Protestantism is nowhere shown more plainly than in the Anglican Church, and in the religious spirit of the English people. It accords with the character of the nation as formed by history to direct all thought and action to practical aims, steadfastly and tenaciously pursuing success, and in all things taking those paths and measures which are short and sure. This innate tendency must seek a moral base, and must construct a system of morals; and it is natural that these moral principles shall seek a sanction in a religious spirit corresponding to their nature. Religion indisputably consecrates the moral principle of activity; its precepts teach us how to live and act; it demands laboriousness, honesty, and justice. This no one will dispute. But, in the practical consideration of religion, we pass directly to the question : What of the faith of those who live in idleness, who are dishonest and false, corrupt, and disorderly, who cannot control their passions? Such men are heathen, not Christian ; he only is a Christian who lives by the law, and in himself bears witness to its power.

This reasoning is logical in appearance. But who has not asked the question : What is the part in the world and in the Church of the wanton and dishonest, who, in the words of Christ, shall take a higher place in the kingdom of heaven than the just according to the law ?

It would be too much to suppose that such religious opinions constitute a positive formula of the Church of England. Such a formula would be a direct negation of the precepts of the Evangel. But such is precisely the spirit of religion among the most zealous and conscientious representatives of the so-called National Established Church, which they defend and extol as the first bulwark of the State, and, as the last expression of the national genius. In English literature, both religious and profane, this view is expressed, sometimes in trenchant words which would excite doubt and almost terror in the mind of a Russian reader.

In a work remarkable for depth and clearness of thought, written evidently by a believer deeply and jealously attached to his Church, the following remarks occur upon religion :—

"Some forms of religion are distinctly unfavourable to a sense of social duty. Others have simply no relation to it whatever, and of those which favour it (as is the case in various degrees with every form of Christianity) some promote it far more powerfully than others. I should say that those which promote it most powerfully are those of which the central figure is an infinitely wise and powerful Legislator whose own nature is confessedly inscrutable to man, but who has made the world as it is for a prudent, steady, hard, enduring race of people, who are neither fools nor cowards, who have no particular love for those who are, who distinctly know what they want, and are determined to use all lawful means to get it. Some such religion as this is the unspoken deeply-rooted conviction of the solid, established part of the English nation. They form an anvil which has worn out a good many hammers, and will wear out a good many more, enthusiasts and humanitarians notwithstanding." — Stephen (Sir James F.), "Liberty, Equality, Fraternity," pp. 305-6. London, 1873.

Such is the conception of religion held by a convinced Anglican churchman. The passage I have quoted is a direct negation of the words of the Evangel, for it says : Happy are the strong and powerful, for they shall possess the kingdom ; to which we reply : Yes, the kingdom of the earth, but not the kingdom of heaven. The author makes no such limitation ; he sees no distinction between the kingdom of heaven and the kingdom of earth. What a terrible and despairing doctrine !

Such tendencies of religious thought were indisputably of the greatest practical value in Protestant countries, especially in England ; and it cannot be denied that Protestantism was a strong and beneficent influence towards social development among the peoples who accepted it, and with whose nature it accorded. But is it not plain that certain races, by their nature, could never accept or submit to it, because they do not find in this doctrine of Protestantism the vital principle of religion? They see not unity but a duality of the religious conscience; not the living truth, but a factitious composition of speculation and falsehood.

"Woe to the weak and fallen ! Woe to the vanquished !" Truly in this life this is inevitable truth, and the voice of worldly wisdom cries to us: Fight, get and hold by force if you would live—in this world there is no place for the weak. But the soul will no more allow the absolute and dogmatic application of this rule to religion than it will accept the terrible Calvinist doctrine that some are predestined from eternity to virtue, to glory, to salvation, and to happiness ; while others, no matter what their lives may be, are condemned from eternity to the abyss of despair and eternal torment.

It is terrible to read those English writers who sound with special emphasis this chord of English Protestantism. Carlyle, for instance, is seized with rapturous emotion through the strength and talent of the conqueror, while he despises the conquered. He honours his strong men as the incarnation of Godhead, and treats with thin, contemptuous irony the weak and unhappy, the incapable and the fallen, crushed by the triumphal chariot of the conqueror. His heroes personify the idea of light and order in the darkness and disorder of the cosmic chaos; they create their own universe; all whom they meet on their path who refuse to submit and to serve, yet have not the strength to resist, are justly and utterly destroyed. Carlyle's extraordinary talents infatuate the reader, but it is painful to read his historical writings, and see the name of God invoked in the struggle of the strong with the weak. The pagans of the classic age, with better sense, sent, by the chariot of the conqueror, a jester, who represented the moral principle, pursuing with his irony, not the conquered but the conqueror himself.

Most painful of all is it to read Froude, the celebrated historian of the English Reformation, and the best representative among historians of the principles of the English people in religion and in politics. Carlyle, at least, is a poet, while Froude speaks in the tranquil tones of the historian, loves dialectics, and knows no iniquity which he cannot justify by dialectics in the interest of a favourite idea. There is no hypocrisy which he does not glorify as truth in his justification of the Reformation and of its protagonists. Unshakeable and fanatical, he holds to the principles of Anglican orthodoxy, the base of which he declares is the recognition of social duty, devotion to the political idea and to the law, and the implacable chastisement of vice and crime and idleness, and all that is designated the betrayal of duty. In human affairs, all this is excellent; but can we make such principles the beginning and end of religion, when we think how the words, duty, law, vice, and crime are variously interpreted day by day, and that men to-day call justice and courage what to-morrow may be condemned as falsehood and crime. For charity and compassion the religion of Froude has no place. How can he reconcile charity with indignation for vice and crime, for the violation of the law? Speaking of the terrible punishments sometimes endured by the innocent as well as the guilty, this stern judge of human affairs eulogises his compatriots as a strong and severe people who know no pity where there is no legal cause for pity, and who, on the contrary, are filled with a sacred and solemn horror of crime, a sentiment which, as it develops in the soul, of necessity hardens it, and results in forming an iron character. The man of severe morality is inclined to compassion only when the disposition to good remains in conflict with evil : in cases of total corruption compassion is unjustifiable, and is conceivable only when in our hearts we confound crime with misfortune. Such, in effect, are the sentiments of Froude.

How the author would have despised us Russians, in whose minds there actually is such confusion, and who from time immemorial have called the culprit unfortunate (*nestchastnui*).

The characters of churches, as the characters of men, and the characters of races, have their merits and defects. The merits of Protestantism are well explained by the history of the German and Anglo-Saxon races. The spirit of Puritanism has created the Britain of the present day. The principle of Protestantism gave to Germany strength, and discipline, and unity. Yet we see with this some defects and tendencies with which we cannot sympathise. As every spiritual force, Protestantism is most inclined to fall where it seeks its firmest spiritual foundation. In aspiring to absolute truth, to the purifying of faith and its realisation in life, it is over-confident of its own righteousness, it is infatuated to idolatry with its justice, and it despises the strange faith which temporises with untruth. Thence springs the danger of hypocrisy and of pharisaical pride. And, indeed, how often do we hear with bitterness from the Protestant world that hypocrisy is the plague of rigorous Lutheranism! On the other hand, while beginning by preaching toleration, and liberty of thought and belief, Protestantism, in its ultimate development, is inclined to fanaticism of a peculiar nature, the fanaticism of the pride of intellect, the fanaticism of a rectitude above all other faiths. Rigid Protestantism treats with contempt every faith which appears to it unclean, uninspired, defiled by the superstition and ritual which it has cast off as the fetters of slaves, the garments of children, the attributes to ignorance. Creating for itself a system of beliefs and ceremonies, it maintains its doctrine as the doctrine of the elect, the enlightened and the rational, and regards all those who hold to the ancient Church as beings of a lower race, who cannot rise to the height of pure reasoning. This contemptuous attitude is expressed unconsciously, but it is only too sensible by the adherents to other faiths. No religion is free from fanaticism, but the height of all absurdity is reached when Lutherans turn to us with such accusations. In spite of the tolerance which is inherent in our national character, we meet, of course, individual cases of exclusiveness and bigotry in religion; but there never has been, and never can be, anything like to that contempt with which rigid Lutherans regard the attributes to our Church, and the qualities of our faith, which to them are incomprehensible, but to us are filled with a deep spiritual significance.

II

The difference between the social spirit and composition of the Anglo-Saxon and the Russian races is noticeable nowhere so much as in the Church. In an English church, more than anywhere else, the thought occurs to the Russian, There are many good things here, yet I am thankful that I was born in Russia. In our churches all social distinctions are laid aside, we surrender our positions in the world and mingle completely in the congregation before the face of God. Our churches for the most part have been built with the money of the people; between rouble and grosh there is no distinction; in all cases our churches are the work and the appanage of the whole people. The poorest beggar feels, with the greatest noble, that the church, at least, is his. The church is the only place (how happy are we to have one such place!) where the poorest man in rags will not be asked, "Why art thou here, and who art thou?" It is the only place where the rich may not say to the poor, "Your place is not beside me, but behind."

Enter an English church and watch the congregation. It is devout; solemn it may be, but it is a congregation of "ladies and gentlemen," each with a place specially reserved; the rich in separate and embellished pews, like the boxes of an opera-house. We cannot help thinking that this church is merely

a reunion of people in society, and that there is place
in it only for what society calls "the respectable."
All use their prayer-books, but each has his own,
which makes it plain that he wishes to be alone
before God, and in no way to sacrifice his individuality. It is said that in the last twenty or thirty
years a remarkable change has taken place in this ;
the places in the churches are to a great extent free,
and access to them is easier than before ; but in
former times, more particularly in the provinces, the
pews were constructed with closed partitions, so that
the occupant might pray in peace, alone, and undis-
turbed by any neighbour. How plainly these dispositions reveal the history of a feudal society, and even
the history of the Reformation in England. "Nobility
and gentry" lead in all, because they possess and
appropriate all. All is bought by conquest, even
the right to sit in church. The celebration of
divine service is a privilege sold at a fixed price.
In England the preferment of clergymen, with right to
fixed incomes, is the hereditary right of "patronage,"
and the power of election to the ministry is the appanage either of the local proprietors or of the Crown,
by virtue not so much of the rights of the State as of
the rights of the feudal possessors. Thus the clergy,
appointed independently of the people, and independent of the people for their maintenance, appear
above it as princes placed above their subjects. The
offices of the Church are, first of all, a "preferment,"
an appanage ; and, it is shameful to say so, this
appanage is the object of traffic. The office of
incumbent may be bought for a certain sum, determined by the capitalisation of the income, as in

our country the positions of attorneys, notaries, and brokers. In any English newspaper you may find a special department for the advertisement of these so-called " preferments," you may see a series of offers of the office of incumbent, with a statement of the income ; the amenities of the position will be praised, the house and its situation described, the price indicated, with the information that the present incumbent is so many years old, and is not likely to enjoy his position long. In London appears a journal (*The Church Preferment Register*) specially devoted to this traffic, with a detailed description of every office, its amenities and revenue, for the information of those who might buy.

We are told that, from the political point of view, every right, personal or social, should be attained by competition alone. This observation may be generally true, but it cannot be applied to the right of praying in church. We must not wonder, then, that the conscience of the people is not satisfied with the constitution of the Church, and that England, the country of an Established State Church, the classic country of theological learning and religious discussion, has become, since the Reformation, the country of dissidence too. The need of religion and the need of prayer in the mass of the people, finding no satisfaction in the Established Church, seek issue in free and independent congregations and in diverse sects. The different sects which flourish in the most insignificant village are innumerable. The Established Church itself is divided into three schools, the so-called High, Low, and Broad Churches, and the partisans of each have their own churches, and will not enter the churches of others. In the smallest villages, with a settled population of no more than five hundred, three Anglican churches may sometimes be found, and, in addition, three Methodist churches of different denominations, distinguished only by verbal subtleties and capricious details, yet cut off from all communion with one another. There will be one chapel for Primitive or Wesleyan Methodists, another for Congregationalists, one for the so-named Bible Christians—these last are also Methodists, who severed their connection some years ago because they opposed the others in believing that those invested in the office of the evangelists ought not to be married. Such a number of churches, large, handsome, and roomy, may be found in a single village. All these sects are distinguished by peculiarities of doctrine, sometimes very subtle and capricious, or altogether absurd, but, apart from differences of doctrine, all are inspired by a desire for a popular Church, free to all, and many by implacable hatred of the Established Church and of its ministers. In addition to these separate sects, in the midst of the Established Church itself a numerous party has been formed under the name of the Free Church Movement. Individuals and societies procure for simple folk the means of participating in divine service ; for this purpose they build special churches, and hire buildings, theatres, sheds, and halls. This movement has produced a visible reaction in the practice of the Established Church, and has forced it to throw its doors more widely open. But is it not strange that in England the masses have been forced to

O

conquer in battle what among us has always been free as the air we breathe?

How often do we hear in Russia strange words about our Church from men who have been abroad, who love to judge everything after the manner of strangers; and, on the other hand, from simple men infatuated with ideals to the estrangement of reality. These men have no limit to their praise of the Anglican and German Churches, and of the Anglican clergy, and to their condemnation of our Church and our clergy. If we believe them, there all is living activity, while among us all is death, rudeness, or sleep; there is work, here ceremonial and inactivity. It is not surprising that people speak thus. Men judge by appearance. To judge by dress is easy, but much thought and observation are needed to learn the spirit and significance of things. Men seize on impressions and cling thereto. There are many for whom the first and final factors in creating impressions are external perfection, manner, dexterity, purity, and respectability. Judged by this standard, there is much to be admired in the Anglican Church, and much to be lamented in our own. Few of us have not met men of the world, and, unhappily, even ecclesiastics, who exalt the simplicity which they find in religion abroad, and condemn our own for "immaturity." Such judgments are as much to be deplored, as the conduct of a young man who, having spent some time in the fashionable world in the midst of the refinements of a metropolis, returns to the village where he has spent his childhood, and looks with contempt on his modest surroundings, and on the rude and simple manners of his family circle.

By nature we are much inclined to be infatuated
with beauty of form, with organisation, with the
external perfection of things. Thence springs the
passion for imitation, and for transplanting to our soil
those foreign institutions which attract us by their
external symmetry. But we forget, or remember too
late, that those institutions were historically evolved ;
they sprang and developed from historical conditions,
and are the logical consequence of the past, created
of necessity. History cannot be changed or evaded ;
and history itself, with its actions, its actors, and
its complex polity, is the product of the national
spirit, as the history of the individual is the product of his living soul. The same may be said of
all systems of church organisation. Therein all
things conform to the spiritual basis whereon they
have grown ; too often charmed with the super-
structure, we neglect the base ; otherwise, we should
not, perhaps, have hesitated to reject this ready-made
symmetry, but with gladness should have clung to
our old and rough form, or deformity, until such day
as our spiritual nature had evolved a new one for us.
In all human institutions the spirit is essential : hence
we should zealously preserve it from distortion and
alloy.

From its dawn to the present day our Church has
been the church of the people, inspired by love, and
all-embracing, without distinction of class. The faith
has sustained our peoples in the day of privation and
calamity, and one thing only can sustain, strengthen,
and regenerate them, and that is faith, the faith of the
Church alone. Our people is reproached with ignorance in its religion ; its faith, we are told, is defiled

by superstition; it suffers from corrupt and wicked practices; its clergy is rude, inactive, ignorant, and oppressed, without influence on its flocks. In this reproach is much truth, but these evils are in no way essential, but temporary and adventitious. They spring from many circumstances, from political and economic conditions, with the disappearance of which they also will disappear. What then is essential? The love of the people for its Church, the conception of the Church as a common possession, a congregation common in all things, the total absence of social distinctions, the communion of the people with the ministers of the Church, sprung from the people, and differing neither in manner of life, in virtues, nor *in failings*, who stand and fall with their flocks. This is a soil which would bring forth rich fruits with good cultivation, with less concern for the amelioration of life than the bettering of the soul, with less desire that the number of churches exceed not the needs of the people than that those needs shall not remain unsatisfied. Is it for us to covet, through rumour from afar, the Protestant Church and its ministers? May Heaven withhold from us the time when our priests shall be officials, placed above the people as princes above their subjects, in the position of men of society with complex needs and desires, while surrounded on every side by privation and simplicity.

By reflection on life we are convinced that for every man in the course of his spiritual development, the thing most precious and essential is to preserve inviolate the simple inborn feeling of humanity in his human relations, and to nourish truth and freedom in his spiritual conceptions and impulses. This is the impregnable fortress which guards and delivers the soul from the onslaught of rank, and from all artificial theories which corrupt insensibly the simple moral sentiment. However precious in some respects these forms and theories may be, when rooted in the soul they corrupt its simple and healthy conceptions and sensations, they confound the notions of truth and untruth, and destroy the roots from which healthy men develop in relation to their fellow-creatures. This is the essential which so often we neglect when seduced by externals. How many men, how many institutions have been perverted in the course of a false development, for these rooted principles in our religious institutions are of all things the most precious. May God prevent them ever being destroyed by the untimely reformation of our Church!

III

We are reproached by Protestants with the formalism of our service, but when we examine their ritual we continue to prefer our own ; we feel that our service is simple and majestic in its deep, mysterious significance. The office of our priest is so simple, that it needs but pious attention to the words he utters and to the actions he accomplishes : from his lips the sacred words are their own interpretation, their deep and mysterious voices reach the souls of all, and unite our congregations in sentiment and in thought. Thus the simplest, most artless man may without exertion repeat the prayers, feeling in

communion with the congregation. The Protestant
service, with all its external simplicity, demands that
the prayers be recited in a certain tone. Only deeply
spiritual and very talented preachers may retain
their simplicity, the immense majority is driven into
that artifice and affectation which we notice first of
all things in Protestant churches, and which produce
in unaccustomed witnesses a sensation of weariness.
When we hear the preacher, with his face turned
to a congregation seated on benches, pronounce
the prayers, lifting his eyes towards heaven, and
crossing his hands conventionally while giving his
words an unnatural intonation, we experience a painful sentiment : how uncomfortable, we think, he must
be ! Still more painful is it when, having ended
the service, he ascends the pulpit and begins a long
sermon, turning from time to time to drink from a
glass of water and to recover breath. Seldom do
we hear in these sermons a living word, and then only
when the preacher is a man of talent or of rare
spiritual nature. For the most part the preachers
are the journeymen of the Church, with extraordinary,
whining voices, infinite affectation, and vigorous
gestures, who turn from side to side, repeating in
varying tones conventional phrases. Even when reading their sermons, which seldom occurs, they have
recourse to gestures, intonations, and intermissions.
Sometimes the preacher, pronouncing a few words
and phrases, cries out and strikes the pupit to give
emphasis to his thoughts. We feel here how faithfully our Church has been adapted to human nature
in excluding sermons from its services. By itself, our
whole service is the best of sermons, all the more

effective since each hears in it, not the words of man, but the words of God. The ideal of that sermon is to lead to faith and love, according to the Scriptures, and not to awaken emotion in a congregation which has come together for prayer.

IV

We are sometimes told that ritual is a trivial and secondary consideration. But there are ceremonies and practices which to abandon would be to deny oneself, for they reflect the spiritual life of man, they express his spiritual nature. In differences of ceremony are most clearly expressed the fundamental and deep diversities of spiritual conceptions hidden in the unrecognised domains of the soul. It is this diversity which prevents the communion and assimilation of peoples of different race, and forms the elemental cause of distinctions of churches and religions. To deny, from the abstract, cosmopolitan point of view, the action of these attractive and repulsive forces, attributing them to prejudice, would be to deny the affinities (*walverwandschaft*) which analogously interact in the relations of individual men.

How remarkable, for instance, are the diversities in the funeral ceremonies of different peoples, and in their conduct towards the bodies of their dead. The Southerner, the Italian, flies the presence of a corpse, and hastens to rid his house of it, committing to strangers the duty of its burial. In Russia, on the contrary, a religious feeling towards the dead body, full of love and tenderness and piety, is a feature of the national character. The immemorial lament for the dead, accompanied by poetical ceremonies and exercises, on our conversion to a new faith was transformed into the solemn prayers of the Church.

Nowhere outside our own country are the burial rites and ceremonies so elaborate; and there can be no doubt that this is an outgrowth of our national character, in special conformity with our nature and our outlook upon life. The features of death are everywhere repulsive and terrible, but we veil them in splendid veils, we surround them with the solemn stillness of contemplative prayer; we chant over them songs in which the terror of stricken nature is relieved by love and hope and pious faith. We do not flee from the presence of death; we adorn it in its coffin; we are drawn to bend our eyes to the abode of the departed soul; we reverence the body, we grant it the last kiss, and watch over it three days and three nights with reading and chanting and prayer. Our funeral prayers are full of beauty and magnificence; they are prolonged by hesitation to surrender to the earth the body tainted by corruption; around the grave not only do we hear the last blessing, but witness a great religious solemnity enacted in the supreme moment of human existence. How dear is this solemnity to the Russian, how well he understands it! The stranger seldom understands it, because —because it is strange. Among us the sentiment of love, defeated by death, expands in the funeral ceremony; the stranger is repelled by the ceremony, and stricken by terror alone.

A German Lutheran resident of Berlin lost in

Russia a dearly-loved sister who belonged to the Orthodox Church. When, on the morning of the burial, he arrived and saw his sister lying in the coffin he was stricken by terror, his heart ceased to beat, the feeling of love and piety which he felt in parting with the dead gave place to repulsion. In this, as in many other things, the German who does not live among us and enter into the depths of our spiritual life, cannot understand us. Nothing repels the Lutheran so much as the adoration of the sacred relics — a practice which to us, who venerate our dead, embrace them, and honour them in burial, seems simple and natural. Not living our life, he sees in this veneration but a barbarous superstition, for us an act of love, the most simple and natural.

Even as he cannot understand our ritual, so we find coarse and repugnant the agitation carried on in Germany and in England for the practice of a new mode of disposing of the dead. It is demanded that corpses shall be buried no more, but burnt in furnaces, specially constructed; and this is required for utilitarian and hygienic reasons. This propaganda is gaining strength, its adherents hold meetings, societies are formed, perfected furnaces constructed at the expense of individuals, chemical experiments made, and funeral marches composed to solemnise the incineration. The demand for cremation is made in the name of science, in the name of civilisation, in the name of social well-being. To us these voices seem to come from a distant world, a world so strange to us, so inhospitable and cold. May God deliver us from dying in the land of strangers, far away from our native Russian soil!

V

He who is truly Russian, heart and soul, knows what the Church of God means to the Russian people. Piety, experience, and respect for religious feelings are not enough in order to understand the import of the Church for the Russian people, or to love this Church as one's own. It is necessary to live the life of the people, to pray with it in congregation, to feel the heart beating in accord, penetrated by the same solemnity, inspired by the same words and the same chants. Thus, many who know the faith only from their private chapels, frequented by select congregations, have no true understanding of the Church, or of religious sentiment, and regard with indifference or repulsion those rites and customs which to the people are especially dear, and constitute the beauty of the Church.

The beauty of the Orthodox Church is its congregation. On entering, we feel that all are united, all is the work of the people, and all is maintained by them. In the Catholic Church, all seems empty, cold, and artificial to the Orthodox worshipper. The priest officiates and reads alone, as if he were above the people, and independent of them. He prays alone from his book, the members of the congregation from theirs; having prayed, and attended one or another part of the service, the congregation departs. On the altar the mass is performed, the worshippers, while present, do not seem to participate by common prayer. The service is addressed to sentiment, and its beauty, if beauty there be, is strange to us, and not our own. The

actions of the service, mechanically performed, to
us seem strange, cold, and inexpressive ; the sacred
vesture is unsightly ; the recitative inharmonious and
uninspired ; the chants—in a strange tongue which
we do not understand—are not the hymns of the
whole congregation, not a cry coming from the
soul, but an artificial concert which conceals the
service, but never unites with it. Our hearts yearn
for our own Church, as we yearn for our homes,
among strangers. How different with us : in our
service there is an indescribable beauty which every
Russian understands, a beauty he loves so much
that he is ready to give up his soul for it. As our
national songs, the chants of our service flow in wide,
free streams from the breasts of the people—the
freer they are the more they appeal to our hearts.
Our religious melodies are the same as among the
Greeks, but they are sung otherwise by our peoples,
who place in them their whole souls. He who would
hear the true voice of this soul must not go where
famous choirs sing the music of new composers ;
he should hear the singing in some great
convent or parish church : there he will hear in
what wide, free streams flows the hymn from the
Russian breast, with what solemn poetry is sung
the dogmatic, what inspiration sings in the canticles
of Easter and Christmas. We hear the word
of our chants echoed by the congregation, it
illumines upturned faces, it is borne over bowed
heads, borne everywhere, for to all the congregation the words and melodies are known from childhood, till the very soul seems to give forth song.
This true, harmonious service is a festival for the

Russian worshipper; even outside his church he preserves its deep impressions, and is thrilled at the recollection of some solemn moment: he is exalted with the harmony, when in his soul echoes again the song of the Easter or Christmas canticle.

In him to whom these words and sounds have been known from childhood, how many recollections and images arise out of that great poem of the past which each has lived, and each still carried in himself! Happy is he who has known these words and sounds and images; who from childhood has found in them the ideal loveliness to which he aspires, without which he cannot live; to whom all is clear and congenial, all lifts his soul out of the dust of life; who in them gathers up again the scattered fragments of his happiness! Happy is he whom good and pious parents have brought in childhood to the house of God, teaching him to pray among the people, and to celebrate its festivals with it! They have built him a sanctuary for life, they have taught him to love the people and to live in communion with it, making the church for him his parents' house, a place of pure and true communion with the people.

But what shall we say of the host of churches lost in the depths of the forests and in the immensity of the plains, where the people understands nothing from the trembling voice of the deacon, and the muttering of the priest?

Alas! the Church is not the cause of this, our poor people is in no way guilty, it is the fault of the idle and thoughtless ministers, the fault of the

ecclesiastical authorities, who carelessly and indiffer-
ently appoint them, sometimes the consequence of
the poverty and helplessness of the people. Happy,
then, is the man in whom burns a spark of love
and zeal for the spiritual life, who leads the forsaken
church back to the world of loveliness and song.
He will truly enlighten with a light in the place of
darkness, he will revive the dead and raise the fallen,
he will save the soul from death, and redeem a multitude of sins. It is for this cause the Russian sacrifices
so much in the building and adornment of churches.
How blindly they judge who condemn him for his
zeal, ascribing it to rudeness and ignorance, fanaticism
and hypocrisy! They ask, Would it not be better to
devote this money to the instruction of the people, to
the founding of schools, to institutions of beneficence?
For these, also, sacrifice is made, but this sacrifice is
another thing, and the pious Russian, with healthy
common-sense, will think twice before opening his
purse in support of formal educational and philanthropic institutions.

As for the Church of God, it pleads for itself, it
is a living institution, an institution of the people.
In it alone the living and the dead are happy.
In it alone all seek light and freedom; in it the
hearts of young and old rejoice, and find rest after
suffering; in it the proud and the lowly, the rich
and the poor, are equal. It is adorned more splendidly
than the palaces of kings; it is the House of God,
and the poor and feeble stand in it as in their homes.
Each may call it his own; it was built, and is maintained, by the roubles, and, what is more, by the
groshes of the people. There all find that refuge

in prayer and consolation which the Russian loves the most.

Such are the sentiments, conscious or unconscious, of the Russian soul towards the Church, such are the sentiments which inspire him to sacrifice for the Church without hesitation or thought. He knows that in this he can make no mistake, and that he gives for a true and holy work.

CHARACTERS

I

MY schoolfellow, Nicander, has always been the
object of astonishment to me. His character, outwardly, was in no way enigmatic, yet I never learnt
to penetrate its nature. Access to him it seemed
would be easy, but when I approached him I felt
between us a troubled, empty space which I never
could bridge, and felt that I should never get
nearer to him. He was on good terms with all, and
all were on good terms with him; he took part in
everything that engaged or interested us; he understood and could speak to anyone on any subject,
yet it seemed that never was he carried away by
enthusiasm for anything. When our conversation
consisted of scandalous stories he seemed always to
have his story ready, but it never seemed original;
when we spoke seriously he always had a wise word;
when we were Liberals, he was never behind in his
Liberalism, yet his words seemed always to have been
taken from a book. When we had committed some
breach of discipline, and were up to our necks in hot
water, he never forsook us — he could not be reproached with cowardice; but, strange to say, after
the trouble had passed, while we were still wet and
wretched, he was dry in a moment. I cannot say
that he was disliked, but intimate friends he had

none. His talents were admired by none, the words
he dropped accidentally never awakened the soul or
elevated the thought; yet all considered him capable,
and although he was always successful, success in him
never awakened envy. He was diligent without being
a book-worm, and his success apparently came to him
without especial effort. No one could remember any
absurd answer he had made: all with him passed
easily and in good order. Our masters regarded him
as the gem of the class; they set him at the head
on all great occasions, and spoke of him as a man
who would go far. They were enraptured by his
answers, by his compositions, by his conduct, and
by his clean and orderly appearance. But I can
remember finding little satisfaction in his compositions and his answers; I admired only the polish
and smoothness of his work, and all that he did
gave me an impression of deficiency and incomplete-
ness, as a breakfast well served from which the guest
arises hungry.

The prophecies of our teachers were fulfilled.
Nicander advanced with great steps on his career;
and when, in a few years, I returned to the capital,
I found him in an important position. In the service
Nicander's name was constantly heard from the lips
of his chiefs with rapturous praise. Everywhere I
heard, "What a capable man!" "What a pen he
has!" And, truly, judged by the general standard,
Nicander was a master of that exposition which his
chief so much admired. But I was again surprised
by the universal praise of Nicander's "expository
powers," when I happened to read some papers he
had prepared. On me these papers created precisely

the same impression as his answers at our school examinations, the impression of a well-served meal at which there was nothing to eat. I was tortured by hunger while others seemed sated and content. In Nicander's papers, in his memoranda and reports, I saw clearly ability only to blunt and seduce the taste, to obscure the kernel of the question, to envelop it in rounded phrases, so that the reader, while losing sight of its essence, should concentrate his attention on the covering, details, and formal attributes ; and, together with this, insistence on the paths by which the matter must progress, dexterously expounded to lead the susceptible reader to the decision required or to some point marked where the matter might be laid aside. It seemed that all was expounded clearly in these rounded phrases ; in reality nothing was clear, all was shrouded in mist ; but the question was settled—on paper at any rate—*e sempre bene.*

Having spent some years in retirement, where from time to time arrived fresh praises of Nicander's ability, I went to the capital again, and found him in occupation of a new and even more important post. Here I had fresh opportunities for examining his work, and admiring his knowledge of affairs which still, as before, seemed to me the product of a strange dexterity. Being older in years and experience, I had learned to understand that there are many things in the working world which are not dreamt of in the philosophy of the young. The features of Nicander's moral physiognomy became clearer to me, and I found in him a curious object of study, not so much by himself, as in the sphere in which he lived and worked. He speaks little, but

P

listens attentively, although apparently with indifference. His features are rarely animated by
interest, but sometimes one may observe a shadow
of unrest when arguments threaten to become too
warm, or when sharp differences of opinion are
expressed. This unrest is changed to agitation if
questions of a delicate nature are introduced, especially when a scandal is threatened. All Nicander's
instincts tend towards the removing of inequalities
in characters, in impressions, in opinions, and towards
the reconciling of contradictions, and the establishment
of concord and tranquillity everywhere. When discussions threaten to pierce to the nature of things,
he becomes alarmed; the application of abstract
principles to individual questions, the search for
fundamental ideas, horrifies him; by experience he
knows that disagreements in fundamental ideas are
the most stubborn and provoking, and he puts in
action all his tactics to reconcile them. It is impossible not to admire the dexterity with which he
draws opponents away from dangerous fields, leading
them to the level plain of trifles, accidents, and
bagatelles. On this field he is master, he finds little
trouble in convincing opponents that they are in
complete agreement, that questions so immaterial as
those which they discuss are unworthy of thought.
His exploits, indeed, are wonderful. He can reconcile
opponents, in appearance separated by an impassable
gulf of contradiction in fundamental opinions. A
struggle, apparently of contending elements, begins.
It seems irreconcilable. Yet in ten minutes Nicander
has filled the gulf with light down and covered it with
brushwood, which the adversaries are crossing, holding

out their hands to one another. Nicander has no
love for fundamental ideas, his experience has not
been in vain. He knows that fundamental ideas are
seldom deeply rooted in the mind, and that it is always
possible to divert the uncertain thought or dim impression from the depths to which it yearns. To attain
this end he has a practice almost infallible : against
the fundamental ideas he places his so-named principles, abstract propositions, and decided opinions,
which are seldom opposed. There are magic words
which throw a spell over us in every discussion, and
no one knows better than Nicander how to bring
them up in the moment of need. Such sayings, like
the classic *Quos ego*, in a moment appease the rising
waves :—" Everyone recognises nowadays," " Modern
civilisation has arrived at this conclusion," " Statistics
prove," " In France, in Prussia, this rule was established
ages ago," " This European scholar, on such and
such a page, declares," " Nowadays no one disputes
that price is determined by relation of supply to
demand," and a number of like aphorisms. Such
are the magic phrases which work enchantment in
our discussions. But the most magical of magic
phrases is "Science tells us—it is admitted by science."
Nicander knows that we fear this word science as
the devil, and dare not contend with it. We know
that it is a stick with two ends, and fear to take
hold of either when he offers it to us. To object
to science would be to raise a host of questions :
What is science? where is it? whence comes it? why?
and a multitude of others which would prolong the
quarrel forever—in which we know we should be lost.
In general, therefore, our discussions end with

"science," and we accept its conclusions without questioning their origin, their import, or their aim.

The more we live the more we learn. It is only now that I begin to understand why our masters praised Nicander so, why to-day all are satisfied with him, and extol his capacity for work. We are told that the genius is he who can answer the questions of the day, who can diagnose the needs of his time and country, and satisfy them. What matters it that these questions are trifling, that these needs are artificial? He is a great man, nevertheless, and, alas, he is a representative of the great workers of our time! Around him is formed a school of like workers. All are polished and respectable, all without difficulty gain the reputation of *capable* men. When I watch them I recall involuntarily the scene from "Faust." '(The spirits vanish without leaving smell.) The marshal in surprise asks the bishop: "Do you smell anything?" "I smell nothing," answers the bishop. Then Mephistopheles explains: "This kind of spirit has no smell, gentlemen" (*Diese art Geister stinken nicht, meine Herren*).'

II

It is with calm, and without repulsion, that I look on Laïs as she passes in her splendid carriage, answering with smiles the salutes of passing notables, or as she sits, half-dressed, half-undressed, at the opera, while the great ladies of society cast at her glances of envy mingled with contempt—a contempt which does not, nevertheless, prevent them quietly appropriating certain features of her manner and of her dress. She bears openly on her face what she is, what she seeks, for what she lives, dresses, and enjoys herself, and she bears her name without hypocrisy, although without shame. When she gazes boldly through her glasses at the great ladies of society her impudence in no way surprises me, or repels me ; her glance seems to say to them, " I am truly that for which you take me, my face is uncovered ; but, you, why do you wear masks ? " I think of the fate of Laïs and pity her ; I ask what circumstances of life have set her on that path, from what class she sprang, and whence she drew that thirst for wild enjoyment. The thought arises, How will this path end for her, to what sad old age will that youth, burnt away in the intoxication of passion, lead ?

Laïs lives in her own circle ; the doors of the salons of society are closed against her. But when in these salons I meet the proud and splendid Messalina my soul revolts : I cannot look on her without indignation. To her the doors of the great world are opened wide ; there is no entertainment where she is not invited and received with honour ; she is beset by a host of young men of great family ; an illustrious name, sumptuous surroundings, and splendid hospitality attract to her salons all who consider themselves as numbered among the elect. All sing praises of her beauty, her taste, her kindness, her gaiety : " Crowned with flowers as the graces, she advances smiling over the blessed earth." But when I ask myself what is the difference between the splendid Messalina and the despised Laïs, alas, I pity Laïs, while for Messalina I feel contempt.

At balls, although many admire her, I look on her with abhorrence. The practice of exposing not only the neck and breast, but the back and arms, goes with her to limits that Laïs herself has not attained, and many of the friends of Laïs cannot repress a smile at the toilette of Messalina. Others assert that no one has heard from Laïs such loose speech and cynical witticisms as have been heard from Messalina to her partner in the mazurka or her neighbour at roulette; but Laïs bears the stamp of infamy, while Messalina rules in the salons of society.

Laïs has no family or home, she stands outside the family circle. Messalina has a husband whose illustrious name she bears, a magnificent house, a cohort of liveried servants on her marble staircase. What is the bond between her and her husband, and why do they live beneath the same roof? This is a secret known to Messalina alone. Her husband is present in her salon, he accompanies her to the salons of others, and protects her with his name. But when in winter you meet Messalina in her troïka, or, in spring, on the noisy boulevard in a splendid carriage with splendid horses, it is not her husband who shares her hours of gaiety and recreation; even in her husband's presence, others stand nearer to her, and behave more freely with her. On meeting Laïs with one of her cavaliers many look aside with shame; but when they meet Messalina with a favourite from the same circle, they bow politely, and whisper among themselves with a smile. O virtue, O honour of society, who shall ever know thy ways!

Messalina is a mother, she has children, but what

are the moral bonds which unite her with her children
no one can tell. She seldom sees them, and seldom
knows their affairs. They live in a special apartment
with their governesses; and at certain hours appear
like butterflies, in costumes of the latest fashion, with
bare hands and legs, to receive from their mother a
kiss, then to return to their rooms. Messalina has no
time to think about children in the excitement in
which her days and nights roll by. Retiring early
in the morning, awakening late, she has hardly time
to collect her thoughts before some guest arrives with
whom she must go for a walk; afterwards she receives
more guests in her salon to discuss the latest
scandals and intrigues, and to draw up programmes
of amusements and entertainments to come. She
dresses in the morning, she dresses for dinner, she
dresses for the opera, she dresses for the ball or
evening party. What is her interest in life? what
are the intellectual and moral springs which keep her
in movement? Where do her thoughts and desires
converge? To these questions you will no longer
seek an answer when you see the hollowness of her
life. On her table lie books which no one has seen
her read. Solitude is intolerable to her, she feels
that she must have society, and why? To seek
incessant distraction. Her life is something in the
nature of an endless holiday, after the manner of
Watteau, with the addition of electric light. The
ordinary mortal, however determined to enjoy his
life, must stumble sometimes upon sickness, grief, or
loss: the mysterious idea of life and death must
sometimes rise before his eyes. To these Messalina
is invulnerable. What does she care for house

and family and children? These are the affairs of
her housekeeper, or, if they cannot otherwise be man-
aged, of her husband.   Sickness?   But she is strong
beyond belief, she has learnt to control her nerves,
and are there not the doctor and strong doses of
chloral.   Grief?   There is no grief which cannot be
dissipated by those who can go to Baden, to Monaco
with its strong excitements, to Paris, where, with the
aid of Worth, one can rid oneself of every woe.   In
some homes shame appears uninvited, but how would
shame dare to cross the thresholds of the splendid
rooms where so many famous and honourable men
gather to eat and drink and make merry, and admire
their hostess; where women in splendid dresses
recount their intrigues and adventures; where from
all sides may be heard the tumult of mutual satisfaction and careless gaiety; where all is forgiven,
save severe devotion to the moral principle of life.
It would seem, old age, at least, is terrible for the
woman of the world!   But then, has not Parisian
science devised good means against the natural decay
of beauty?   How many old women are there who
appear young by the aid of false blushes, false skins,
false hair, and even false bodies?   But death, at any
rate, stands behind the shoulders of all—death—death
—mais—franchement, après tout—who now thinks of
death?

Yet there is one point whence threatens a tempest
of dread.   All is false in the life and surroundings of
Messalina.   The luxury around her, her house with
its sumptuous appointments, the majestic servants
who crowd her staircases, her thousand toilettes—all
these are illusions which may vanish in an hour.   For

years her home has not belonged to her ; she and her
husband have long lost all account of their debts ; for
years the bills sent to her from shops have formed a
chaotic heap, which no one would attempt to order.
Their estates are mortgaged, the day of public sale
is appointed, their factories stop work, they are beset
by money-lenders with demands and actions. But
at the critical moment their troubles vanish by enchantment, their estates are freed, their factories work
again, their creditors disperse as conquerors seized
by inexplicable panic, and Messalina announces a
ball, which is attended by select guests, gushing with
rapturous praise of her splendour, taste, and magnificence. For not one of her guests is it secret that
all this splendour is a figment, yet all, as moths, fly
to the bright light and sumptuous luxury, asking
not whose it is and whence it comes ; all are satisfied,
all are charmed, for such are the bonds of friendship
which bind a crowd thirsty for enjoyment and excitement, and together worshipping the idol of vanity.
Once, when it seemed that ruin was near for
Messalina, and there was no salvation, what pity-
ing words were heard about her in salons ! "Have
you heard—poor Messalina—things are going very
badly with them. I am told that they have only
twenty thousand roubles income left, it is terrible, it
is beggary, is it not?" Is it possible to allow the
ruin of such a house? From all sides come inter-
cession and entreaty, and then, as if by a magician's
wand, a favouring wind brings great sums for the
settlement of her affairs. Shall we wonder then that
Messalina has no trouble or fear? Proudly she walks
through the world looking into the eyes of all: how

often when we meet her do we recall the lines from
Racine's " Phèdre,"

" . . . . Dieux, qui la connaissez
Est-ce donc sa vertu que vous récompensez ! "

Messalina and her kind live upon the mountain-tops,
and never descend into the valleys. We look up-
wards towards them with astonishment, and ask, How
do they breathe the air of the mountain-tops without
being stifled ? Or are they, as the Olympians, nourished on ambrosia ? They see and hear only those
like themselves, and all the work, the troubles, the
joys of the lower world rise up to them in a misty
picture, as the distant buzzing of insects. Is it
possible that poverty and pain can penetrate their
gilded palaces, not as ideas or images, but in the
concrete forms of suffering men ? Can they feel sympathy for such? God preserve us from condemning all
as evil: many are good, full of the best intentions; their
misfortune is that they can never examine themselves.
Time for introspection there is none in the revolution
of a day dedicated from hour to hour to the search
for enjoyment and distraction, to the conventional
duties and conventional proprieties of the circle in
which they turn. Some, when conscience awakens,
curse their manner of life, and say, "To-morrow I
will begin to live as a human being." But this
to-morrow never comes ; to-morrow, the inexorable,
enchanted circle draws up a new list of pleasures and
conventional obligations.

One of the subtlest of arts is the art of self-deception and of lulling conscience to sleep ; and this art
humanity has practised well from the beginning of

time. It is not strange then, that many have attained perfection. Those who live the conventional life of a restricted circle cannot find rest in the thought that they have no concern with the lives of ordinary mortals, with beggary, privation, and misery. They feel it necessary to prove that nothing human is strange to them. With this object, institutions of beneficence have been founded — a splendid means to clear the consciences of individual men. These institutions exist by themselves, and, like other institutions, work by statute and regulation, while the individual man, with his conscience, his feelings, his personal energy of will, lives freely alone, and all unhappiness which would spoil his life, shackle his liberty, or occupy his time, is sent to the *institution*.

By means of this inspired contrivance, in the enchanted circle where Messalina rules poison is turned into food, from bitterness sweetness proceeds, and the work of benevolence, the work of pity, the work of mutual sympathy among the children of dust in the name of the high spiritual principle of love, is turned into a social entertainment—a fair of all the vanities.

Thus Messalina appears as the protectress of the poor, the benefactress of suffering humanity, the patroness of the charity bazaar. I have seen her standing in a blaze of electric light, to the sound of a splendid orchestra, at a stall ingeniously built in the magnificent salon of a great house. She looked dazzlingly lovely in a splendid toilet just received from Paris, and worth an unimaginable sum. Around her thronged buyers, attracted by her glances and her smiles, her profits every day awakening envy in the neighbouring stalls. She leaves her post with the proud consciousness of duty fulfilled, with the emotion of a new triumph, although her receipts, as those of her companions, do not equal the price of the toilette which she wore. The thought involuntarily occurs: What an immense sum might have been collected if we could have put together the values borne upon the shoulders of these resplendent ladies!

In this assembly there is no place for Läis, and why, indeed, should she be there? Läis is a despised being, and her infamy is notorious. Yet once there was one such as she who bore in herself the fire of love through long wandering on the way of evil. Long and deeply had she sinned, yet all her sins were forgiven because she had loved much, although in ignorance where to place her love until that day when at last she met with the true principle of all love. But whom, except herself, has Messalina ever loved, what fire does she bear in herself?

III

There are men with arid and limited minds, whom, nevertheless, we may take seriously, because they have firm, decided views—a certain character which constantly reveals itself. There are able and interesting men whom we never take seriously, because they have no firm opinions, but only sensations which perpetually change. Such very often is the nature of artistic men, their lives are a constant play of shifting sensations, the expression of which sometimes goes to virtuosity. In the expression of their views they deceive neither themselves nor their hearers; like talented actors, they adopt a role to which they abandon themselves with true art. But when in real life they are called upon to act, it is impossible to foresee how they will direct their action and express their will, or what colour they will give to their words in the moment of crisis.

Such constitution of thought and feeling is unhappily familiar among us, more particularly among people by nature gifted. The artistic faculties develop, while those clear and defined ideas which sustain mankind in life and action are absent. With such men all is impression. They are inspired by every medium into which they accidentally fall; they are preachers and prophets of every idea which they find current there. Falling into endless inconsistency, to-day contradicting to-morrow, they learn dexterously to reconcile their inconsistencies, and pass from one to another, skilfully playing with subtleties of thought and sentiment. In politics and administration such men, often unconsciously, become opportunists, practised in sailing with every wind from whatever quarter it may blow, and of drawing inspiration from every wind which is favourable to them. Among statesmen in Parliament, among attorneys and advocates examples of this are common; inspired by the impression of the moment, the man who but yesterday was the stern, inexorable enemy of injustice, to-morrow appears as its apologist; he will defend with ardent, inspired conviction ideas entirely inconsistent; he will find features of beauty to-day in that which yesterday he condemned for its moral deformity.

The attribute to the talented actor is susceptibility to inspiration by his part and capacity for entering into the soul and character of the person whom he personates. But if the actor can abandon himself to his art, if he is able to live again in the characteristic adventures of the individual he represents, it is because before him is a mass of observers whose souls unite with his own; and, inspired by his part, he is, at the same time, inspired by the souls of his audience. This is the cause of the attractiveness of acting, which grows to a passion almost, both in the actor and in his audience. It is the same with every speaker in public assemblies when advocating ideas or doctrines; inspired by his subject, he is at the same time inspired by the medium on which he acts, and, while never abdicating his personality, this personality aspires to awaken in the medium sentiments of sympathy and enthusiasm. Such aspirations may lead a talented nature to passion; unrestrained he seeks a scene for his art, practising it everywhere, in great assemblies, in the conversations of the salon and the study; adapting himself to the nature of his audience, and inspired by the colour of its opinions.

Such actors abound in all deliberative and legislative assemblies. It may be said that they constitute the majority which decides all matters of moment. As a counterbalance, we have men of serious action and firm opinions, but these are seldom strong in words; they cannot wield the weapons which their opponents, the men of impressions and sensations, make use of with ease. The more numerous the assembly, the more heterogeneous its composition, the less is it able to examine the nature of questions, to comprehend their data, to distinguish their truth or falsehood, and the more is it likely to be carried away by sensation, sometimes the sensation of the moment which a speaker has produced. Few approach questions with conscience or after preparatory study; the majority either has no precise apprehension of the question, or approaches it with prejudice and preconception. In such assemblies the artist in words is master of emotions. Skilfully armed with his disposition of facts and figures, casting upon them light or shadow according to his own views, he seduces some by pathos, entangles others by irony, and holds the field against all who struggle for truth, yet who cannot arm themselves with phrases, but work with a strong chain of logical reasoning. Their arguments are inaccessible to a majority drawn by sensations; the more conscientious they are—the more they feel the moral responsibility for their opinions—the harder it is to conquer the irresponsible majority, which lacks conscience, for how can there be conscience in a crowd without unity or wholeness, united only in the numbering of votes? This numbering of votes unhappily serves as the final criterion of truth, and the final sanction of conclusions which sometimes determine the gravest questions of State.

IV

The avarice typified in Molière's "Harpagon" has many varieties which have been little investigated.

It is strange that hitherto no humorist has called attention to that peculiar species of avarice, the avarice of time. For it is a subject rich in interest.

As Molière's miser amasses wealth and trembles over it, this other miser economises time, not to employ it productively, but to admire his capital as the miser takes pleasure in his hoard of gold. Gold would live if a living soul possessed it. In the hands of a true man it would become a mighty instrument of fruitful productiveness and of wise beneficence, for, as every other force, money requires circulation. The English tell us that "Time is money." A living man must put it into circulation, and expend it productively, without parsimony or extravagance.

Society is rich in these extreme types. On one hand, we find too many idle forces, and too much squandering of time by men who know not what to do with it ; and the meeting of men of this type with men of action who value their time is a situation not devoid of absurdity. On the other hand, we often meet with misers of time, and, unhappily, meet with them sometimes among men of business, and even among men in authority.

In such men the dread of losing time some- times degenerates to a nervous irritation, which forces them to lock themselves up from the world, and to regard as thieves and robbers all those who approach them on actual work with explanations or requests. This explains the difficulty of seeing some men of authority on the most necessary affairs. The only means of communication with them is by letter. Written communications have a soothing effect, although the routine work inseparable from correspondence wastes more time than any personal interview. In this, perhaps, we may find the cause of the immense development of correspondence in our time. Ask such a man why he treasures his time and secludes himself so jealously. He will answer that every moment is precious. But if we examined more closely how he employs those moments we could only wonder at the cause of his self-seclusion from life, from men, from living action—the cause of his sitting like Harpagon over his hoarded gold.

V

Xenophon, in his recollections of Socrates, records the instructive history of a young Athenian of under twenty years of age, who wished to become a statesman, and began zealously to deliver speeches to the public, in the hope of attaining popularity. At last he came to Socrates, who said, " I hear, Glaucon, that you wish to take part in the direction of State affairs?" "Yes, that is my ambition." "It is a splendid career," said Socrates, "to govern a State —what infinite good you can do to your native land! What honour you will gain for yourself and for your house! You may attain celebrity in Athens; yes, and not in Athens only! Themistocles was famous even among the barbarians. Excellent! But I think you will admit that such honours are not given for nothing; something must be done to deserve them ?" " Undoubtedly," Glaucon hastened to reply. "Tell me," continued Socrates, "with what would you begin, for instance?" The young man made

Q

no answer; he had never thought of how he would begin. "Let us see, we are told that of all things wealth is the most necessary for the State. You, of course, would do your utmost to increase the revenue?" "Unquestionably." "I am curious to know how you would begin. You know, of course, from what sources the treasury receives its revenue, what sums it receives, and from what quarters?" The young man was compelled to admit that he did not know exactly. "Well, in such a case, tell me what expenditure you think superfluous and what you would wish to curtail." "I confess I have never had time to think about this in detail. But it seems to me, Socrates, that we need not trouble about this when we can fill our treasury at the expense of our enemies." "Quite true; but for this we must first conquer the enemy; we must be stronger than he. If he be stronger, it is he who will fill his treasury from ours. If you rely upon war you must know exactly our strength and the strength of the enemy. Can you tell me the strength of our forces on land and sea, and the strength of the forces of the enemy?" "I cannot tell them out of my head at a moment's notice." "That does not matter," answered Socrates; "if you have them noted somewhere let us go and examine them." But Glaucon had no memoranda. "Very well," began Socrates again, "I see that we must abandon this subject; its time has not yet come. But, of course, you know of all that relates to the internal security of the State; how many posts of police there are, how many are required, where they are lacking, where there are too many, and where they may be diminished?" "To tell the truth," answered Glaucon, "I should have abolished them all if it had depended on me. For what purpose does our police serve, and why should we maintain it, when everywhere robbery takes place, so that no man feels safe?" "What! Why, if we abolished the police, then thieves would plunder at free will in the open day. But can you truly say, from your own knowledge, that our police is of no use?" "So it seems to me; everyone says that it is so." "No, Glaucon, you must not be satisfied with seeming; you must know exactly." Glaucon was forced to assent. "Come now," said Socrates, "you wish to rule the State. Do you know how much wheat is needed by the inhabitants of our city in a year, what is our home production, and how much we have to buy abroad?" "How should I know this, Socrates?" answered the young man. "You ask so many questions that it would be a great labour to reply to them." "But, Glaucon, you cannot govern your own house without knowing this, and it is harder to govern a State than a household. Go to your uncle's house, which is in disorder. Begin with it—manage your uncle's house, and you will then find the knowledge and the strength you lack." "I should willingly undertake it, but my uncle will not listen to my advice." "What!" cried Socrates, "you are not able to convince your uncle, yet you imagine that you are able to convince all Athens, your uncle among them!" The discussion ended; the young man reflected, began to study, and ceased to make speeches in the assemblies of the people.

It is well to recall this old, simple tale at the present

day, when the earth is overrun by Glaucons, who aspire
to political careers by beginning with all manner of
reforms ; when young men, who have scarcely left the
benches at school, often without success, hasten to compose, in questionable grammar, projects for new legislation, and to deliver speeches swollen with inflated
phrases.   In the past there was a Socrates to whom
parents might send their young aspirants when they
saw them made ridiculous by empty eloquence.
In our unhappy age there is no Socrates, and if
there were, our Glaucons would not go near him or
listen to his advice.   To audiences like themselves
resound the empty speeches of inflated orators,
filled with impudence and unfailing assurance.
Their projects are received without criticism, and
awaken admiration instead of contempt.   Before
them rise the easy steps of that desired staircase
which they ascend on the stilts of phrase.

VI

When first reflection awakens in man, the desire
to define himself, to determine his place in life, to
make his ideal of life accord with his activity awakens
also.   The restless mind trembles in the midst of an
eternally shifting, various, and inconstant activity,
in the midst of a changing circle of aspirations,
impressions, and desires.   The thinking mind desires
a resting-place in this uncertainty ; a point on which
to affirm the *balance* of life, to create for itself a
character.

There are fortunate men who attain this equi-

librium at once without great effort. Making no
deductions or conclusions, asking no questions—why?
whence? for what purpose? such men themselves unconsciously find in action a decision of all questions.
Their ideas correspond to their organic requirements, and settle equably in the soul, never opposing
their wishes or sensations. Their interests are
restricted by a circle of action which they choose
for themselves, and which they wish not to transcend.
In ordinary life this type is often met with, awakening sympathy everywhere, for the simplicity of its
relations to life generally imparts to it a character of
directness and sincerity. It is true that this type
presents little interest on the lower grades of its
development, because we do not find in it creative
force. But on the higher steps, it numbers men
of culture, of developed intellect, who may be
numbered among those of well-balanced life. They
do not aspire to creation, but are generally masters
of thought and action; and are gifted with the capacity of assimilating, understanding, and transmitting
creative thought, because they possess *talent.* Their
nature makes possible a harmonious union of life and
work, ideas and images; and their thoughts, while
never ceasing to work, never aspire to destroy this
harmony. This class numbers a multitude of men
who acquire honourable celebrity in administrative
work, in literature, in art, in science. And their
work is precious, because they educate the thought
and taste of society; not in the name of creative,
but of accepted ideas and images. They accomplish
a great work with small pretensions. They inspire
imitation through sympathetic tendencies of mind,

but they cannot create new schools, or attract enthusiasts to a new gospel.

Others strive to form an equilibrium in life by conscious efforts of will. All reasoning in man begins from the knowledge of good and evil. The sensations of evil and error produce in the soul perplexity, from which the human mind seeks an issue ; and, dissatisfied with the instinctive feeling sufficient for others, it flies to the aid of reason to find a path to the attainment of truth. Thus are formed rationalists, who seek to attain truth in the duality of human nature. General principles, accepted on the blind confidence of the intellect, constitute for them impregnable propositions, with which they attempt to classify all the phenomena of life. The reason which they worship becomes a divinity, solving all questions of practical life, and their convictions they regard as the conclusions of truth, which every rational being must accept. Such tendencies of mind sometimes develop to the fanaticism of formal logic. The fanatical worshipper of abstract principles acknowledges nothing that will not accord with his system of speculation, and he is in no way embarrassed by the plain facts and phenomena of actuality. I see, he replies, but I do not believe. Among the higher specimens of this type we find philosophers, theologians, moralists, naturalists, whose one desire is to reconcile with reason not only all that they see, think, and feel, but all that others think and feel, and even things that never were thought, but may somewhere occur or appear. The highest representatives of this type were Auguste Comte and Stuart Mill, both true patterns of abstract thinkers with absolute faith in the infallibility of reason and analysis.

Such are the great! The lower varieties found in the different domains of knowledge and action are very different in nature, and of late their number has multiplied immeasurably. Pretended philosophers appear, investing themselves with some fashionable religion or philosophical doctrine, or founding schools themselves simply by denying the ideas accepted by those around them. All, however, imagine that they drink from the spring of universal knowledge — in politics, in science, in philosophy. By its nature reason is an art, and feeds on the artistic instinct. The mind is naturally inclined to build more or less symmetrical edifices of proofs, deductions, and conclusions. By some this instrument is used to subserve their passions, their caprices, and their material interests, while others are drawn by passion to licence in speculation, and strive to accord in formal unity the whole domain of observation. This passion is one of the strongest that rules mankind. To the number of the first belong the passionate propagandists of social and religious ideas who wish to reform humanity—of such is the upper grade. On the lower steps stand sophists of all kinds, who employ their arts in defence or advocacy, at the impulse of caprice, or for the sake of selfish interests. To this class belong advocates and journalists of the baser sort.

Men of this type seek to establish harmony in their souls by means of the balancing and co-ordination of its ideal elements. But there are minds which, having evolved certain ideas from within, or adopted

them from without, seek to subordinate all other ideas
to them, and what they cannot subordinate refuse to
recognise or accept.   These are, indeed, the fanatics
of preconception.   So convinced are they of the truth
of their convictions that they worship them, and,
when the real truth appears, reject it as they reject
phenomena irreconcilable with their conceptions of
truth.   Pursuing one idea to its extreme limits, they
refuse to regard any other idea, or consider other
facts or phenomena.   Having affirmed thus their lives
on the basis of a favourite idea, they reject violently
all ideas and sentiments irreconcilable with it, but
cannot, nevertheless, annihilate them; and often those
rejected forces, in spite of theories and a faith which
knows no limits, continue to determine their activity,
their personal relations, and their feelings to real life.
These sentiments, concealed in the depths of the
human soul—sentiments which such men will not for
anything recognise — unconsciously manifest themselves in their actual lives, although they have rejected
and buried them.   This is especially noticeable where
the dominant idea is sharply opposed to the ideas
accepted in the sphere around it.   Thus we see that
the atheist, whose denial of religion goes to hatred,
falls into gross superstition in his domestic life, or
creates himself a faith from the refuse of those forms
he has rejected.   The theorist who, by his theory of
the struggle for existence, condemns as falsehood
and evil all beneficence, when he sees poverty hastens
to relieve it ; the ardent apostle of free love, who denies
all marriage and family life, shows himself a tender
and careful husband and father; the fanatical advocate
of celibacy and asceticism rejoices at the birth of

children ; the fiercest foe of wealth and of capital
lets no occasion pass for the increase of his capital
and his wealth. Such phenomena, so common among
us, serve as a striking exposure of the falsehood of
all theories constructed independently of life. The
fatal duality of human nature is everywhere revealed;
on the tongue is a proud and triumphant word ; the
deeds correspond in no way. In the depths of the
souls of men, both great and small, hypocrisy is
concealed. When evil appears clothed in the vest-
ments of religion and philanthropy we are horrified.
But in addition to such conscious and shameless
hypocrisy, how often is unconscious hypocrisy revealed, when men, blinded by pride, glorify their faiths
and speculations as the images of truth, flattering
their hearts with a multitude of worshippers and
disciples, who bear their gospels to the four winds.
Sometimes these disciples develop the system of
their master, with new applications of its essential
ideas, as formulas destined to enlighten humanity, to
reveal to it the mystery of the Godhead, of the world,
and of life, and to reform, in the sudden light of truth,
religion, and art, and science, and philosophy. More
often the pupils do a vain service to their master by
building a system on the fallacies and imperfections
of his doctrine.

What are the impulses which drive the human mind
to such narrowness and extremity? Some characters
by nature are inclined to contradiction and to protest
against received opinions and convictions rooted in
the social polity, or existing and consecrated by
tradition. This innate tendency may degenerate to
fanaticism when seeking issue and satisfaction. At its

prompting, the subtle thinker elaborates a system of
tenuous dialectics, which serves as an instrument for
the attainment of his ends—that is, the conversion of
others to what, with all the energy of a strained will,
he regards as truth.   Immersed in scientific theories,
in doctrines of religion or sociology, the mind strives
to extract from them a truth which no one sees ; and
on this truth aspires to establish unity of science,
faith, and life.   Another, the seeker after truth, lost in
the study of the Gospel, and seeking there an ideal of
religious truth, rejects as incompatible all but a few
words and phrases.   On these scattered fragments he
builds himself the temple of a new faith, proclaims
it as the revelation of his own intellect, and charms
disciples from that multitude which wanders over the
world, seeking to affirm on unity its scattered thoughts
and desires.   From the time when man began to see
and think upon the phenomena of social life, the
host of such prophets has been innumerable, sowing among peoples of different faiths not love, but
infinite hatred and intolerance.

Among the higher representatives of this class we
cannot but observe much genial imagination and ingenuity.   The architect of ideas is everywhere a master
of art ; seduced by external symmetry he builds his
house ; he is charmed by its form and harmony,
and ignores the essential absurdity of the materials.
Such, for instance, was the system of the inspired
madman, Fourier.   All the higher creators of such
systems were distinguished as artists in thoughts and
words.   It is remarkable that few of them took part
in the realisation of their theories ; most were satisfied
with proclaiming their teaching, troubling little about

its consequences. Having worked upon the letter of
their doctrine, they send it out into the world to care
for itself, where, seizing minds in a state of transition,
it creates fanatical advocates, who seldom attempt to
realise, but extend and proclaim it, according to their
own interpretations. Often the most fanatical preacher
of anarchy proves a quiet citizen, a wise parent, and a
virtuous man, while his pupils and adherents do sanguinary deeds by virtue of his teaching and in his
name. The prophet of Socialism issues works, delivers
speeches, and maintains his own welfare, while his
teaching incites the people to infamous misdeeds. The
prophet troubles little how many lives have been ruined
by his doctrine, how many falsehoods have been sown
in unripe minds, how many new misfortunes he has
brought upon humanity, how many feeble, trusting
souls he has destroyed. Why should he think of
this? Has he not faith in his formula for the unity
of human life, which early or late is destined to
regenerate the world?

Ours is a time of restless and wandering thought, a
time richly abounding in abnormal and unbalanced
minds. In all ages the life of man has been afflicted
with violence, injustice, falsehood, and misfortune ; but
never so widely as to-day was opened before us the
infinite roll of evil and untruth. It is not surprising
that among such unhealthy sentiments the mind,
seeking an ideal, should lose itself, and, finding no
issue, be compelled to cleave a way. And woe to
it if it find no issue save denial, indignation, and
protest ! The path of negation too often leads to
fictitious formulas of life : engendering new falsehoods in the mind, while striving with other formulas,

it exhausts itself in fruitless denials, until it in turn gives way to some new doctrine. One after another stretch infinite files of men seeking an answer to Pilate's question: What is truth? And he only who is of the truth may find in himself an answer without search.

POWER AND AUTHORITY

In human souls there exists a force of moral gravity which draws them one to another; and which, made manifest in the spiritual interaction of souls, answers an organic need. Without this force mankind would be as a heap of sand, without any bond, dispersed by every wind on every side. By this inherent force, without preparatory accord, are men united in society. It impels them out of the crowd of men to seek for leaders with whom to commune, whom to obey, and whose direction to seek. Inspired by a moral principle, this instinct acquires the value of a creative force, uniting and elevating the people to worthy deeds and to great endurance.

But for the purposes of civil society this free and accidental interaction is not enough. The natural instinct of man seeks for power in unbroken activity, to which the mass, with its varied needs, aspirations, and passions may submit; through which it may acquire the impulse of activity, and the principles of order; in which it may find amid all the subversions of wilfulness a standard of truth. Thus, by its nature, power is founded on truth, and inasmuch as truth has as its source the All-High God and His commandments written indelibly in the consciences of all, we find a justification in their deeper meaning of the words, "There is no power but of God."

These words are addressed to subjects, but they apply with equal force to power itself, and O, that all power might recognise their import! Power is a great and terrible, because it is a sacred thing. This word *sacred* (*svyastchennui*) in its primitive signification means *elect* (*otdyelennui*), dedicated to the service of God. Thus, power exists not for itself alone, but for the love of God; it is a service to which men are dedicated. Thence comes the limitless, terrible strength of power, and its limitless and terrible burden.

Its strength is unlimited, not in the material acceptation of the word, but in its spiritual meaning, because it is the strength of reason and of creation. The first act of creation was the appearance of the light and its separation from darkness. Thus, the first act of power must be the finding of truth and its discrimination from falsehood; on this is founded the faith of the people in power, and the gravitation towards it of all mankind. Many times and everywhere this faith has been deceived, but its fount remains intact, and cannot dry up, because without truth no man can live. From this also springs the creative force of power, the strength to attract just and rational men, to animate them, and to inspire them to work and to great deeds. To power belongs the first and last word—it is the alpha and omega of human activity.

While humanity exists it will not cease to suffer, sometimes from power, sometimes from impotence. The violence, the abuse, the folly and selfishness of power raise rebellion. Deceived by their ideals of power, men seek to dispense with it, and to replace it by the authority of the law. This is a vain fancy.

In the name of the law arise a multitude of un-authorised factions, which struggle for power, and the distribution of power leads to violence worse than that which went before. Thus poor humanity, searching for an ideal organisation, is borne on the waves of an infinite sea, without a guide, without a harbour in sight.

To live without power is impossible. After the need of communion the need of power is of all feelings most deeply rooted in the spiritual nature of man. Since the day duality entered into his soul, since the day the knowledge of good and evil was vouchsafed to him, and the love of good and justice rose in his soul in eternal conflict with evil and in-justice, for him there has been no salvation save to seek sustenance and reconciliation in a high judge of this conflict ; in a living incarnation of the principle of order and of truth. And, whatever may be the disenchantment, the betrayal, the afflictions which humanity has suffered from power, while men shall yearn for good and truth, and remember their helplessness and duality, they can never cease to believe in the ideal of power, and to repeat their efforts for its realisation. To-day, as in ancient times, the foolish say in their hearts : There is no God, no truth, no good, no evil ; and gather around them pupils equally foolish, proclaiming atheism and anarchy. But the great mass of man-kind stands firm in its faith in the supreme principle of life, and, through tears and bloodshed, as the blind seeking a guide, seeks for power with imperishable hope, notwithstanding eternal betrayal and disillusion.

Thus the work of power is a work of uninter-

rupted usefulness, and in reality a work of renunciation. How strange these words must seem
beside the current conception of power! It is natural,
it would seem, for men to flee and to avoid renunciation. Yet all seek power, all aspire to it; for power
men strive together, they resort to crime, they destroy one another, and when they attain power they
rejoice and triumph. Power seeks to exalt itself, and
falls into the strange error that it exists for itself and
not for service of men. Yet the immutable, only true
ideal of power is embodied in the words of Christ:
"Whosoever of you will be the chiefest shall be
servant of all." These words pass through our heads
as something in no way concerning us, as especially
addressed to a vanished community in Palestine. In
reality, they apply to all power, however great, which,
in the depth of conscience, does not recognise that the
higher its throne, the wider the sphere of its activity,
the heavier must become its fetters, the more widely
must open before it the roll of social evils, stained
by the weeping of pity and woe, and the louder must
sound the crying and sobbing of injustice which
demands redress. The first necessity of power is
faith in itself and in its mission. Happy is power
when this faith is combined with a recognition of
duty and of moral responsibility! Unhappy is it
when it lacks this consciousness and leans upon itself
alone! Then begins the decay which leads to loss
of faith, and in the end to disintegration and
destruction.

Power is the depository of truth, and needs, above
all things, men of truth, of clear intellects, of strong
understandings, and of sincere speech, who know the

limits of yes and no, and never transcend them, whose thoughts develop clearly in their minds, and are clearly expressed by their words. Men of this nature only are the firm support of power, and its faithful delegates. Happy is the power which can distinguish such men, appreciate their merit, and firmly sustain them! Unhappy is the power which wearies of such natures, promoting men of complaisant character, flexible opinions, and flattering tongues!

The just man is one complete in himself, who tolerates no duality. He looks straight in the faces of others; his eyes reflect one image, one thought, one feeling. His presence is calm and unterrified, and his words change not. His thoughts accord with his character, and are expressed, not tentatively, but without regard for the mental susceptibilities or the desires and caprices of others. His words are simple, and seek no crooked paths or cunning methods to convert others to doctrines which he does not trust himself.

How different is the man of unstable thought, the flatterer, with a double soul. He looks in your face, but in his eyes you see not him, but another, and know not which to believe. He speaks, and while his words are ardent and eloquent, his mind is busy considering whether the impressions he creates are in accord with your caprices and desires. If you assent he will yield his opinions to you, declaring that you are their author, that he has taken them from you. He will seize your casual words as they are uttered, invest them with definite forms, and express them as concrete thoughts and firm opinions. The abler such a man the more skilfully

R

he will exploit and direct you. You are embarrassed —you hesitate; he has a solution ready to relieve you from your embarrassment and to lead you into the calms of complacency. You hesitate to define the truth—he has reasons and formulas ready to convince you that what you questioned is absolutely true.

Paper will tolerate all things—so says an old proverb, spoken in a time when learning was almost wholly literary and paper served as the chief material and instrument of chicane. Since then a great change has taken place. Paper remains, but oral speech is master, and modern chicanery seeks as an instrument the words of innumerable orators. A new school has been founded, in which the ignorant as well as the learned and able may acquire the art of speaking well on everything, of proving the truth or falsehood of what they will, and of carrying on a skilful game by playing with the susceptibility of their audiences. A new class has sprung up to fill the ranks of practical workers, of administrators, of judges and schoolmasters. He is a happy man who, having passed through this school, has yet preserved clear thoughts, a conscientious judgment, and the ability to recognise truth in the midst of the host of abstract propositions, and the formulas of modern sophistry—in a word, who, having passed through the school of dissimulation, has been able to remain sincere.

Men in authority must always remember the dignity of power. Dignity once forgotten, power decays, and relations to subordinates are falsified.

With dignity is coincident, and should be inseparable, that simplicity which is necessary to impel
subordinates to work, to inspire them with interest in their duties, and to maintain with them
sincerity of relations. The consciousness of dignity
engenders also freedom in relations to men. Power
must be free within the limits of the law; being
conscious of its worth, it need not consider the
appearances it makes, the impressions it creates,
or the conduct it should observe in its relations
to men. But the consciousness of merit must be
inseparable from the recognition of duty; as the
recognition of duty is enfeebled, the consciousness
of merit swells, till, swollen beyond measure, it
degenerates to a disease which may be called the
hypertrophy of power. As this disease advances
on its course, power may fall into a moral
obscurity, in which it considers itself as independent
and as existing for itself alone. Then begins the
disintegration of power.

While preserving the dignity of power, authority
must not forget that it serves as a mirror and
example for all its subordinates. As the man in
authority conducts himself, so those who will
succeed him are preparing to conduct themselves
in their relations to others, in their methods
of work, in their regard for their work, in their
tastes, in their standards of propriety and im-
propriety. It would be wrong to imagine that
power, when it takes off its robe of authority,
may without danger mingle in the daily life of
the crowd in the fair of human vanity.

Nevertheless, while cherishing his dignity, the

leader must as steadfastly guard the dignity of his subordinates. His relations to them must be founded on trustfulness, for, in the absence of trustfulness, there can be no moral bond between him and them. He is a foolish man who fancies that he can know and judge all things without intermediaries and independently of the knowledge and experience of his subordinates; who wishes to decide all questions by his word and command, without recourse to the thoughts and opinions of those who stand directly beneath him. Such men, recognising their helplessness without the knowledge and experience of their subordinates, often end by becoming altogether dependent upon them. Still worse is the case of the leader who falls into the fatal habit of tolerating no objections or contradictions; and this is the attribute not only of narrow minds, but often of able and energetic, but vain and over-confident men. A conscientious worker must avoid everything absolute and arbitary in his decisions, the fruit of these is indifference— the poison of democracy. Power must never forget that papers and reports represent living men and living works, and that life itself demands and expects decisions and directions which conform with its nature. Truth must be in the leader himself, in his sincere, conscientious, and practical views of work, and truth also corresponding to the social, moral, and economic conditions of the national life and the national history. Such truth is absent where the ruling principle of power is abstract theory, detached from life with its manifold conditions and needs.

The wider the field of the activity of a leader, the

more complex the mechanism of government, the more he needs subordinates capable of work, and able to combine in single directions to a common end. Men are needed in all times and by all governments, but perhaps more than ever to-day. In our time governments must consider a multitude of forces now rising and affirming themselves—in science, in literature, in the criticism of public opinion, in social institutions with their independent interests. Ability to find and to choose men is the first essential attribute to power ; the second is ability to direct them and to establish due discipline upon their activity.

The choice of men is a matter of labour, and the ability to distinguish their capacities an art acquired with trouble only. Unhappily, power seeks often to shirk this labour, and is satisfied with external symptoms of ability. The proofs most often demanded are diplomas of courses of higher education, acquired by means of examinations. This test, it is well known, is quite untrustworthy, for its value depends upon a multitude of adventitious circumstances, and it cannot prove the knowledge, while it proves still less the capacity of candidates for the work they are to undertake. But it serves to deliver power from the labour of studying men itself. Guided by such untrustworthy tests, power falls into errors fatal to its work. Capacity and knowledge, even education, in no way depend upon the completion of courses of study on the multitude of subjects which compose the regimen of the schools. The numberless examples of clever students who have turned out good-for-nothing, and of distinguished men of action who failed as students, demonstrate the contrary.   Often the capacity of men is discovered only the moment they deal with the living realities of work ; until then, science in the form of lessons and lectures leaves them indifferent, because they find in it no actual interest.   Such has been the history of many eminent public men.

The head of a great administration with a wide sphere of activity cannot act with success if he tries, beyond due measure, to extend his immediate authority over all the component departments of his administration, and over all the details of work.   The most energetic and experienced man may waste his strength, and confound the issues of work among his subordinates, if he pay the same attention to trifling details of routine work as to those essential questions which it is his duty generally to direct. His place is above all work, whence he may survey the whole horizon of subordinate activity ; by descending personally into the byeways of administration he breaks the measure of his work and of his strength, he loses his capacity for comprehensive survey, he destroys the division of labour necessary in all practical affairs, and weakens the interest of his subordinates in their work and their sense of moral responsibility for their appointed tasks.   A supreme leader mistakes if he reserves to himself the choice of men not only depending from him directly, but the secondary officials subordinate to the heads of the different departments of his administration.   In such cases he undertakes a labour beyond his strength, to the detriment of his work, merely for the satisfaction of his own will and absolute authority.

The head of every department is responsible for the success of the work entrusted to him ; to deprive him of the right of selecting his collaborators personally is to relieve him of responsibility for the successful issue of his labours, to weaken his authority, and to restrict his free action within the lawful limits of his power.

Unhappily, as the moral principle of power decays, the chief becomes possessed by the fatal passion of patronage, the passion of playing the protector, and of sharing places high and low. The spread of this vice, hypocritically covered with the veil of generosity and benevolence, is one of the greatest evils of our time. Too often this benevolence is mingled with servility to the great who desire to do kindnesses to their clients. Unhappily, benevolence such as this flourishes only at the expense of the public welfare, at the expense of the efficient organisation of the public service, and, finally, at the expense of the treasury and of the people. Let power once forget itself, and it loses the sentiment of the greatness of its service, and that consideration for the public welfare to which it is called.

The chief motive of favouritism is flattery, an ancient source of temptation, which attacks not only weak, but also strong natures, for the art of flattery is inexhaustible in the variety of its methods. One of its subtlest courses is the insinuation to men in authority that all creative power proceeds from them, that all reforms originate in them, that all the successes of subordinates are by them inspired. Thus, little by little, the flatterer becomes a welcome guest ; he appears a capable man, and creates in his patron an impression of attachment. When once the disposition of a chief to such agreeable conduct is observed, to acquire his good opinion becomes a customary part of the internal economy of his department.

But men with clear outlooks on life, who have trained themselves and their wills to reasoned work, clearly knowing to what they aspire, are free in their relations to their fellow-men, and in this freedom of relations find full opportunity for judging character. They know the strong and able when they see them, for they are in no way alarmed by the thought that their dignity suffers injury from the dignity of others. They have attained power, but they have not lost their freedom.

But men unprepared for power by disciplined work and disciplined character lose their freedom in their relations to men. The external dignity of power corrupts them and steals away their strength, because they do not join with it worthiness of soul and understanding, and do not value worthiness of soul in others, but take alarm at it. They feel themselves free only with men of mean spirits and worldly instincts, who flatter them with flattery adapted to their tempers and tendencies. Thus is formed about the chief a body of confidential friends and favourites, from which he is able at will to select men for the work of his administration. Himself undisciplined by labour, he has no clear conception of what labour means and what is its value; each thought strange to him he appropriates as his own, and issues in his name.

To the motive of favouritism is joined the motive of

comradeship. The relations established in early life
at school, in the amusements of youth, and in military
life, create among men ties, founded less on sympathy
of intellect than on the habit of constant association.
But among many habit is the chief guiding principle of life and action, both in personal and in public
affairs. Thus, when a friend appears as a candidate
for some appointment, the choice is determined by
personal favour, or anxiety for a man with scanty or
disordered means, sometimes without consideration
whether the candidate be suited to his work, or
whether he be capable of protecting the interests to
be entrusted to him. Still nearer to the favour of a
leader than his friends are his relations, often numerous,
who seek to carve out careers in some of the services,
and regard provision for this as the moral duty of their
powerful kinsman.

The most precious gift of a statesman is ability to
organise. It is a talent seldom met—a talent inborn,
which no study will produce. Of men of this character
it may be said as was said of poets, *nascuntur, non
fiunt.* It is enough to reflect how many different
abilities are needed to constitute the organising
talent. Strength of imagination must unite to the
capacity of promptly choosing the means of realisation. A comprehensive and foreseeing intellect is
demanded, resolution in action, ability to seize the
proper moment, to embrace rapidly the details of all
work, without losing sight of its fundamental principles. Fine observation of men and knowledge of
character are indispensable ; knowledge of whom to
trust, and experience that the best of men are not free
from low instincts and interested motives.

Happy is the statesman who recognises such talent, and makes no mistake in his choice. Error is easy; and cases are not few where statesmen have mistaken for organising talent great intellect and eloquence. Yet these qualities are not only distinct, but almost incompatible. Logical development of thought and dialectical ability seldom go with ability to organise, while the man ready to devise means of action is not often capable of the demonstrative exposition of the plans which have developed in his mind. The organising talent is made manifest in work alone, while eloquence, acting on the mind by means of reason, and by criticism of the opinions of others, attracts men at once, and evokes instantaneously enthusiasm and admiration.

Great and sacred is the vocation of power. Worthy of its mission, it animates men, it lends their activity wings, it holds up to all a mirror of justice, energy, and worth. To see such power, to feel its inspiring influence, is a great happiness for every man who loves truth, and yearns for light and virtue. But, unhappy is he who seeks power and cannot find it, or finds instead the pretended power of majorities, the power of mobs—despotism in the mirage of freedom. More deplorable is it still to see power lost to the sentiment of duty and to the knowledge of its calling; power fulfilling its work unconsciously and formally, under the shield of its dignity. The same forms of procedure remain, the wheels of the mechanism turn as before, but the spirit of life is not in them. Little by little is enfeebled the will to choose men prepared and capable for their work, till men are no longer chosen at all, but appointed at random through casual impulses and fortuitous interests. Then vanish the traditions of procedure preserved by tried and devoted workers. The school in which the young were trained by the experience of the old is destroyed, while those who undertake the work for the sake of personal interest or to build their careers, shifting ceaselessly in the eager chase for advancement, leave behind them no abiding trace of their labours.

In all practical activity art is needed as a factor of animation. This art is acquired by rational and conscientious labour, which in its turn has need of a guide also. Thus, every institution established for practical work must at the same time be a school, in which the younger generations of workers may study the art of their work, under the guidance of their elders. On this are affirmed the essential interests of every work and the moral forces which animate it. With such conditions an institution may develop and be perfected, keeping before itself a clear horizon ; a path whereby to advance. But when institutions, restricted to the vulgar paths of formalism, decay and become moribund, they cease to be schools of art, and remain mere machines, around which hireling labourers pass in succession. The horizon is obscured, aspiration dies, and progress ceases. Such may be the fate of the new institutions which multiply with the increasing complexity of political and civic life. Such is the fate of the school, with its multitude of pupils, masters, and subjects of study, when its chairs are filled by teachers unprepared and incapable, who make their teaching a trade for the sake of bread; the spirit of life departs, and the institution becomes incapable of educating and training the young generation. Such is the fate which overtakes the institutions of justice, however complex and perfect their procedure may be, when they cease to be schools for the cultivation of knowledge and experience in jurisprudence; the forms wither and die, the spirit of life vanishes, and justice becomes a mere machine, operated by hirelings.

The conceptions formed of power by those who seek it are various as the passions and aspirations of mankind. The masses, whose speculations are restricted to their daily life, are possessed by a desire to improve their condition, without any other considerations. Among others, the ruling impulse in the search for power is ambition. The self-love of every man, however insignificant by nature, is susceptible of rapid and infinite development, and may attain monstrous dimensions. Each, however small, sees others with still less capacity, who, under favourable circumstances, have contrived to climb to the roof of some building, and look complacently down on the masses that crawl upon the earth. To belong to the congregation, even of these *dii minorum gentium*, is seductive for the little man; then he sees on the horizon buildings higher still, and from his little perch how pleasant it is to see a higher roof, to climb to it, and to see on the far horizon the clouds on which the *dii majorum gentium* are enthroned! There have been many cases of elevation such as this.

Such are the planes on which aspire the imaginations of the mediocre and the little. Seldom does one of them ask himself, "Who am I? Am I capable of the work which I undertake with my elevation? Can I accomplish it? And how shall I answer for it?" And such questions are quickly dimmed in the light of an imaginary glory; the questioner compares himself with many enthroned around him, and regains his shaken confidence.

Leaving these lower paths, how varied and exalted, and, alas, how deceptive are all the aspirations to power! Knowledge of two things is essential for the consecration of a man in power. The first is shown in the eternal precept, "Know thyself"; the other, "Know thy surroundings." Both are necessary to the conscious expression and execution of the human will, to influence on the wills of others, and to creation on whatever field of action, great or small. Action takes place in the world of reality; the laws of reason are at the same time the laws of nature and of life. He who ignores these laws and will not submit to them is unworthy of his work.

The imagination of man, nourished on the vague although ennobling aspirations of the spirit, but neglected by reality, exalts to infinite heights the human soul, impelling men to conceive themselves capable of work, by painting before them illusory pictures of happiness and truth. Thus is engendered a deceptive confidence, which by slow degrees may develop into faith in a destiny. And when with this faith is joined the adoration of abstract ideas and axioms, which, as seemingly they work by themselves, apparently only need application to human relations to renovate the world in order and equity, this confidence acquires the nature of dogmatism, and, by inciting the mind, begets a passionate aspiration to power, avowedly in the name of the higher principles of truth and virtue, but in reality in the name of the overgrown self.

" I will command," says the aspirant to power, "and my word will work wonders," for he fancies that words of command, as a magic wand, can act by themselves. Poor man, before he commands he has first to learn to obey! Before he has given orders, he must learn to hear them, and to listen to questioning. He must pass through the school of duty, where each in his place and time must faithfully and duly play his part in harmony with the parts of a host of others. He must learn to remember that orders do not spring forth armed as Minerva from the head of Jupiter, but are the last links in an infinite chain of reasoning ; an infinite chain of causes and effects.

The imaginations of benevolent men draw pictures of good works ; they wish to do good and to serve as instruments of good. Alas, goodness is but a little way on the path to the doing of good ! Even he who wishes to do good after the precept of the Evangel out of his own estate, will at last be taught by experience that the doing of good to men in its truest sense is a wearying and burdensome task. How much more difficult is it to do good out of the capital of power with which men are invested ! It is well for a man if when thinking of himself and of his power he does not for a minute forget that power belongs to him for the sake of the general welfare and for the benefit of the State ; that in his sphere of action the little store of strength he has cannot and must not be transformed into a horn of plenty, from which to scatter liberal gifts and many rewards. It is well if he does not forget that the power entrusted to him by the State to judge the merits of men, the justice of things, and the lawfulness of needs which cry for help, cannot, and must not, in his hands be perverted into favouritism and protection, for the temptation is strong to good men and to vain men, and goodness and vanity too often are joined. How sweet it is to meet on all sides grateful and affectionate glances ! The seduction of this vanity may lead power to extreme weakness, to the confusion of merit and capacity with baseness and stupidity, to the demoralisation of subordinates by the general hunt for promotion and by an increased desire for honours, rewards, and monetary gratifications.

The first essential of righteous power is "a just standard." It gives the strength to judge by merit, and to allot to each a task no higher and no lower than his deserts. It teaches the preservation of human dignity in self and in others, and the distinction of faults which may not be tolerated from human weaknesses which ask for indulgence and care. It maintains all power in allegiance to its high calling, impelling and inspiring it to study the men and the work confided to its charge. It gives steadfastness to the orders that issue from power, and to the words of power a creative force. And he who has lost this standard through idleness or indifference forgets that the work which he neglects is a work of God.

W. H. WHITE AND CO. LIMITED, RIVERSIDE PRESS, EDINBURGH.

By GRANT ALLEN.　　　*Demy 8vo, Cloth,* **20s.** *net.*

The Evolution of the Idea of God:

An Enquiry into the Origins of Religions.

SOME PRESS OPINIONS.

The World:

" This book, the outcome of twenty years of thought and ten years of writing, is certainly one of the most important contributions to the history of the human mind which the last decade has given us. . . . We have no space to trace further the unfolding of these suggestive ideas, which are developed and illustrated with a brightness uncommon in books of serious purposes. The present work, Mr Allen says, is but a sketch which will be filled in and amplified if the public is sufficiently interested."

The Daily Chronicle:

" The sympathetic spirit in which Mr Allen treats a delicate and complex subject should have kindly consideration from those to whom the story of man's beliefs and guesses about the unseen makes appeal. . . . A book which is the outcome of careful scholarly research."

The Times:

" One of the most ambitious and not the least successful of Mr Allen's works. . . . It is needless to say that the book is clever, showing marks of wide reading, ingenuity, and a certain *verve*—one might say dash—and that it attracts by the very reason that the writer is cumbered with few doubts or misgivings as to the soundness of his theories. . . . The true student will profit much by Mr Grant Allen's erudition and his criticisms of the work of his predecessors."

Mr H. G. WELLS, in the *Daily Mail*:

" A work of extraordinary interest and suggestion. . . . It is on the whole a worthy treatment of an immensely interesting subject, a book for the intelligent general reader; one of the books that bristle with the always plausible, and frequently convincing, reason why."

The Scotsman:

" It will be understood by every one that the subject Mr Allen has chosen would be handled by him in a thoroughly scientific manner, and in absolute independence of all theological theories. . . . The writer has collected an immense number of facts bearing on the development of religion, and has put them together in a most interesting way. The more educated part of the world is prepared for a work like this, and we have no doubt it will be read by many with the deepest interest."

GRANT RICHARDS,

9 HENRIETTA STREET, COVENT GARDEN, W.C.

Letters from Julia;

or

Light from the Borderland;

A Series of Messages as to the Life beyond the Grave received by Automatic Writing from One who has gone before.

Edited by W. T. STEAD.

Second Edition. 16mo, *Cloth,* **2s.**

AN EXTRACT FROM Mr STEAD'S PREFACE.

" Automatic writing is writing that is written by the hand of a person which is not under control of his conscious mind. The hand apparently writes of itself, the person to whom the hand belongs having no knowledge of what it is about to write. It is a very familiar and simple form of mediumship, which in no way impairs the writer's faculties or places his personality under the control of any other intelligence. This writing may proceed from his subconscious mind, or it may be due to the direct action of in-dependent but invisible intelligences. What is certain is, that it does not emanate from the conscious mind of the writer, who often receives messages containing information as to past events of which he has never heard, and sometimes perfectly accurate predictions as to events which have not yet happened. It was in this way that I began to receive the communications, some few of which are collected in this little volume. All the 'Letters from Julia' were received by me in the same manner. Sitting alone, with a tranquil mind, I consciously placed my right hand, with the pen held in the ordinary way, at the disposal of Julia, and watched with keen and sceptical interest to see what it would write. The bulk of the first series was written as letters from Julia to Ellen. They were written as from one friend to another, beginning and ending just as if the writer were still in the body instead of having to rely upon the loan of my hand. The second series was written for publication at irregular intervals. The first series is really a compost of extracts from letters which were written every week for nearly six months, with some interculated observations made to me at the time of writing. The second series is composed of the communications written as printed at the dates given in the text."

GRANT RICHARDS,

9 HENRIETTA STREET, COVENT GARDEN, W.C.

PUBLICATIONS & ANNOUNCE-
MENTS OF MR. GRANT RICHARDS
AT No. 9 HENRIETTA STREET
COVENT GARDEN, LONDON

BOOKS NOW READY, ARRANGED IN ORDER OF PRICE

35s. net.
English Portraits.

20s. net.
Evolution of the Idea of God.

10s. 6d.
H. R. H. The Prince of Wales.

7s. 6d.
In Court and Kampong.

6s.
True Heart.
Wheel of God.
Cattle Man.
Aunt Judith's Island.
Actor-Manager.
Studies in Brown Humanity.
Linnet.
Wooings of Jezebel Pettyfer.
Ape, the Idiot, and other People.
Yellow Danger.
Blastus.
Logic : Deductive and Inductive.
African Millionaire.
"Old Man's" Marriage.
Book of Verses for Children.
Flower of the Mind.
Laughter of Jove.

5s. net.
Hannibal.
Porphyrion.
Versions from Hafiz.
Inferno of Dante.
St. Botolph.
Pioneers of Evolution.
Limbo.
Poems by A. and L.

5s.
Plays : Pleasant and Unpleasant.
Bishops of the Day.
Cakes and Ale.
Real Ghost Stories.
Old Rome and the New.
Tom, Unlimited.
Rubaiyat of Omar Khayyam.

3s. 6d. net.
The Wind in the Trees.
Grant Allen's Guides.
Spikenard.
Hernani.

3s. 6d.
Convict 99.
Where Three Creeds Meet.
Little Stories about Women.
One Man's View.
Paul's Stepmother.
Subconscious Self.
Tenth Island.

3s. net.
Realms of Unknown Kings :
    Buckram.
Politics in 1896.

2s. 6d. net.
Tabulation of the Factory Laws.
Aglavaine and Selysette.
English Portraits : Parts.

2s. 6d.
Ethics of Browning's Poems.
Peakland Faggot.

2s. net.
New Zealand.
Realms of Unknown Kings :
    Paper.

2s.
Letters from Julia.
Ethics of the Surface Series.
Cub in Love : Cloth.

1s. 6d.
Dumpy Books.
Cub in Love : Paper.

1s.
Labour in the Longest Reign.

ANNOUNCEMENTS

〜 〜 〜

A new volume will be added to Mr. GRANT ALLEN'S series of Historical Guides.

Venice

Three volumes in the series have already appeared, PARIS, FLORENCE, and CITIES OF BELGIUM; and ROME and CITIES OF NORTHERN ITALY are in preparation. Of the general need for the series, the Morning Post *says :—*

"That much-abused class of people, the tourists, have often been taunted with their ignorance and want of culture, and the perfunctory manner in which they hurry through, and 'do' the Art Galleries of Europe. There is a large amount of truth, no doubt, but they might very well retort on their critics that no one had come forward to meet their wants, or assist in dispelling their ignorance. No doubt there are guide-books, very excellent ones in their way, but on all matters of art very little better than mere indices ; something fuller was required to enable the average man intelligently to appreciate the treasures submitted to his view. Mr. Grant Allen has offered to meet their wants, and offers these handbooks to the public at a price that ought to be within the reach of every one who can afford to travel at all. The idea is a good one, and should ensure the success which Mr. Allen deserves."

Grant Allen's Historical Guides are bound in green cloth, with rounded corners, to slip into the pocket. Fcap. 8vo. 3s. 6d. each, net.

New Fiction

Author of " The Black Mass," " The Trespasses of Two," etc.

True Heart

Being Passages in the Life of Eberhard Treuherz,
Scholar and Craftsman, telling of his Wanderings
and Adventures, his Intercourse with People
of Consequence to their Age, and how ·
he came scatheless through a
Time of Strife

While doing his best to retain ample romantic interest, Mr. Breton's intention has been to present a true picture of the time rather than to produce a mere novel of incident.

In One Volume, 6s.

∿　∿

BY GEORGE EGERTON

Author of " Keynotes," " Discords," etc.

The Wheel of God

Hitherto "George Egerton's" books have been made up of short stories. "The Wheel of God" is her first long novel, and deals with woman's life both in America and in England. Its note is one rather of reaction than of revolt.

In One Volume, 6s.

∿　∿

BY G. B. BURGIN

Author of " ' Old Man's ' Marriage," " Tuxter's Little Maid," etc.

The Cattle Man

In One Volume, 6s.   [*Ready.*

4

New Fiction

BY LEONARD MERRICK
Author of "One Man's View," "Cynthia," etc.

The Actor-Manager

Mr. Merrick writes of theatrical life in London and the provinces from a fulness of knowledge: he has been both actor and dramatist. His story here is that of an actor's progress, social and artistic, and of the clash of ideas with the hard necessity of the box-office.

In One Volume, 6s.

BY HUGH CLIFFORD
Author of "In Court and Kampong."

Studies in Brown Humanity

Being Scrawls and Smudges in Sepia, White, and Yellow

Mr. Hugh Clifford, who occupies the important post of British Resident at Pahang in the Malay Peninsula, achieved considerable success with his first book, "In Court and Kampong," of which this book is in some sense a continuation, dealing as it does with the tragic, eventful lives of the varied peoples among whom lies his work.

"The chief aim is to portray character, to reveal to the European thoughts, passions, and aspirations which unfold themselves but slowly even to him who for long years has lived the life of his Asiatic associates in places remote from the sound of western civilisation. . . . In this effort Mr. Clifford has achieved a considerable success ; and as he writes also in a bright style, which has a distinctly literary flavour, his work is not less welcome for the information which it gives than interesting as a story-book."—*Athenæum* on "In Court and Kampong."

In One Volume, 6s.

BY GRANT ALLEN

Linnet: a Romance

The story of a Tyrolese peasant-girl who becomes a great singer. The scenes are laid in the Tyrol, in London, Monte Carlo, and elsewhere: the treatment varying between the idyllic and the novel of society.

In One Volume, 6s.   [*June.*

5

New Fiction

By MARIE AND ROBERT LEIGHTON

Convict 99

A True Story of Penal Servitude

With 8 Full-page Illustrations by STANLEY L. WOOD.
In One Volume, 3s. 6d.

❧ ❧

By HALDANE MACFALL

The Wooings of Jezebel Pettyfer

Being the Personal History of Jehu Sennacherib Dyle,
Commonly called Mashcen Dyle

A realistic story of West Indian negro life, written with sympathy and knowledge, Mr. Macfall having held, for a considerable period, a commission in a West Indian regiment. "He has aimed at giving us," says *The Literary World* in an advance note on the book, "negro views of life, negro religious prejudices, and negro superstitions. The hero is a Zouave, and the chief characters are negroes—acting and living like negroes—and not, as in most books of the kind, travesties of the white man."
In One Volume, 6s.

❧ ❧

By DR. J. CAMPBELL OMAN

Where Three Creeds Meet

A Tale of Indian Life

In One Volume, 3s. 6d.

❧ ❧

By W. T. STEAD

Blastus, the King's Chamberlain

A reprint, with a new introduction of considerable length, of an old Christmas number of the *Review of Reviews*, long out of print. In the tale, Mr. Stead made the experiment of prophesying the immediate future of a prominent politician whose identity is only thinly veiled. Events have given that prophecy an extreme interest, which Mr. Stead's new introduction greatly enhances.

In One Volume, 6s.

6

New Fiction

The Ape, the Idiot, and other People

Mr. Morrow, an American, has produced here a collection of short stories of the weird, the horrible, and the grotesque, reminding us now of Robert Louis Stevenson, now of Edgar Allan Poe, and now of Mr. H. G. Wells, but retaining at the same time a note of his own that is likely to make his volume a considerable success.

In One Volume, 6s.

∽ ∽

By M. P. SHIEL

Author of " Prince Zaleski," etc.

The Yellow Danger

The plot of this story is laid in the present year, the first chapters dealing with those incidents in the Far East that have so fluttered the chancelleries of the West. A great leader—half Chinese, half Japanese —unites the yellow races, and conceives the idea of setting the nations of Europe at war by giving to the three great Continental powers vast tracts of Chinese land. The policy of the " open door " forces England to fight the coalition, and, as a result, the object of the East is achieved —Europe is decimated and enfeebled, lying open to the locust swarm of the yellow races (the " Yellow Danger " of the *Spectator*). And then—then England saves the world. Although dealing with so vast a subject, there is no lack of personal interest and individual incident in Mr. Shiel's work.

In One Volume, 6s.

∽ ∽

By F. C. CONSTABLE

Author of " The Curse of Intellect."

Aunt Judith's Island

A Comedy of Kith and Kin

A satirical novel of society and European politics. In Aunt Judith the author has added to that gallery of resourceful women (which already is graced by Mrs. Poyser and Betsy Trotwood, Gainor Wynne, Old Pummeloe, and Mrs. Major O'Dowd) a millionaire with pronounced views on Socialism and enough opportunism to stock three Prime Ministers. How Aunt Judith reconciles the various branches of her family, and conducts the Concert of Europe, one must read the story to discover.

In One Volume, 6s.

Drama

By GEORGE BERNARD SHAW

Plays: Pleasant and Unpleasant

I. Unpleasant. II. Pleasant.

With special Portrait in photogravure of the Author.

The existence of a number of unpublished and unperformed plays by Mr. Shaw has been, for some time past, discussed with the interest which his work never fails to arouse. Mr. Shaw has his own views about the printing of work intended for the stage: he holds that the mere printing of the "prompt copy" is insufficient, and that "the institution of a new art" is necessary. So, in the two volumes now in the press, the customary meagre stage directions and scenic specifications will be found replaced by finished descriptions, vivid character-sketches, physiologic notes, sallies, and comments, in which the author's literary force is as conspicuous as in the dialogue. There is a lengthy introduction to the first volume, and prefaces to each play.

In Two Volumes. Fcap. 8vo. Cloth. 5s. each.

[*Ready April* 6.

∽ ∽

By VICTOR HUGO

Hernani

Translated into English Verse, with an Introduction
By R. FARQUHARSON SHARP.

Small 4to. Boards. 3s. 6d. net. [*Ready.*

∽ ∽

By LOUISA SHORE

Hannibal

With Portrait in photogravure of the Author.

Mr. Frederic Harrison writes: "I have read and re-read 'Hannibal' with admiration. As a historical romance, carefully studied from the original histories, it is a noble conception of a great hero. . . . The merit of this piece is to have seized the historical conditions with such reality and such truth, and to have kept so sustained a flight at a high level of heroic dignity."

Crown 8vo. Cloth. 5s. net. [*Ready.*

Poetry

By LAURENCE BINYON

Author of "London Visions"

Porphyrion and other Poems

Crown 8vo. Cloth. 5s. net. [*Ready.*

❧ ❧

By WALTER LEAF, LL.D.

Versions from Hafiz

An Essay in Persian Metre

"For Hafiz, at least as much as for any poet," says Dr. Leaf in his introduction, "form is of the essence of his poetry," and an attempt is here made "to give English readers some idea of the most intimate and indissoluble bond of spirit and form" in his odes. "And with it all one must try to convey some joint reminder of the fact that Hafiz is, as few poets have been, a master of words and rhythms."

Small 4to. Linen. 5s. net. *Also ten copies on Japanese vellum, numbered and signed by the Author,* 21s. *net.* [*Ready.*

❧ ❧

By EUGENE LEE-HAMILTON

Author of "Sonnets of the Wingless Hours," etc.

The Inferno of Dante translated with Plain Notes

Mr. Lee-Hamilton's aim has been to secure *a line-for-line translation.*

Fcap. 8vo. Half Parchment. 5s. net. [*Ready.*

❧ ❧

By LAURENCE HOUSMAN

Author of "Gods and their Makers," etc.

Spikenard

A Book of Devotional Love Poems

With Cover designed by the Author.

Small 4to. Boards. 3s. 6d. net. [*Ready.*

❧ ❧

By W. P. REEVES

Agent-General for New Zealand

New Zealand, and other Poems

Fcap. 8vo. Paper Wrapper. 2s. net. [*Ready.*

Poetry

By KATHARINE TYNAN (MRS. HINKSON)

The Wind in the Trees

A Book of Country Verse

Fcap. 8vo.   Cloth.   3s. 6d. net.

❧ ❧ . ❧

English Portraits

A SERIES OF LITHOGRAPHED DRAWINGS

BY

WILL ROTHENSTEIN

With an Introduction by the Artist, and Short Texts
by various hands.

❧ ❧

The following Portraits are included in this Collection,
each from sittings specially given to Mr. Rothenstein :—

Mr. Grant Allen	Sir Henry Irving
Mr. William Archer	Mr. Henry James
Lord Charles Beresford, M.P.	Mr. W. E. H. Lecky, M.P.
Mr. Robert Bridges	Professor A. Legros
Mr. Walter Crane	Mrs. Meynell
Right Rev. Dr. Creighton	Mr. A. W. Pinero
Mr. Sidney Colvin	Sir Frederick Pollock
Mr. George Gissing	Mr. Charles Ricketts
Marchioness of Granby	Mr. John Sargent, R.A.
Sir F. Seymour Haden	Mr. Charles Haselwood Shannon
Mr. Thomas Hardy	Mr. George Bernard Shaw
Mr. W. E. Henley	Miss Ellen Terry

"Admirably life-like, . . . and the style of publication makes it very attractive."
—*Speaker.*

"The drawings are lithographs, rough sketches rather than elaborate drawings, but
they show that Mr. Rothenstein has thoroughly mastered his method, and knows how
to use it with most commendable self-restraint.   They are admirable examples of the
style of drawing which he has made his own, and which has much to recommend it."
—*Scotsman.*

Folio.   In Buckram Cover specially designed by
the Artist.   35s. net.

Also in Parts, each containing Two Portraits.

2s. 6d. net.   [*Ready.*

History

By The Rev. A. G. B. ATKINSON, M.A.

St. Botolph, Aldgate

The Story of a City Parish, compiled from the Record Books and other Ancient Documents. With a Supplementary Chapter by the Vicar

Crown 8vo. Cloth. 5s. net. [*Ready.*

❧ ❧ ❧

By TEMPLE SCOTT

A Bibliography of Omar Khayyam

With Prefatory Note by EDWARD CLODD, Ex-President of the Omar Khayyam Club.

Fcap. 8vo. Buckram. 5s. net.

❧ ❧

EDITED BY W. T. STEAD

Letters from Julia

Or, Light from the Borderland: a Series of Messages as to the Life beyond the Grave received by Automatic Writing from one who has gone before

16mo. Cloth. 2s.
[*Second Edition ready.*

11

ALLEN, GRANT.

Linnet: a Romance. Crown 8vo. Cloth. 6s.

The Evolution of the Idea of God: an Inquiry into the Origins of Religions. Demy 8vo. Buckram. 20s. net. [*Second Edition.*

Grant Allen's Historical Guides:

Paris. [*Ready.*
Florence. ,,
Cities of Belgium. ,,
Venice. [*In preparation.*
Rome. .,
Cities of Northern Italy. ,,

Fcap. 8vo. Cloth. 3s. 6d. each, net.

"Good work in the way of showing students the right manner of approaching the history of a great city. . . . These useful little volumes."—*Times.*

"Those who travel for the sake of culture will be well catered for in Mr. Grant Allen's new series of historical guides . . . There are few more satisfactory books for a student who wishes to dig out the Paris of the past from the immense super-incumbent mass of coffee-houses, kiosks, fashionable hotels, and other temples of civilisation, beneath which it is now submerged. Florence is more easily dug up, as you have only to go into the picture galleries, or into the churches or museums, whither Mr. Allen's guide accordingly conducts you, and tells you what to look at if you want to understand the art treasures of the city. The books, in a word, explain rather than describe. Such books are wanted nowadays. . . . The more sober-minded among tourists will be grateful to him for the skill with which the new series promises to minister to their needs."—*Scotsman.*

"Mr. Grant Allen, as a traveller of thirty-five years' experience in foreign lands, is well qualified to command success in the task he has set himself, and nothing in the two volumes under notice is more striking than the strong sense conveyed of his powers of observation and the facility with which he describes the objects of art and the architectural glories which he has met and lingered over. . . . It would be a pity indeed were his assiduous researches and the fruits of his immense experience, now so happily exemplified, to pass unnoticed either by 'globe trotters' or by students of art and history who have perforce to stay at home."—*Daily Telegraph.*

"No traveller going to Florence with any idea of understanding its art treasures, can afford to dispense with Mr. Grant Allen's guide. He is so saturated with information gained by close observation and close study. He is so candid, so sincere, so fearless, so interesting, and his little book is so portable and so pretty."—*Queen.*

"Not only admirable, but also, to the intelligent tourist, indispensable. . . . Mr. Allen has the artistic temperament. . . . With his origins, his traditions, his art criticisms, he goes to the heart of the matter, is outspoken concerning those things he despises, and earnest when describing those in which his soul delights. . . . *The books are genuinely interesting to the ordinary reader, whether he have travelled or not, and unlike the ordinary guide-book may be read with advantage both before and after the immediate occasion of their use.*"—*Birmingham Gazette*

Grant Richards's Publications

An African Millionaire: Episodes in the Life of the Illustrious Colonel Clay. With over Sixty Illustrations by Gordon Browne. Crown 8vo. Cloth. 6s. *[Fifth Edition.*

"It is not often that the short story of this class can be made as attractive and as exciting as are many of the Colonel's episodes. Let us be thankful for these, and hasten to commend 'An African Millionaire' to the notice of all travellers. We can imagine no book of the season more suitable for an afternoon in a hammock or a lazy day in the woods. And the capital illustrations help an excellent dozen of stories on their way."—*Daily Chronicle.*

"For resourcefulness, for sardonic humour, for a sense of the comedy of the situation, and for pluck to carry it through, it would be difficult to find a more entertaining scoundrel than Colonel Clay."—*Daily News.*

"This book is a good example of Mr. Grant Allen's talents. It is only a collection of tales describing how a very rich man is again and again victimised by the same adventurer, but it has not only plenty of dramatic incident, but of shrewd and wise reflection, such as is seldom found in the modern novel."—Mr. JAMES PAYN in the *Illustrated London News.*

ALMA TADEMA, LAURENCE.

Realms of Unknown Kings: Poems. Fcap. 8vo. Paper Wrapper. 2s. net. Buckram. 3s. net.

ANSTEY, F.

Paleface and Redskin, and other Stories for Boys and Girls. With Illustrations by Gordon Browne. *[In preparation.*

ATKINSON, A. G. B., M.A.

St. Botolph, Aldgate: The Story of a City Parish, compiled from the Record Books and other Ancient Documents. With a Supplementary Chapter by the Vicar. Crown 8vo. Cloth. 5s. net.

BELL, R. S. WARREN.

(*See* Henrietta Volumes.)

BINYON, LAURENCE.

Porphyrion and other Poems. Crown 8vo. Cloth. 5s. net.

BRETON, FREDERIC.

True Heart: a Novel. Crown 8vo. Cloth. 6s.

BROOK, EMMA.

A Tabulation of the Factory Laws of European Countries, in so far as they relate to the Hours of Labour and Special Legislation for Women, Young Persons, and Children. Demy 8vo. Half Cloth. 2s. 6d. net.

BURGIN, G. B.

The Cattle Man : a Novel.
"Old Man's" Marriage : A Novel. (A Sequel to "The Judge of the Four Corners.")
Crown 8vo. Cloth. 6s. each.

"Mr. Burgin's best qualities come to the front in '"Old Man's" Marriage.' . . . Miss Wilkes has nearly as much individuality as any one in the story, which is saying a good deal, for reality seems to gather round all the characters in spite of the romance that belongs to them as well . . . the story is fresh and full of charm."—*Standard.*

"Mr. Burgin's humour is both shrewd and kindly, and his book should prove as welcome as a breath of fresh air to the weary readers of realistic fiction."—*Daily Telegraph.*

"'Old Man's' Marriage is told with such humour, high spirit, simplicity, and straightforwardness that the reader is amused and entertained from the first page to the last. Once I had begun it I had to go on to the end ; when I put it down it was with a sigh to part with such excellent company. . . . As thoroughly enjoyable and racily written a story as has been published for a long time."—Mr. COULSON KERNAHAN in the *Star.*

"It would be difficult to speak too highly of the delicate pathos and humour of this beautiful sketch of a choice friendship in humble life. . . . A study at once simple and subtle and full of the dignity and sincerity of natural man."—*Manchester Guardian.*

CLIFFORD, HUGH (British Resident at Pahang).

Studies in Brown Humanity: Being Scrawls and Smudges in Sepia, White, and Yellow. Crown 8vo. Cloth. 6s.

In Court and Kampong : Being Tales and Sketches of Native Life in the Malay Peninsula. Large Crown 8vo. Cloth. 7s. 6d.

"Mr. Clifford undoubtedly possesses the gift of graphic description in a high degree, and each one of these stories grips the reader's attention most insistently. The whole book is alive with drama and passion ; but, as we have said, its greatest charm lies in the fact that it paints in strikingly minute detail a state of things which, whether for good or ill, is rapidly vanishing from the face of the earth."—*Speaker.*

"These tales Mr. Clifford tells with a force and life-likeness such as is only to be equalled in the stories of Rudyard Kipling. Take, for instance, the gruesome story of the were-tiger, man by day and man-eater by night. . . . Every one of these tales leaves its impression, dramatic yet lifelike. Moreover, they are valuable as giving a picture of strange, distorted civilisation which, under the influence of British residents and officials, will soon pass away or hide itself jealously from the gaze of Western eyes."—*Pall Mall Gazette.*

CLODD, EDWARD.

Pioneers of Evolution from Thales to Huxley,

with an intermediate chapter on the Causes of Arrest of the Movement. With portraits in photogravure of Charles Darwin, Professor Huxley, Mr. A. R. Wallace, and Mr. Herbert Spencer. Crown 8vo. Linen. 5s. net. *[Second Edition.*

"We are always glad to meet Mr. Edward Clodd. He is never dull; he is always well informed, and he says what he has to say with clearness and incision. . . . The interest intensifies as Mr. Clodd attempts to show the part really played in the growth of the doctrine of evolution by men like Wallace, Darwin, Huxley, and Spencer. Mr. Clodd clears away prevalent misconceptions as to the work of these modern pioneers. Especially does he give to Mr. Spencer the credit which is his due, but which is often mistakenly awarded to Darwin. Mr. Clodd does not seek in the least to lower Darwin from the lofty pedestal which he rightly occupies; he only seeks to show precisely why he deserves to occupy such a position. We commend the book to those who want to know what evolution really means; but they should be warned beforehand that they have to tackle strong meat."—*Times.*

"There is no better book on the subject for a general reader, and while its matter is largely familiar to professed students of science, and indeed to most men who are well read, no one could go through the book without being both refreshed and newly instructed by its masterly survey of the growth of the most powerful idea of modern times."—*Scotsman.*

CONSTABLE, F. C.

Aunt Judith's Island: a Comedy of Kith and Kin. Crown 8vo. Cloth. 6s.

DANTE.

(*See* Lee-Hamilton.)

DIXON, H. SYDENHAM ("Vigilant" of the *Sportsman*).

From Gladiateur to Persimmon: Turf History for Thirty Years. With portraits. Demy 8vo.

DUMPY BOOKS FOR CHILDREN.

Edited by E. V. Lucas, and with End-papers designed by Mrs. Farmiloe. 18mo. Cloth. 1s. 6d. each.

1. The Flamp, the Ameliorator, and the Schoolboy's Apprentice: Three Stories. By Edward Verrall Lucas.

2. Mrs. Turner's Cautionary Stories.

EGERTON, GEORGE.

The Wheel of God: a Novel. Crown 8vo. Cloth. 6s.

ETHICS OF THE SURFACE SERIES.

1. The Rudeness of the Honourable Mr. Leatherhead.
2. A Homburg Story.
3. Cui Bono?

By Gordon Seymour. 16mo. Buckram. 2s. each.

"The stories are remarkable for their originality, their careful characterisation, their genuine thoughtfulness, and the sincerity of their purpose. They certainly open up a fresh field of thought on the problems set by the philosopher of the superficial, problems which, though they seem to lie on the surface, strike their roots deep down into human life; and they make us think for ourselves (though perhaps somewhat gropingly), which is more than can be said for the general run of modern novels."—*Pall Mall Gazette.*

"An able and well-written little bit of fiction. . . . Amongst the short descriptive portions of the book there are some excellent examples of graceful prose, and if the dialogues occasionally resolve themselves into disquisitions on life and society too elaborate for the reader who is chiefly concerned to get the story, they will repay the reader who can appreciate the analysis of delicate shades of thought and feeling."—*Aberdeen Free Press.*

FLEMING, GEORGE.

Little Stories about Women. Crown 8vo. Cloth. 3s. 6d.

"All novel readers must welcome the decision which has caused these stories, many of which are gems, to appear in volume form. . . . Story is hardly the name to employ in the case of these impressionist pictures. They have the suggestive merit of the school and none of its vagueness."—*Morning Post.*

"It is impossible to read 'Little Stories about Women' without a feeling of blank astonishment that their author should be so very little more than a name to the reading public. . . . It is difficult to imagine anything better in its way—and its way is thoroughly modern and up to date—than the first of the collection, 'By Accident.' It is very short, very terse, but the whole story is suggested with admirable art. There is nothing unfinished about it, and the grip with which the carriage accident which opens it is presented never relaxes."—*World.*

GILCHRIST, R. MURRAY. (*See* Sylvan Series.)

HENRIETTA VOLUMES, THE.

The Cub in Love: in Twelve Twinges; with Six additional Stories. By R. S. Warren Bell. With Cover by Maurice Greiffenhagen. Tauchnitz size. 1s. 6d. (*Copies also obtainable in Cloth. 2s.*)

"Light and amusing withal is Mr. Warren Bell's sketch of a very young man suffering from the bitter-sweet of an unrequited affection. . . . The Cub seems to be a near relation of Dolly (of the 'Dolly Dialogues'), and the sprightliness of his dialogue makes him worthy of the kinship."—*Pall Mall Gazette.*

"The book makes excellent reading for travelling or a holiday, or, indeed, for any occasion on which amusement is the thing desired. If the subsequent volumes of the Henrietta series are up to this standard, there need be no question of their success."—*Scotsman.*

"This is one of the most brightly written books we have read for some time. . . . We cannot conceive a more enjoyable book for a couple of hours' reading at the seaside."—*Belfast Evening Telegraph.*

Grant Richards's Publications

HOUSMAN, LAURENCE.

> **Spikenard:** a Book of Devotional Love Poems. With Cover designed by the Author. Small 4to. Boards. 3s. 6d. net.

H.R.H. The Prince of Wales: an Account of His Career, including his Birth, Education, Travels, Marriage, and Home Life and Philanthropic, Social, and Political Work. Royal 8vo. Cloth. 10s. 6d. With one hundred Portraits and other Illustrations.

HUGO, VICTOR.

> **Hernani:** a Drama, translated into English Verse, with an Introduction by R. Farquharson Sharp. Small 4to. Boards. 3s. 6d. net.

LEAF, WALTER, LL.D.

> **Versions from Hafiz:** an Essay in Persian Metre. Small 4to. Linen. 5s. net. (*Also Ten Copies on Japanese Vellum, numbered and signed by the Author, 21s. net.*)

LEAKE, MRS. PERCY.

> **The Ethics of Browning's Poems.** With Introduction by the Bishop of Winchester. Fcap. 8vo. Cloth. 2s. 6d.

LEE, VERNON.

> **Limbo and other Essays.** With Frontispiece. Fcap. 8vo. Buckram. 5s. net.

"The brilliant and versatile writer who adopts the pseudonym of Vernon Lee affords a dainty feast to her readers in this charming little volume."—*Times.*

"For charm, that 'delicate and capricious foster-child of leisure,' Vernon Lee's latest work, small as it is, is the equal of anything that she has yet produced."—*Morning Post.*

"This little volume might be called a manual of the cultivated soul adventuring among masterpieces of art and natural beauties. It brings to the enjoyment of these a power of association which traverses seas and years, and refreshes the mind with images summoned from the recesses of memory. They are pitched in a pleasant conversational way, frankly, even daringly, personal, and are strewn with vivid descriptions of Italian scenes and places."—*Manchester Guardian.*

"'Limbo and other Essays' is amongst the most welcome of recent books. . . . Few essayists see so many beautiful things as Vernon Lee, and fewer still, having seen them, say so many beautiful things about them."—Mr. RICHARD LE GALLIENNE in the *Star.*

LEE-HAMILTON, EUGENE.

> **The Inferno of Dante translated with Plain Notes.** Fcap. 8vo. Half Parchment. 5s. net.

18

LE GALLIENNE, RICHARD.

Rubaiyat of Omar Khayyam: a Paraphrase from several Literal Translations. From the press of Messrs. T. and A. Constable of Edinburgh. Long Fcap. 8vo. Parchment. 5s. Also a very limited Edition on Japanese Vellum, numbered and signed by the Author. 15s. net. [*All sold.*

LEIGHTON, MARIE CONNOR and ROBERT.

Convict 99: a Novel. With Eight full-page Illustrations by Stanley L. Wood. Crown 8vo. Cloth. 3s. 6d.

LOWNDES, FREDERIC SAWREY.

Bishops of the Day: a Biographical Dictionary of the Archbishops and Bishops of the Church of England, and of all Churches in Communion therewith throughout the World. Fcap. 8vo. Cloth. 5s.

"While the assembly of nearly 200 Bishops of the Anglican Communion at the Lambeth Conference makes the publication of the volume at the present time especially opportune, Mr. Lowndes's work is likely to command a more permanent interest. It gives a full and lucid sketch of the career of each Bishop, without any suggestion of partisan bias on the part of the author."—*Times.*

"Few works of reference could be more acceptable to Churchmen of the present time. . . . Plenty of dates of the right sort, as well as matters of more human interest."—*Guardian.*

"The work is thoroughly up to date, as one may see from the Episcopal events of 1896 and 1897 here recorded. It abounds in personal incidents and anecdotes not to be found elsewhere, and evidently derived from original and accredited sources. . . . Much valuable information on Church matters generally incidental to Episcopal administration."—*Morning Post.*

"Mr. Lowndes has spared no pains to make his compendium as perfect as possible. . . . This book is, as far as we can know, the first of the kind that has been published, and supplies, in good time, a want that would have soon become urgent."—*Standard.*

"Valuable for reference on account of much of the information contained in the neatly got-up volume being supplied by the prelates themselves."—*World.*

"The book should be bought and read at once. There is no Churchman whom it will not interest, and it contains a sufficiency of blank spaces to admit of MS. additions, which may record the inevitable changes brought about by death or by translation. Mr. Lowndes deserves our very cordial thanks for a piece of work which few would have undertaken, and none could have achieved more perfectly."—*Sheffield Daily Telegraph.*

LUCAS, EDWARD VERRALL.

A Book of Verses for Children. With Cover, Title-page, and End-papers designed in colours by F. D. Bedford. Crown 8vo. Cloth. 6s.

[*Third Edition.*

(*See also* Dumpy Books for Children.)

MACFALL, HALDANE.

The Wooings of Jezebel Pettyfer: a Novel.
Crown 8vo. Cloth. 6s.

MAETERLINCK, MAURICE.

Aglavaine and Selysette: a Drama in Five Acts.
Translated by Alfred Sutro. With Introduction by
J. W. Mackail, and Title-page designed by W. H.
Margetson. Globe 8vo. Half Buckram. 2s. 6d. net.

"To read the play is to have one's sense of beauty quickened and enlarged, to be
touched by the inward and spiritual grace of things. . . . Mr. Sutro is the most
conscientious, and at the same time the most ambitious, of translators; not content
with reproducing the author's thought, he strives after the same effect of language—
the plaintive note, the dying cadence, the Maeterlincked sweetness long drawn out.
And more often than not he succeeds,—which is saying a good deal when one considers the enormous difficulties of the task."—Mr. A. B. WALKLEY in the *Speaker*.

"The book is a treasury of beautiful things. No one now writing loves beauty as
M. Maeterlinck does. Sheer, essential beauty has no such lover. He will have
nothing else."—*Academy*.

"Mr. Alfred Sutro's careful and delicate translation of M. Maurice Maeterlinck's
new play gives readers of English every opportunity of appreciating a work which,
so to speak, is at the tip of the century. . . . The book, as a whole, is perhaps the
best yet published by which an English-speaking stranger to M. Maeterlinck could
make his acquaintance."—*Scotsman*.

MERRICK, LEONARD.

The Actor-Manager: a Novel. Crown 8vo.
Cloth. 6s.

One Man's View: a Novel. Cr. 8vo. Cloth. 3s. 6d.

"A novel over which we could at a pinch fancy ourselves sitting up till the small
hours. . . . The characters are realised, the emotion is felt and communicated."—
Daily Chronicle.

"An uncommonly well-written story. . . . The men in the book are excellent, and
the hero . . . is an admirable portrait."—*Standard*.

"Mr. Leonard Merrick's work is exceptionally good: his style is literary, he has
insight into character, and he can touch on delicate matters without being coarse or
unpleasantly suggestive. 'One Man's View' is keenly interesting. . . . 'One Man's
View' is one of those rare books in which, without a superfluous touch, each character
stands out clear and individually. It holds the reader's attention from first to last."—
Guardian.

MEYNELL, ALICE.

The Flower of the Mind: a Choice among the
best Poems. With Cover designed by Laurence
Housman. Crown 8vo. Buckram. 6s.

"Partial collections of English poems, decided by a common subject or bounded
by the dates and periods of literary history, are made more than once in every year,
and the makers are safe from the reproach of proposing their own personal taste as a
guide for the reading of others. But a general Anthology gathered from the whole
of English literature—the whole from Chaucer to Wordsworth—by a gatherer intent
upon nothing except the quality of poetry, is a more rare attempt."—*Extract from
Introduction*.

MORROW, W. C.
> **The Ape, the Idiot, and other People**. Crown 8vo. Cloth. 6s.

OMAN, DR. J. CAMPBELL.
> **Where Three Creeds Meet**: a Tale of Indian Life. Crown 8vo. Cloth. 3s. 6d.

READ, CARVETH, M.A.
> **Logic : Deductive and Inductive**. Crown 8vo. Cloth. 6s.

REEVES, W. P.
> **New Zealand, and other Poems**. Fcap. 8vo. Paper Wrapper. 2s. net.

ROTHENSTEIN, WILL.
> **English Portraits** : a Series of Lithographed Drawings. With an Introduction by the Artist, and Short Texts by various hands. Folio. In Buckram Cover designed by the Artist. 35s. net. Or in Twelve Parts, 2s. 6d. each, net. (*See p.* 10.)

"The portraits, which are of a large portfolio size, are vivid likenesses, and their appearance is a gratifying indication of the revival of lithography in fine art."—*Aberdeen Free Press.*

"The introductory examples fulfil to the full the promises made in the publisher's announcements, and it is certain that the series will be keenly appreciated by art lovers."—*Dundee Advertiser.*

SCOTT, TEMPLE.
> **A Bibliography of Omar Khayyam**. With a Prefatory Note by Edward Clodd. Fcap. 8vo. Buckram. 5s. net.

SCHWARTZE, HELMUTH.
> **The Laughter of Jove**: a Novel. Cr. 8vo. Cl. 6s.

SEYMOUR, GORDON.
> (*See* Ethics of the Surface Series.)

SHAW, GEORGE BERNARD.
> **Plays : Pleasant and Unpleasant.**
> I. Unpleasant.   II. Pleasant.
> With special Introduction, Prefaces to each Play, and a portrait of the Author in photogravure. Fcap. 8vo. Cloth. 5s. each.
> (*See also* Politics in 1896.)

Grant Richards's Publications

SHIEL, M. P.

> **The Yellow Danger:** a Novel. Crown 8vo.
> Cloth. 6s.

SHORE, ARABELLA and LOUISA.

> **Poems by A. and L.** Crown 8vo. Cloth. 5s. net.

SHORE, LOUISA.

> **Hannibal:** a Poetical Drama in Two Parts. New
> Edition. With Portrait. Crown 8vo. Cloth. 5s. net.

SPENCER, EDWARD ("Nathaniel Gubbins").

> **Cakes and Ale:** a Memory of Many Meals; the
> whole interspersed with various recipes, more or
> less original, and anecdotes, many veracious. With
> Cover designed by Phil May. Small 4to. Cloth. 5s.
> *[Third Edition.*

"Exceedingly readable, clever, and, moreover, highly informative. . . . From racy chapter to racy chapter the reader is irresistibly carried on. . . . The mistress of the house will read it carefully for the sake of the valuable recipes and hints, and mine host will esteem it for the smart style in which it is written, and for the plenitude of humour displayed in anecdote, story, and reminiscence."—*Dundee Advertiser.*

"Allow me to say that it is a little book on a great subject that deserves to occupy an honourable place in every library, on the same shelf as Kettner's 'Book of the Table,' Sala's 'A Thorough Good Cook,' and perhaps that over-praised but undoubtedly entertaining classic, 'Gastronomy as a Fine Art,' by Brillat-Savarin."—*Sporting Life.*

"This little volume should have its place among the wedding presents of every bride."—*Lady's Pictorial.*

"There are many useful hints on table matters, and the recipes are all eminently practical. No country house should be without it."—*Guardian.*

STEAD, W. T.

> **Real Ghost Stories:** a Revised Reprint of the
> Christmas and New Year Numbers of the
> "Review of Reviews," 1891-92. With new Intro-
> duction. Crown 8vo. Cloth. 5s.

> **Letters from Julia; or, Light from the Border-
> land:** a Series of Messages as to Life beyond the
> Grave received by Automatic Writing from one who
> has gone before. 16mo. Cloth. 2s. *[Second Edition.*

22

STILLMAN, W. J.

The Old Rome and the New, and other Studies. Crown 8vo. Cloth. 5s.

SYLVAN SERIES, THE.

A Peakland Faggot: Tales told of Milton Folk. By R. Murray Gilchrist. Fcap. 8vo. Cloth. 2s. 6d.

"Not only are the sketches themselves full of charm and real literary value, but the little volume is as pleasant to the eye and to the touch as its contents are stimulating to the imagination. . . . We do not envy the person who could lay down the book without feeling refreshed in spirit by its perusal. . . . We cannot give our readers better counsel than in advising them to procure without delay this charming and cheery volume."—*Speaker.*

"We have no hesitation in saying that this is the very best work which Mr. Gilchrist has given us. As studies of Black Country character it is superb. In fact he is a master of our feelings and emotions in this daintily produced little volume, and ' A Peakland Faggot ' will solidify that reputation which he has been steadily building up of late years. The style is thoroughly poetic. . . . Our hearty congratulations to Mr. Murray Gilchrist upon this performance—the magic he has used is the magic of true genius."—*Birmingham Gazette.*

"The writer who gives us glimpses into the psychology of the poor and illiterate ought always to be welcome. . . . Mr. Murray Gilchrist has introduced us to a new world of profound human interest."—Mr. T. P. O'CONNOR in the *Graphic.*

"I have read no book outside Mr. Hardy's so learned in such minutiæ of country ' wit ' and sentiment."—Mr. RICHARD LE GALLIENNE in the *Star.*

TROUBRIDGE, LADY.

Paul's Stepmother, and One Other Story. With Frontispiece by Mrs. Adrian Hope. Crown 8vo. Cloth. 3s. 6d.

"There is a fine natural interest in both these stories, and Lady Troubridge recounts them so well and gracefully that to the critical reader this interest is greatly enhanced."—*Dundee Advertiser.*

"It is with a genuine feeling of pleasure that the reader will linger over ' Paul's Stepmother,' a story that one is inclined to wish were longer. . . . The pathos of the situation is treated with real feeling, and there is not a discordant note throughout the story. . . . Both stories are marked as the work of a fine and cultured writer."—*Weekly Sun.*

TURNER, ELIZABETH.

(*See* Dumpy Books for Children.)

WALDSTEIN, LOUIS, M.D.

The Subconscious Self and its Relation to Education and Health. Fcap. 8vo. Cloth. 3s. 6d.

WARBOROUGH, MARTIN LEACH.

Tom, Unlimited: a Story for Children. With Fifty Illustrations by Gertrude Bradley. Globe 8vo. Cloth. 5s.

Grant Richards's Publications

WEBB, SIDNEY.

Labour in the Longest Reign (1837 - 1897).
Issued under the Auspices of the Fabian Society.
Fcap. 8vo. Cloth. 1s.

"It is, considering the source from which it comes, a singularly temperate and just review of the changes in the lot of the labourer which the reign has brought."—*Scotsman.*

"Mr. Sidney Webb has set forth some expert and telling comparisons between the condition of the working-classes in 1837 and 1897. His remarks on wages, on the irregularity of employment, on hours of labour, and on the housing of the poor, are worthy of earnest consideration."—*Daily Mail.*

WHELEN, FREDERICK (Editor).

Politics in 1896. With Contributions by H. D. Traill, D.C.L. ; H. W. Massingham ; G. Bernard Shaw ; G. W. Steevens ; H. W. Wilson ; Captain F. N. Maude ; Albert Shaw, and Robert Donald. Globe 8vo. Cloth. 3s. net.

"For more reasons than one Mr. Whelen's Political Annual, of which the present is the first issue, deserves a welcome. Not only does it constitute a handy work of reference, that besides merely enumerating the political wants of the past year shows also the light in which they are regarded by various shades of public opinion, but it calls for recognition as a record of the development of political thought, that, if regularly issued, will be of value to the future historian. . . . The book has attractions for those who wish to understand the various ideas actuating contending parties, and such readers will certainly find entertaining matter in the several contributions."—*Morning Post.*

"Mr. Whelen has undertaken a difficult task, but the volume which he has just issued is a very interesting and useful retrospect, and all who are interested in contemporary affairs will be glad to know that it is intended to be an annual. The plan is simple and comprehensive. . . . Mr. Whelen has done a useful work in starting this adventure, and we wish him all success."—*Daily Chronicle.*

"Those who can afford it, which includes at least every Labour Club, ought to possess a copy for their library."—Mr. KEIR HARDIE in the *Labour Leader.*

WHITTEN, WILFRED.

London in Song: an Anthology of Prose and Poetry inspired by London. With an Introduction. Crown 8vo. Buckram. 6s. [*In Preparation.*

WILLSON, BECKLES.

The Tenth Island: Being some Account of Newfoundland ; its People, its Politics, and its Peculiarities. With an Introduction by Sir William Whiteway, K.C.M.G., Premier of the Colony, and an Appendix by Lord Charles Beresford. Globe 8vo. Buckram. 3s. 6d. With Map.

Printed by R. & R. CLARK, LIMITED, *Edinburgh.*